50 SOCIAL STUDIES STRATEGIES FOR K–8 CLASSROOMS

50 SOCIAL STUDIES STRATEGIES FOR K–8 CLASSROOMS

THIRD EDITION

Kathryn M. Obenchain
The University of Texas at Austin

Ronald V. Morris
Ball State University

Boston Columbus Indianapolis New York San Francisco Upper Saddle River
Amsterdam Cape Town Dubai London Madrid Milan Munich Paris Montreal Toronto
Delhi Mexico City Sao Paulo Sydney Hong Kong Seoul Singapore Taipei Tokyo

Editor in Chief: Paul A. Smith
Acquisitions Editor: Kelly Villella Canton
Editorial Assistant: Annalea Manalili
Vice President, Director of Marketing: Quinn Perkson
Senior Marketing Manager: Darcy Betts
Marketing Assistant: Robin Holtsberry
Project Manager: Holly Shufeldt
Senior Art Director: Jayne Conte

Cover Designer: Suzanne Duda
Manager, Cover Visual Research & Permissions: Karen Sanatar
Cover photo: Shutterstock
Full-Service Project Management: Aparna Yellai, GGS Higher
    Education Resources, PMG
Printer/Binder: Courier/Kendallville
Cover Printer: Lehigh-Phoenix Color Corp.
Text Font: Galliard

Library of Congress Cataloging-in-Publication Data

Obenchain, Kathryn M.
    50 social studies strategies for K–8 classrooms / Kathryn M. Obenchain. — 3rd ed.
        p. cm.
    Includes bibliographical references.
    ISBN-13: 978-0-13-705015-4
    ISBN-10: 0-13-705015-1
    1. Social sciences—Study and teaching (Elementary)—United States—Handbooks, manuals, etc. 2. Social sciences—study and teaching (Middle school)—United States—Handbooks, manuals, etc. I. Morris, Ronald V. II. Title.
III. Title: Fifty social studies strategies for K–8 classrooms.

LB1584.O24 2011
372.83'044—dc22

2009047637

10 9 8 7 6 5 4   Upper Saddle River, New Jersey   Columbus, Ohio

Allyn & Bacon
is an imprint of

www.pearsonhighered.com

ISBN 10:   0-13-705015-1
ISBN 13: 978-0-13-705015-4

This book honors my family for their unending love and support. In particular, it is in memory of the love, unquestioning support, faith, and humor of my late parents, Keith G. and Nannabelle H. Obenchain.

Kathryn M. Obenchain

This book is in honor of my father, Peyton R. Morris:
- who introduced me to the wonders of northern Michigan
- my longtime skiing companion
- a friend who makes the long drives with me
- who introduced me to Greenbriar Mountain.

Ronald V. Morris

CONTENTS

Introduction   xiii

**Summary of the National Council for the Social Studies
(NCSS) Curriculum Strands**   xv

PART I   General Social Studies Instructional Strategies   1

1 Community Building   2

2 Establishing a Democratic Classroom   6

3 Developing Multiple Perspectives   10

4 Concepts: Development and Attainment   14

5 Discovery Learning   19

6 Inquiry Learning   23

7 Questioning   27

8 Primary Sources   30

PART II   Specific Social Studies Instructional Strategies to Advance
Content Knowledge and Skills Development   35

9   Archeological Digs   36

10   Architecture and Landscape Design Significance   40

11   Case Studies   44

12   Cemetery Studies   47

13   Community Maps   51

14   Custom Boxes   55

15   Decision Trees and Decision Grids   59

16   Digital Storytelling   64

17   Discerning Qualifications   68

18   Field Trips of Distinction   73

19   Flannel Boards   78

20   Folk Culture   81

21   Games   86

22   Genealogies   89

23   Globes   93

24   Graphic Organizers   97

25   Guest Speakers   103

26   Historical Characters   107

27   Historical Reenactments   111

28   Home Living Centers   116

29   Interactive Bulletin Boards   119

30 Learning Centers   122

31 Literature Book Clubs   127

32 Media Literacy   131

33 Mini-Society   136

34 Mock Trials   140

35 Model Factory   144

36 Museum Exhibits   148

37 Music History   152

38 Newspaper Making   155

39 Oral Histories   159

40 Pen Pals   163

41 Readers' Theater   167

42 Role Playing   171

43 Sand Table Maps   175

44 Service-Learning   179

45 Story Boards   183

46 Time Lines   186

47 Trash Trail   190

48 Traveling Ambassador   194

49 Video Productions   197

50 Webquests   200

PREFACE

We considered multiple audiences while writing this text. We wanted to fill it with ideas—well-explained, useful, and meaningful ideas that teachers could use to engage their students in learning social studies. This book is of interest to undergraduate elementary and middle school teacher education students as an additional source and reference in their methods class and in their first years of planning social studies instruction in their classrooms. It is also helpful to experienced elementary and middle school teachers in the social studies field or in graduate classes looking for teaching ideas. We hope teacher educators find this book useful as a companion to a more standard methods textbook because of the number and variety of strategies provided.

This book contains 8 general and 42 specific teaching and learning strategies. These materials were designed for use in the K–8 classroom, and we encourage readers to adapt these strategies to fit their particular classroom configuration and needs. Included in the strategies are multiple types of assessment tools so that readers have options in assessing their students. Further, the commitment to pragmatic instructional practices and multiple examples complements our commitment to research in the social studies field.

All of the strategies are organized in the same fashion. Each strategy includes an Introduction, which provides a brief description of the strategy and a rationale as to why it is particularly beneficial. Where appropriate, we have included historical, practitioner, theoretical, and/or research support for the use of the strategy in social studies. Procedural Recommendations provide a simple outline of how to prepare for and facilitate or direct the strategy. The section on Applications and

GRADE LEVELS	NCSS CURRICULUM STRANDS
✓ K–2	I Culture
✓ 4–5	VI Time, Continuity, and Change
✓ 6–8	IV Individual Development and Identity

Ideas includes either a classroom example or implementation ideas. The third edition also includes a new section on Assessment for each strategy. This section may include an assessment tool, reference to an assessment task in another strategy, or a brief assessment-related discussion. Each strategy includes References and Resources, which lists any combination of scholarly support, additional readings and information, and/or helpful organizations. This list helps teachers examine how others have successfully used similar strategies in their classrooms to expand and deeply understand the strategy beyond what is presented in this text. Finally, each strategy now contains a Web Sites section offering additional resources and examples. In addition, the 42 specific strategies contain additional information. Before the introduction to each specific strategy, are two indicators. One indicator highlights the grade level target(s) of the strategy. While many of the strategies are pertinent across grade levels, each strategy includes notations of K–2 (primary), 3–5 (intermediate), and/or 6–8 (middle level). The second indicator highlights the link to appropriate National Council for the Social Studies (NCSS) national curriculum standards. These Roman numerals I through X directly reference the organization of the NCSS curriculum standards. A brief overview of these standards follows the Introduction of this text.

The strategies presented in this text should help teachers plan effective social studies lessons using multiple types of student groups, as well as the diversity of learners in our classrooms. We believe students enjoy social studies more when they experience a variety of instructional strategies. With individuals, small groups, or large groups, the students and teacher should have plenty of ideas for enriching the social studies curriculum. We are interested in hearing from the readers about additions they would like to see in future editions of this text. Finally, we hope these strategies will encourage teachers to continue to create intellectual and enjoyable social studies experiences for their students.

NEW TO THE THIRD EDITION

The writing process rarely ends, and this is true with this text. From the moment we finished the first edition, we began to think of revisions for the second edition. And, as soon as the second edition was sent to print, we began to think of ways to improve the third edition. The ideas for revisions have come from many sources: our university students, teachers we work with, K–8 students who help us learn how certain strategies work for them, our evolving scholarship, and, of course, the dedicated reviewers. In addition, the world in which we live and teach, changes. The large changes we have made to the third edition are outlined below.

- **NEW organization of text** begins with **eight** (instead of three) **overarching strategies,** organized conceptually, followed by **42 Social Studies-specific strategies** to prepare for and then implement meaningful social studies teaching and learning. This is a two-fold change. We have expanded the content of overarching strategies; and, we have reorganized it. We believe that the new conceptual organization provides social studies teachers with the basic organizational foundational principles necessary for establishing a social studies classroom.
- **New Primary Sources (Strategy 8)** represents a combination of three related strategies (Artifacts, Public Records, and Private Records) in the previous edition to improve organization and make room for new strategies. This strategy has also been moved to the overarching strategies, representative of the foundational importance of using primary sources of evidence in the social studies classroom.
- **Revised Field Trips (Strategy 18)** reflects a combination of Field Trips of Distinction and Virtual Field Trips strategies from the previous edition, done to more thoroughly explore the topic of field trips for students in one place and to allow for some new strategies. This also illustrates the shared philosophical goal of the two previous strategies. By synthesizing the two strategies into a new one, we are able to better articulate what is important about planning, participating in, and evaluating a field trip, whether virtual, in one's neighborhood, or at a great distance.

- **Five new strategies,** 3. Developing Multiple Perspectives and 7. Questioning in Part I and 16. Digital Storytelling, 37. Music History, and 50. Webquests in Part II, introduced to offer current ideas and strategies to enhance the 21st Century classroom. These new strategies reflect the growing diversity of perspectives and experiences present in our students; and the growing availability of resources in the classroom. Access to both perspectives and resources has been technologically revolutionized in ways that were not practically possible to teachers a few years ago.

- **NEW!** Each strategy now includes an **Assessment section** that provides an **assessment tool or assessment discussion**, demonstrating how assessment tasks vary with varied learning goals. The inclusion of assessment to each strategy is a substantial change to this edition. We believe it illustrates the multiple approaches to assessment tasks, as well as providing a discussion of what is not practically assessed.

- **Revised!** The *Applications and Ideas* section with each strategy provides either **a classroom example or additional applications for the strategy**. This is another substantial change. Many of the strategies now contain multiple examples or applications, across grade levels. We believe this assists the pre-service teacher in seeing how to transfer the strategy into multiple grades and multiple content situations.

- **Revised!** A list of websites appears with every strategy under the References and Resources section. Finally, we have always included references and resources within each strategy. This has been revised in two ways, and is reflective of evolving access to information. In many strategies, we have reduced the number of article and/or book references. In addition, we have now added websites to every strategy.

We hope that these major changes, along with our more minor revisions, are helpful to you in teaching social studies in your classrooms.

ACKNOWLEDGMENTS

Special thanks to Mrs. Nadine Roush and her fifth-grade class at Amelia Earhart Elementary School in Lafayette, Indiana. Experiences in Mrs. Roush's classroom provided the examples for the Establishing a Democratic Classroom, Concepts: Development and Attainment, Mini-Society, and Traveling Ambassador strategies. Mrs. Roush exemplifies a master social studies teacher. It is always a treat and honor to spend time in her classroom. Also, thanks to Christopher Koch, a University of Nevada, Reno graduate assistant, for his help with third-edition revisions.

KMO

Thanks are due to Ms. Darlinda Rogers for providing the photographic example of the Interactive Bulletin Board.

RVM

We also gratefully acknowledge the feedback offered by colleagues and students and by the reviewers who provided much insight for this third edition. In particular, the reviewers provided detailed feedback and guidance for us—we sincerely thank them: Alison Black, State University of New York at Oneonta; Michelle D. Cude, James Madison University; Carol Klages, University of Houston–Victoria; Denise M. Littleon, Norfolk State University.

INTRODUCTION

What is social studies and why is it important for our students to learn social studies? Social studies is "that part of general and liberal education that specializes in the education of an effective democratic citizen" (Engle & Ochoa, 1988, p. 3). That general and liberal education is usually interpreted as history and the social sciences and often includes the behavioral sciences and humanities. As a distinct discipline, a hallmark of social studies is the integration of history and the social sciences. The debate continues as to whether that integration deepens understanding or is too broad for any depth of understanding. Some strategies in this book reflect substantial integration; others stand alone on their historical, geographical, or economic foundations. However, we have kept the purpose of social studies in mind as we explained these strategies.

The purpose of social studies education is the development of effective citizens of a democratic republic in an increasingly interdependent and diverse world (Barr, Barth, & Shermis, 1977; Engle & Ochoa, 1988; NCSS, 1994; Ochoa-Becker, 2007). Citizenship education generally includes a balance among knowledge, skills, and values or dispositions. As we considered what to include in this text, the balance stayed in the forefront of our thoughts. Many strategies in this text focus more on skill development—research skills, interpersonal skills, communication skills, democratic participation skills, and so on—rather than on specific content or values (see NCSS, 1994; National History Standards, 1996; and Sehr, 1997, for a discussion of skills). Our inclusion of content comes from the direct link to the NCSS curriculum strand and through the examples included. The values and dispositions are more implicit than explicit. They include values such as justice (e.g., how we live justly in our classroom) and individual rights (e.g., how we protect our rights as learners, as well as how we respect the rights of our classmates). In addition, these strategies reflect a record of research that examines the best practices in social studies, and on elementary and middle school education, and pertinent research from the social sciences and humanities disciplines. In addition, these strategies reflect a long practitioner base of classroom implementation across the country and over time. Students who engage in educational experiences that promote democratic citizenship development and encourage social understanding should be able to promote and uphold democracy as it changes and grows in the 21st century.

REFERENCES

Barr, R. D., Barth, J. L., & Shermis, S. S. (1977). *Defining the social studies (Bulletin 51).* Washington, DC: National Council for the Social Studies.

Engle, S. H., & Ochoa, A. (1988). *Education for democratic citizenship: Decision making in the social studies.* New York: Teachers College Press.

National Council for the Social Studies (NCSS). (1994). *Curriculum standards for social studies: Expectations of excellence (Bulletin 89).* Washington, DC: Author.

National Center for History in the Schools. (1996). *National standards for history.* Los Angeles: National Center for History in the Schools.

Ochoa-Becker, A. (2007). *Democratic education for social studies: An issues-centered decision making curriculum.* Greenwich, CT: Information Age Publishing.

Sehr, D. (1997). *Education for public democracy.* Albany, NY: State University of New York Press.

SUMMARY OF THE NATIONAL COUNCIL FOR THE SOCIAL STUDIES (NCSS) CURRICULUM STRANDS

THE TEN THEMES

Following are the 10 themes that form the framework of the social studies standards.

I Culture.   The study of culture prepares students to answer questions such as: What are the common characteristics of different cultures? How do belief systems, such as religion or political ideals, influence other parts of the culture? How does the culture change to accommodate different ideas and beliefs? What does language tell us about the culture? In schools, this theme typically appears in units and courses dealing with geography, history, sociology, and anthropology, as well as multicultural topics across the curriculum.

II Time, Continuity, and Change.   Human beings seek to understand their historical roots and to locate themselves in time. Knowing how to read and reconstruct the past allows one to develop a historical perspective and to answer questions such as: Who am I? What happened in the past? How am I connected to those in the past? How has the world changed and how might it change in the future? Why does our personal sense of relatedness to the past change? This theme typically appears in history courses and others that draw on historical knowledge and habits.

III People, Places, and Environments.   The study of people, places, and human environment interactions assists students as they create their spatial views and geographic perspectives of the world beyond their personal locations. Students need the knowledge, skills, and understanding to answer questions such as: Where are things located? Why are they located where they are? What do we mean by "region"? How do landforms change? What implications do these changes have for people? In schools, this theme typically appears in units and courses dealing with area studies and geography.

Source: National Council for the Social Studies. (1994). *Curriculum standards for social studies: Expectations of excellence (Bulletin 89)*. Washington, DC: Authors, pages x–xii reprinted by permission.

IV Individual Development and Identity. Personal identity is shaped by one's culture, by groups, and by institutional influences. Students should consider such questions as: How do people learn? Why do people behave as they do? What influences how people learn, perceive, and grow? How do people meet their basic needs in a variety of contexts? How do individuals develop from youth to adulthood? In schools, this theme typically appears in units and courses dealing with psychology and anthropology.

V Individuals, Groups, and Institutions. Institutions such as schools, churches, families, government agencies, and the courts play an integral role in people's lives. It is important that students learn how institutions are formed, what controls and influences them, how they influence individuals and culture, and how they are maintained or changed. Students may address questions such as: What is the role of institutions in this and other societies? How am I influenced by institutions? How do institutions change? What is my role in institutional change? In schools, this theme typically appears in units and courses dealing with sociology, anthropology, psychology, political science, and history.

VI Power, Authority, and Governance. Understanding the historical development of structures of power, authority, and governance and their evolving functions in contemporary U.S. society and other parts of the world is essential for developing civic competence. In exploring this theme, students confront questions such as: What is power? What forms does it take? Who holds it? How is it gained, used, and justified? What is legitimate authority? How are governments created, structured, maintained, and changed? How can individual rights be protected within the context of majority rule? In schools, this theme typically appears in units and courses dealing with government, politics, political science, history, law, and other social sciences.

VII Production, Distribution, and Consumption. Because people have wants that often exceed the resources available to them, a variety of ways have evolved to answer such questions as: What is to be produced? How is production to be organized? How are goods and services to be distributed? What is the most effective allocation of the factors of production (land, labor, capital, and management)? In schools, this theme typically appears in units and courses dealing with economic concepts and issues.

VIII Science, Technology, and Society. Modern life as we know it would be impossible without technology and the science that supports it. Technology brings with it many questions: Is new technology always better than old? What can we learn from the past about how new technologies result in broader social change, some of which is unanticipated? How can we cope with the ever-increasing pace of change? How can we manage technology so that the greatest number of people benefit from it? How can we preserve our fundamental values and beliefs in the midst of technological change? This theme draws upon the natural and physical sciences, social sciences, and the humanities and appears in a variety of social studies courses, including history, geography, economics, civics, and government.

IX Global Connections. The realities of global interdependence require understanding the increasingly important and diverse global connections among world societies and the frequent tension between national interests and global priorities. Students will need to be able to address such international issues as health care, the environment, human rights, economic competition and interdependence, age-old ethnic enmities, and political and military alliances. This theme typically appears in units or courses dealing with geography, culture, and economics, but it may also draw upon the natural and physical sciences and the humanities.

X Civic Ideals and Practices. An understanding of civic ideals and practices of citizenship is critical to full participation in society and is a central purpose of the social studies. Students confront such questions as: What is civic participation and how can I be involved? How has the meaning of citizenship evolved? What is the balance between rights and responsibilities? What is the role of the citizen in the local community, the nation, and the world at large? How can I make a positive difference? In schools, this theme typically appears in units or courses dealing with history, political science, cultural anthropology, and fields such as global studies, law-related education, and the humanities.

PART I

General Social Studies Instructional Strategies

There are eight broad strategies for social studies teaching and learning introduced in this first section of the book. All are reflective of John Dewey's ideas of experiential education and attend to the overarching goals of a social studies education, that is focused on providing students with the necessary knowledge, skills, and dispositions required of citizens in a democratic society. These strategies span grade levels and the separate academic disciplines that are a part of social studies. The first three strategies of community building, establishing a democratic classroom, and developing multiple perspectives are much more than individual strategies. Rather, they provide a process for creating a certain kind of social studies classroom where students are active participants in the classroom and where the democratic ideals of justice, diversity, rights, and responsibilities are valued. The strategies of concept development and attainment and questioning both provide the opportunity to promote abstract thinking in our students. And combined with the student-centered broad strategies of discovery learning and inquiry learning, they require higher-level thinking. Students have multiple opportunities in these four strategies to include their specific interests and questions. In addition, teachers have numerous opportunities to incorporate these four strategies in most social studies units. Finally, the strategy of primary sources is familiar to most social studies teachers who attend to history methodology, and it is an acknowledgment of the central role that history learning plays in many K–8 social studies classroom. Primary sources are evidence used by historians to interpret the past and are common in social studies materials at all levels. Taken together, these eight overarching strategies provide opportunities to gain knowledge (e.g., primary sources and inquiry learning), enhance skills (e.g., discovery learning, questioning, inquiry learning, and establishing a democratic classroom), and develop democratic dispositions (e.g., inquiry learning, developing multiple perspectives, establishing a democratic classroom, and community building).

1
Community Building

INTRODUCTION

A community is often thought of as a town or city; however, physical proximity is not an essential component; it can be a classroom, school, neighborhood, or a global community. In essence, communities are defined by the commitments of their members or citizens. Having a connection to others and being able to work cooperatively and productively for the betterment of all are requirements for public democratic participation. In a healthy classroom or school community, students and teachers respect each other, are able to work together, and are comfortable in disagreeing with one another. Unfortunately, by the time they enter school, very young students have already developed stereotypes that can be a barrier to developing positive relationships with others. While students are social beings, developing, nurturing, and maintaining a sense of community require skills unfamiliar to some students. As the United States becomes more diverse, our schools reflect this diversity in multiple ways (language, ethnicity, and exceptionality). It becomes even more important to create a classroom in which the individual and collective talents brought by students are recognized and appreciated.

This strategy introduces a process for building a sense of community in the classroom. It should be noted that community building is somewhat cyclical. Students may move back and forth between community-building phases as they tackle different classroom experiences or as they build different, smaller communities (e.g., through cooperative group work). Shaw (1992) identifies four main phases in community building: inclusion, influence, openness or trust, and community. It is helpful to split inclusion, the first phase, into two phases—introduction and inclusion. This allows for distinct attention to each of these important elements. Healthy communities rarely evolve through happenstance. Rather, healthy classroom communities develop through the learning experiences and instructional strategies designed by the teacher.

PROCEDURAL RECOMMENDATIONS

- Introductions are an important first step and should be done early in the school year. Find creative ways to help students first learn and use each other's names and then learn something about one another. This becomes even more important when all students have moved to a new school (e.g., from elementary to middle school). It is also important when there are just a few new faces within a sea of familiar ones.

- Inclusion addresses that feeling many have when entering a class or a party. Will they be like me? Will someone talk to me? Activities that nurture group spirit and help students better know the lives and experiences of their classmates are appropriate in this phase. Knowing classmates' names is a part of this, but additional work is required to get to know individuals and make them feel "included." The term *inclusion* is typically associated with special education and refers to the practice of including children with special needs in the general classroom. As described in this strategy, the term *inclusion* refers to the broader perspective. In this strategy, inclusion refers to the perspective of involving each student, including those with special needs, in the life of the classroom. This entails social and academic conversations and decisions.

- When students have influence, they believe that what they say is heard and respected by others. For example, when the class or a small group is making a decision, students who contribute to the conversation should believe that their opinions are heard and valued. This does not mean that each student should believe he or she will get his or her way in every decision, but rather that each voice is heard, respected, and considered. Using the decision-making grid (see Strategy 15) is one way to help students learn both individually and in groups how to make thoughtful decisions.

- The phase of openness/trust occurs almost simultaneously with influence. For a student to believe his or her opinion is valued, he or she must trust the group and feel comfortable in sharing expertise, opinions, and questions. This involves risk, particularly with middle grade students because of the emotional turmoil of early adolescence. Experiences in this phase include those that teach students concrete ways to acknowledge the contributions of others such as summarizing, eye contact, and other nonverbal reinforcement.

- Community is achieved when a group of students know one another, include one another, and consider and acknowledge one another.

APPLICATIONS AND IDEAS

In a middle school enrichment class on leadership, coauthor Kathryn Obenchain wanted her students to become acquainted. The students had come from different schools, and most had never met. One of the first activities Obenchain conducted was Leadership Bingo, a simple variation of the traditional bingo game in which students must approach one another and obtain signatures in order to cover all of the squares on the bingo sheet. Each person could sign another's bingo sheet only once. This was a small class, so only 9 squares were needed. A larger class might have 12 or 15 squares. On this bingo sheet, the squares included items or characteristics of democratic participation and leadership that the students would study over the next two weeks. Introducing these characteristics helped to begin academic conversations; it also got the students talking to one another by providing a topic for conversation. Figure 3.1 is a sample Leadership Bingo sheet that students could use to obtain the signatures of other students who can fulfill the requirements of the different squares.

A second example builds on introductions and promotes inclusion. Conducting school interviews, which is recommended at the beginning of a school year and particularly appropriate in a new school setting (e.g., as part of the transition to middle school), is one way to promote cooperation among students within the classroom as well as connections to the school community. Begin by taking a class inventory of particular talents that each student has, such as running audio or video equipment, keyboarding, easily approaching people, writing well, and so on. This inventory may be used for a number of projects throughout the year, with students adding to their own talents or suggesting talents of others.

Set the inventory aside, and hold a discussion about what students want to know about their school and the people who are there. This discussion will be different in every setting. What students want to know in a newly constructed school will be different from what new middle-school students

FIGURE 3.1 SAMPLE LEADERSHIP BINGO SHEET

LEADERSHIP BINGO: LEADERS FOR THE TWENTY-FIRST CENTURY

Name a historical figure who displayed courage. name _____	Find someone who says she/he is a good listener. name _____	Name a current public figure who is civil to those who believed differently. name _____
Find someone who believes he or she is a good compromiser. name _____	Name a leadership characteristic that the President of the United States displays. name _____	Find someone who can name a U.S. senator from his or her state. Give the state. name _____
Find someone who displays leadership in his or her school and tells you about it. name _____	Find someone who displays leadership in his or her community and tells you about it. name _____	Find someone who can name a person in his or her community who is a leader and can describe how that person leads. name _____

want to know. Once students have determined what they want to know, the class works to group the topics according to who in the school might know the answer. It is appropriate and advisable to approach more than one person for some topics. For example, if students want to know how to get involved in school clubs, they could approach different club sponsors as well as older students already in clubs. This phase serves the purpose of categorizing the topics while also determining whom the students wish to interview.

The next phase requires the teacher to put heterogeneous interview teams together, using the talent inventory to build diverse, multitalented teams. Each team (with five students maximum) is assigned one or two people to interview and cooperatively works to develop interview questions, decide on the interview format (audio, video, etc.), schedule and conduct the interviews, and synthesize the interview data. Each team then presents the results of its interview(s) to the entire class and/or other classrooms.

This activity could easily be modified for much younger children, still building on introductions and promoting inclusion. Young children could still interview one another, asking very basic questions about their new classroom or school community. Questions such as "What is your favorite thing to do at home? What is your favorite thing to do at school?" provide information for a teacher to facilitate the creation of a classroom list of talents and skills. As with the previous example, this can be used as springboard to a discussion of what the students want to know about the school and how some of their talents and skills could help find answers to their questions. If a few students report that their favorite thing to do is play soccer or another sport and if the students want to know what they will be doing in school in addition to their classroom work, the teacher can invite the physical education teacher to explain upcoming activities. In this instance, students get to know one another and another teacher.

ASSESSMENT

The goal of this strategy is to create and promote a classroom community. Academic assessment and evaluation of students for this strategy, and in particular the examples provided, is inappropriate for a few reasons. One, building community is an ongoing process that occurs throughout the school year. Two, while individual students can be evaluated on criteria such as "plays well with others," building a classroom community is a collective, not individual goal.

REFERENCES AND RESOURCES

Kieff, J. (2005). Let's talk about friendship: An anti-bias unit on building classroom community. *Childhood Education, 82*(2), 98–K.

Nicholas, S. N. (1997). Community building in the classroom: A process. *Journal of Humanistic Counseling, Education & Development, 35*(4), 198–298.

Nielsen, L. E., Finkelstein, J. M, Schmidt, A., & Duncan, A. (2008). Citizenship education: Engaging children in building community. *Social Studies and the Young Learner, 21*(1), 19–20, 22–23.

Obenchain, K. M., & Abernathy, T. V. (2003). 20 ways to . . . build community and empower students. *Intervention in School & Clinic, 39*(1), 55–60.

Rule, A. C., & Kyle, P. B. (2009). Community-building in a diverse setting. *Early Childhood Education Journal, 36*(4), 291–295.

Schniedewind, N., & Davidson, E. (2006). Open minds to equality. A sourcebook of learning activities to affirm diversity and promote equity. (3rd ed.). Milwaukee, WI: Rethinking Schools.

Shaw, V. (1992). *Community building in the classroom*. San Juan Capistrano, CA: Kagan

Cooperative Learning. This text more fully describes the phases or stages of community building. It also includes many instructional strategies to implement during each phase.

Web Sites

These Web sites contain classroom community-building activities and/or examples of successful community-building programs.

Youth Learn
http://www.youthlearn.org/learning/teaching/community.asp and
http://www.youthlearn.org/learning/teaching/climate.asp

PTA
http://www.pta.org/2219.htm

2

Establishing a Democratic Classroom

INTRODUCTION

Most elementary school classrooms contain a posted list of rules and policies that guide and govern activity in that classroom. One way to link the social studies curriculum to this list of rules and to develop student ownership of the rules and the classroom community is to include the students in the process of rule making. This is an opportunity to link the process of classroom rule making to the rights and responsibilities of citizens in a democratic society. Citizens and/or their representatives deliberate over important issues. The classroom version of this process addresses an essential role for schools and the primary responsibility of social studies—democratic citizenship education. Reflecting Dewey's philosophical belief that classrooms are embryonic communities or societies, classroom life should simulate life in the broader and adult community. From a learning perspective, students better understand and then commit to the rules when they participate in the process—they develop a deeper understanding as well as ownership of the process and outcome. When carried out early in the year, this process helps to build a sense of community (see Strategy 1) as students share with the teacher and one another their needs as learners. Rule making also serves as an informal assessment in citizenship education for the teacher, as he or she learns what civic knowledge, skills, and attitudes students are bringing into the classroom.

PROCEDURAL RECOMMENDATIONS

- Arrange for rule making to occur very early in the year, preferably the first week of school, to set the tone and parameters for class. Avoid telling students they will be "making the rules." This remark has the potential for subverting the process, and students often proceed straight to likes and dislikes from previous classroom rules. To avoid students jumping to the end, allow plenty of time over several days for everyone to invest in the process.
- Begin by leading a brainstorming session on what kind of classroom environment is necessary for you to teach and students to learn in the best way possible. Students may bring up issues related to the kind of setting in which they do their homework at home or the need to have

difficult things explained in more than one way. Perhaps they note that they like to be able to ask a classmate for help or that a quiet environment is helpful. Create a lengthy list, asking for the contributions of all students.

- After the initial brainstormed list, post the list somewhere in the classroom and encourage students to individually add to it over the course of a few days. This creates the opportunity for students to reflect on what does and does not help them learn as they participate in the regular classroom day.

- Referring to the brainstorm list, ask students, "What does a classroom that includes these characteristics look and sound like?" Facilitate a discussion about the physical and emotional space. This includes the behaviors, practices, and attitudes you and your students display. For example, if "quiet study time" is listed as a necessity for students to succeed, then a classroom in which classmates do not disturb others' study time is a desired goal.

- When this list is complete, ask students how they can ensure that these behaviors and attitudes are present. Through questioning, introduce the idea of setting some ground rules that will lead to a learning environment that will benefit everyone.

- Ask students to summarize, categorize, and convert the list of "needs" into rules. For example, "need to be heard when asking a question," "room shouldn't be too noisy when we're doing individual or group work," and "the teacher should be available to help us" could be synthesized into "Quietly raise your hand." This synthesis will take time, dialogue, and effective questioning.

- Encourage students to use positive statements in creating rules and to avoid "don't," "can't," and other prohibitions. As one fifth grader put it, "The rules tell us what we can do, not what we can't do. This way we know how we should behave."

- Develop no more than five to seven general rules. (This requires substantial synthesis of student comments.) It is easier for the teacher and students to remember fewer, yet meaningful, rules.

- Post the rules in clear view of the students. Beginning early in the year, consistently refer to the rules when students are behaving in ways that promote a quality learning environment.

- Another aspect to this is to be very clear with students about the consequences of violating the rules, and there should be consequences. For the teacher and students to invest so much time in the process, and then not honor the process, is disrespectful to those involved. The development and posting of consequences can also involve the students in much the same way as the creation of the rules.

APPLICATIONS AND IDEAS

Rule making in Mrs. Roush's class is an important annual ritual. A few years ago, during the first week of school, she asked her students to list what each of them individually needed from her and from their classmates in order to succeed in fifth grade. Mrs. Roush also included what she needed from the class in order to successfully teach all of them. With 22 students and 1 teacher contributing, this list became long. It included very specific items such as "I need a few minutes every morning to talk with my friends before I can concentrate on school" and general items such as "I need to be respected." Mrs. Roush then asked students to describe what a classroom would be like if all of these needs were met. She asked them to think about the physical arrangement of teacher's and students' desks and student actions and activities, such as how they treat people and property as well as the noise level in the classroom. Students created a narrative of what a great day in their classroom would be like. They wrote about where they would sit, when and to whom they would talk, how they would do their work, how Mrs. Roush would teach, and what they would do to help one another learn.

With the list and narrative complete, Mrs. Roush linked the process they had just gone through with democratic citizenship and the rights and responsibilities of citizens. She asked them to compare their classroom to a city or country. She also introduced the democratic values of individual rights and the common good, noting that every community must find a balance between protecting each individual and promoting the good of the whole. She brought up a few issues from the student list. One person said she studied best with her favorite music playing. Several other students, however, said they needed a fairly quiet place to study. Mrs. Roush asked the students to think about how they would protect the rights of all when wishes or needs of individuals were different.

From this conversation, Mrs. Roush and her students developed a list of positively stated rules. It was quite a challenge to combine the many specific wishes and needs of students into a general list that each student understood. Their list of rules follows:

1. Show respect for others and for yourself.
2. Be helpful.
3. Take care of our community.
4. Be prepared for class.
5. Behave appropriately in class.
6. Listen, follow directions, and do your best.

Once the list was complete, the class reviewed it several times; Mrs. Roush also encouraged students to provide concrete examples of each rule. Behaviors related to the third rule include picking up trash from the floor; not writing on desks; treating games, books, and school equipment respectfully; and making sure the water faucet is shut tightly to conserve water. As a result of the time Mrs. Roush took to create classroom rules and the meaningful involvement of the students, the rules became a part of her classroom culture. Mrs. Roush and the students gently reminded one another when they were not living up to the rules. Comments such as "Please respect my right to study," "I'm doing my best and that is what I'm supposed to do," and "Can I offer you some help?" were made frequently and with great courtesy.

ASSESSMENT

There are many ways to assess the knowledge and skills associated with democratic citizenship. A traditional multiple-choice examination can assess specific knowledge. A performance checklist used at various times throughout the day or week can assess students' use of democratic citizenship skills (e.g., negotiation, mediation, deliberation). However, assessing individuals in the process of establishing a democratic classroom through the strategy described above would be difficult to do, as this is a collective process. The assessment is the set of rules; the evaluation is the usefulness and appropriateness of the rules.

REFERENCES AND RESOURCES

Bicard, D. F. (2000). Using classroom rules to construct behavior. *Middle School Journal, 31*(5), 37–45.

Dewey, J. (1916/1944). Democracy and education. New York: Free Press.

Horsch, P., Chen, J., & Nelson, D. (1999). Rules and rituals: Tools for creating a respectful, caring learning community. *Phi Delta Kappan, 81*(3), 223–227.

Miller, S. A. (2001). Tips for creating classroom rules. *Scholastic Early Childhood Today, 15*(6), 8.

Rightmyer, E. C. (2003). Democratic discipline: Children creating solutions. *Young Children, 58*(4), 38–45.

Rosen, L. (1999). Civic education in the elementary school. *Streamlined Seminar, 18*(2), 1–4.

Schimmel, D. (1997). Traditional rule-making and the subversion of citizenship education. *Social Education, 61*(2), 70–74.

Thornberg, R. (2008). "It's not fair!"-Voicing pupils' criticisms of school rules. *Children & Society, 22*(6), 418–428.

Web Sites

Education World is a Web site offering a variety of classroom ideas. The link below accesses one article about the creation of classroom rules in collaboration with students.
http://www.educationworld.com/a_lesson/lesson/lesson274.shtml

Read.Write.Think. is a joint project of the International Reading Association and the National Council for the Teachers of English. The link below accesses one specific lesson plan that utilizes children's literature in the process of classroom rule making.
http://www.readwritethink.org/lessons/lesson_view.asp?id=991

3

Developing Multiple Perspectives

INTRODUCTION

Social studies is the study of human beings throughout time and around the world (see http://www.socialstudies.org/standards/introduction for a complete discussion of the definition of social studies). It is the study of what they believe, how they feel, and what they do. As adults, it is obvious that people believe, feel and do things differently. It is not so obvious for our elementary and middle school students. Their worlds are often defined by what they see and how they see it. If a perspective is introduced that is not a part of their experience or prior learning, they may dismiss it as wrong or as not real. The ability to recognize the existence of multiple or diverse perspectives, as well as the ability to develop multiple perspectives, is an essential component of social studies in a democracy. Democratic societies are diverse in many ways, and diversity is a strength and essential component of a strong, multicultural democracy (Marri, 2003; Parker, 1996). Diversity includes racial, ethnic, gender, and religious diversity. It also includes diversity of opinion. In other words, different people, who have studied and thought a great deal about an issue, may believe very differently about that issue. They believe differently for numerous reasons. Perhaps their prior life experiences have differed, they have examined different evidence, and/or they value different things. The last three U.S. presidential elections illustrate that different Americans view the same situations or issues (e.g., the economy, stem cell research) from very different perspectives; and they make decisions based on those differing perspectives. It is essential for students to develop an awareness of, and respect for, the right of others to have diverse opinions. Students may not agree with those diverse opinions, but it is important to know that they exist.

PROCEDURAL RECOMMENDATIONS

- Developing multiple perspectives in a lesson does not follow a lock-step procedure. Rather, it is a conscious decision by the teacher to teach students the existence of multiple or diverse perspectives as well as how to develop multiple perspectives. The list below includes important points for the teacher to consider.
- Determine the objective for the lesson. It may be to develop an awareness of multiple perspectives or the ability to construct multiple perspectives. In an extended lesson, it could be both. In most instances, the examination of, or development of, multiple perspectives will be situated within some other social studies content. A lesson on Revolutionary America that includes the perspectives of Loyalists' and Patriots' views of independence and war (for example, see Scheurman, 1998), a pen pal exchange with students from another state or

10

nation in which ideas about the environment are explored and compared, or even a classroom vote on which book to read next provides an opportunity for the teacher to explicitly address multiple perspectives.

- A key component is to make the awareness of, or development of, multiple perspectives an explicit objective. Being explicit is a reminder to the teacher to introduce and reinforce the ideas and associated vocabulary.
- For younger students, choose something concrete that they can personally experience, such as the example found below in Applications and Ideas. Older students, too, can benefit from a personal experience but will also be able to explore multiple perspectives in a more abstract manner.
- Be cautious that students do not see this as approval for an anything-goes attitude. Not all opinions are weighted equally. Informed opinions, diverse informed opinions, are given more weight than uninformed opinions, whether they are the same or diverse.
- This leads to the need to reinforce the need for resources and evidence to support opinions.

APPLICATIONS AND IDEAS

For young students, multiple or diverse perspectives may be introduced with a mapping activity. Typically, maps are seen from a bird's-eye view. That is, the kinds of maps that students often use are as if we were above the setting. We look down onto the landscape and see the tops of buildings, trees, bodies of water, or whatever other setting the map represents. Young students can experience this by standing on a chair and looking down at the items on their desk or by standing up and looking down at various items on the floor.

One group of second graders began exploring multiple perspectives by arranging a variety of common school items on their desks, including books, paper, crayons, markers, a juice box, and a ruler. Working with a partner, one student acted as a spotter for the second student, who stood on the chair with a pencil, paper, and clipboard. The paper had the cardinal directions and the outline of the desk on it. The students standing on the chairs looked down onto the desk and sketched the items onto the paper. All of the items had well-defined edges, so they were relatively easy to sketch and put in the correct position. Once the items were sketched, each pair of students reviewed the items to make sure all of the items were accounted for and were on the map. The students were reminded that they were to only draw what they could see from where they stood. For example, a juice box looks like a small rectangle when observed from above. From the bird's-eye position, the student cannot see the name of the juice box because it is not on the top. Once each pair of students was satisfied with their work, they got a new piece of paper. The student who served as the spotter for the first map drew the second perspective. However, instead of drawing from a bird's-eye view, this student got on her knees, so that her eyes were level with the desk and the entire width of the desk was observable, and began to sketch only what was observable from this very different perspective. Once this student finished her sketch, the pair of students reviewed it for completeness, with another reminder that the sketch should contain only what was observable from where the student doing the sketch was kneeling or squatting. In this sketch, the juice box looks completely different from the prior map and is partially obscured by a book that is lying on the desk in front of it. Each pair of students was then asked to compare their sketches for similarities and differences. During class discussion, different students pointed out that each pair drew a representation of what was on the same desk and that nothing on the desk was moved, removed, or added. They also pointed out that even though the same things were on the desk, their sketches did not always show the same items. The bird's-eye view map showed everything that was visible from above but missed items that were under other items. One group pointed out that when two books of the same size were stacked on top of each another, the student drawing from the bird's-eye view observed only one book. Yet when the second student drew from a kneeling position, she was able to see the spines of both books. A second group pointed out the different views of the juice box. Throughout the discussion, the teacher used the terms *perspective* and *different views* to familiarize students with vocabulary. This was just an opening activity; in a future lesson, students explored different perspectives by looking at how characters in a story viewed the same event differently.

Older students go into much more depth with multiple perspectives. For example, when studying a historical event, students examine different primary and secondary sources in order to see how the same event was viewed differently. When studying current events, older students may compare how different media sources report the same event. This examination, while reinforcing multiple perspectives, also reinforces the need to be aware of, and to critically question, the perspective of all media sources.

ASSESSMENT

The assessment of students' abilities to discern among multiple perspectives and their ability to develop multiple perspectives may be assessed through a variety of tasks and evaluated through different types of scoring guides. An analytical scoring rubric, such as the one in Strategy 38, or a performance checklist, such as the one in Strategy 28, would work. Of course, either option would need to be modified for the specific task and specific goals.

REFERENCES AND RESOURCES

Burstein, J. H., & Hutton, L. (2005). Planning and teaching with multiple perspectives. *Social Studies and the Young Learner, 18*(1),15–17.

Epstein, T., & Shiller, J. (2005). Perspective matters: Social identity and the teaching and learning of national history. *Social Education, 69*(4), 201–204.

Fournier, J. E., & Wineburg, S. S. (1997). Picturing the past: Gender differences in the depiction of historical figures. *American Journal of Education, 105*(2), 160–185.

Henning, M. B., Snow-Gerono, J. L., Reed, D., et al. (2006). Listening to children think critically about Christopher Columbus. *Social Studies and the Young Learner, 19*(2), 19–22

Jetty, M.(2006). History through red eyes: A conversation with James Loewen. *Phi Delta Kappan, 88*(3), 218–222.

Levstik, L., & Barton, K. C. (200X). *Doing history: Investigating with children in elementary and middle schools* (2nd ed.). Mahwah, NJ: Erlbaum.

Marri, A. (2003). Multicultural democracy: Toward a better democracy. *Intercultural Education, 14*(3), 263–277.

McCormick, T. M. (2008). Fear, panic, and injustice: Executive Order 9066—A lesson for grades 4–6. *Social Education, 72*(5), 268–271.

Parker, W. C. (1996). "Advanced" ideas about democracy: Toward a pluralist conception of citizen education. *Teachers College Record, 98*(1), 104–125.

Scheurman, G. (1998). Revisiting Lexington Green. *Social Education, 62*(1), 10–18

Web Sites

The official site of the Colonial Williamsburg Foundation
(**http://www.history.org/history/teaching/enewsletter/volume2/february04/teachstrategy.cfm**)

details the storytelling teaching strategy and notes that storytelling is one way to incorporate multiple perspectives into the social studies curriculum.

The National Council for the Social Studies (NCSS) Web site has made a 2002 article, entitled "World Religions and Personal Tolerance" available to all at **http://downloads.ncss.org/lessons/worldreligions.pdf.**

The article provides a middle school example for exploring and developing multiple perspectives.

4

Concepts: Development and Attainment

INTRODUCTION

One key in moving social studies learning from the memorization of disconnected names, dates, and facts to a meaningful understanding of important issues in the human experience is to organize social studies around concepts. Concepts are typically single words, like *democracy, interdependence, justice, power, pioneer, movement, change,* and *map.* These words all describe a larger category of meaning. Concepts are typically very easy for students to find examples of; however, they are much more difficult to define because of their abstractness. For example, many of our students can provide concrete examples of what is fair or just, but they are not always able to define and understand fairness or justice in its abstract form or to be able to apply the concepts across multiple situations and academic disciplines. Consider the concept of movement, important in the study of geography as the movement of ideas, people, and goods are examined. But movement is also used to describe work toward change in social and political settings, like the Women's Rights Movement. Movement on a political issue is described as a change in position. These varied examples utilize the concept and conceptual definition of movement.

Although the theoretical work on concept development and concept attainment in social studies is over 40 years old, Hilda Taba's (1967) work is seminal. Concept development is an inductive approach in which the concept is not initially named. Rather, through a facilitated process students identify characteristics of something concrete they have observed or experienced, group similar characteristics together, and then create a descriptive name. Concept attainment, on the other hand, is a deductive approach. Students are given the name of the concept and then examine a variety of examples and nonexamples of the concept in order to better understand the nuances of the concept. Lessons utilizing both the concept development and concept attainment models assist in student understanding.

PROCEDURAL RECOMMENDATIONS

- Determine what social studies concepts are to be developed and examined and for what purpose. In making this decision, consider the age and experience of your students as well as the social studies curriculum for their particular grade level. Knowing the students' developmental levels and their background experience will guide your selection of materials. Recall that the traditional social studies curriculum works on the expanding horizons model, as earlier grades focus on more local and current issues. As students progress, their social studies horizon broadens to include issues more distant in both time and location. Also consider whether the concepts will be developed for one particular unit of study in social studies or will provide a framework for the entire year's curriculum. For broad-based social

14

studies concepts, consider using the National Council for the Social Studies (1994) curriculum strands, which are conceptual. For example, strand VI, Power, Authority, and Governance, is comprised of the three concepts of power, authority, and governance. In the example provided below, the teacher, Mrs. Roush, used *CIVITAS*, published by the Center for Civic Education (1991). The *CIVITAS* text describes what it means to be a citizen in a democratic republic such as the United States. *CIVITAS* examines such concepts as patriotism, individual rights, the common good, diversity, truth, justice, and equality. It also includes the historical and philosophical foundations of citizenship in such a society as well as a description of basic ideals or concepts.

- The use of this text also provides some foundational knowledge for Mrs. Roush. For your own classroom, once you have chosen the concepts, identify resources that will assist you in examining your own understanding of the concept to check for your own conceptual understanding as well as any misconceptions.

- Consider all of the resources available to students in their study. If they are to look for historical examples, they should examine historical documents, including primary sources. If they are to find more recent examples, newspaper and television archives—accessed through the Internet—will be helpful. If they are looking for current examples, resources are limitless. To meet the needs and match the abilities of a variety of learners, consider multiple kinds of text, including photographs, posters, and audio and video recordings in addition to the more traditional language-based text resources. Choose a wide variety of language-based text resources, addressing the varied reading levels of students in the classroom.

- The steps below describe a traditional concept development lesson. The classroom example describes a concept attainment lesson.

- Begin with a whole-group introduction to the concept under study. Typically, concept lessons explore one concept at a time. The introduction can be a simple brainstorm, beginning with the prompt of "Tell me everything that comes to mind when you hear the word [i.e., the concept] patriotism." Record all of this information on the board or on chart paper so that students have easy access to the information. This step is often called *List*.

- Place students in groups of four or five.

- Ask each group to copy the results of the brainstorming session and categorize or group all of the similar items from the brainstorm. The number of categories and how the categories are created are the decision of each small group of students. This step is often called *Group*.

- Once each group finishes categorizing all of their terms, ask them to create a name for each category. For example, the patriotism group may have the categories of "symbols" and "individual actions." Every item from the brainstorm should fit into a category, and no category should be labeled "miscellaneous." This step is often called *Label*.

- Introduce additional information to each group. This information should expand and challenge students' understanding of the concept under study—for example, a newspaper story about an individual who violates the law because it is unjust (e.g., persons who supported the Underground Railroad, helping enslaved persons escape to the North). The materials should encourage in-depth reading and discussion of the information under examination. Detail the resources and reference materials available for group use. Make all of the resources available to students so that time is spent in discussion rather than searching for materials. It is appropriate for students to continue their search in a focused manner, but provide enough materials for students to develop that focus. Depending on your objectives, each group can be given all of the same materials to examine, some of the same and some different materials, or each group may have its own unique set of materials.

- After the discussion of the new material, have each group return to its list of categories and examples under each category. Should additional categories and/or information be added? Should the name of the category (i.e., the label) be changed? The groups should make adjustments as needed.

- There is an additional option at this stage. Bring the entire class back together to revisit the original brainstorm. Allow each group to suggest new words or terms that they believe are appropriate based on their examination of evidence. Once this is done, the small groups can decide how much of the new whole-group information to incorporate into their own categories.

- Have the groups review the categories and determine which ones are essential to the concept or ideal and which ones are not essential. That is, patriotism includes all of these categories (essential); patriotism may include these categories (nonessential). For example, justice includes fairness (essential), but justice does not always mean treating people exactly the same (nonessential).

- The groups take the terms that are essential to the concepts under study and write a definition of the concept using those terms.

- The groups then reexamine their materials to determine if their definitions are comprehensive but not overly broad. This is an appropriate time for students to compare their definition to the definitions written by other experts.

- Finally, the groups share and compare the results of their learning to those of their classmates. This may be done in a variety of ways—oral (e.g., reports, songs), visual (e.g., posters), or electronic (e.g., PowerPoint). The following example details one way for students to present their work.

APPLICATIONS AND IDEAS

In Mrs. Roush's fifth-grade classroom, students are introduced early in the school year to several core democratic ideals; these ideals are also concepts. These include patriotism, justice, truth, diversity, and individual rights, among others. These ideals are taught as foundations for strong and active democratic citizenship. Because these ideals anchor the fifth-grade curriculum, Mrs. Roush wanted to make sure that her students were familiar with the concepts and were comfortable examining different types of information that illustrate each. In an earlier concept attainment lesson (Taba, Durkin, Fraenkel, & McNaughton, 1971), Mrs. Roush introduced the terms, defined the selected democratic ideals (concepts), and examined examples and nonexamples. Students made posters with definitions, synonyms, and antonyms of the ideals.

Because students' exposure to these abstract ideals had been limited and Mrs. Roush wanted these ideals to frame her curriculum, she developed another concept attainment lesson to help students build on their prior experiences with these abstract ideals through additional concrete examples. She placed students in small groups and gave each group a large sheet of poster board. She assigned to each group one of the democratic ideals under study, directing the students to define the democratic ideal. Students then examined a local newspaper to find three national and three local examples of their democratic ideal in practice. In addition, students identified and detailed three examples of the democratic ideal occurring in their classroom. Students displayed all of the information they gathered on the poster.

One group examined the democratic ideal of truth. A student selected a lost-and-found advertisement describing a "found" puppy. She explained to her group that this was an example of truth because the person who found the puppy could have just kept it. Instead, the person was being truthful about ownership by placing an advertisement and searching for the real owner.

This process was typical of each of the small groups. Students proposed articles or classroom examples, the groups discussed and evaluated each item, and they eventually settled on the items for the posters. Each group presented its poster to the rest of the class. Mrs. Roush and other students asked questions about each group's choices. They also compared interpretations when two groups chose the same newspaper article as an example of two different democratic ideals; for example, one group selected a celebrity's disclosure about a serious illness as an example of the celebrity's truthfulness about a private matter, while a second group used the same article to illustrate the ideal of the common good. The second group's rationale was that, by disclosing and talking about illness, the celebrity was helping people by making them aware of the disease and the need for additional medical research related to it.

ASSESSMENT

A simple performance checklist can assess students' understanding of the example above. The teacher can observe students at work in their groups, as they present to the entire class, and with some oral questioning to determine students' understanding.

Criteria	Observed (y/n)	Notes related to specific evidence provided of understanding/misunderstanding
Concept is defined including the criterial attributes/essential elements		
National examples of the concept are provided & explained		
Local examples of the concept are provided & explained		
Classroom examples of the concept are provided & explained		
Nonexamples of the concept are identified and evaluated during questioning		

REFERENCES AND RESOURCES

Beck, T. A. (2008). Behind the mask: Social studies concepts and English language learners. *Social Education, 72*(4), 181–184.

Bisland, B. M. (2005). Walls, towers, and sphinxes: Multicultural concept construction and group inquiry. *Social Studies and the Young Learner, 17*(4), 8–12.

Cannon, M. W. (2002). Concepts and themes: A learning odyssey. *Gifted Child Today, 25*(3), 24–29.

Center for Civic Education. (1991). *CIVITAS.* Calabasas, CA: Author. This text may be difficult for some students to read. However, it is an excellent teacher resource.

Endacott, J. (2005). It's not all ancient history now: Connecting the past by weaving a threaded historical concept. *Social Studies, 96*(5), 227–231.

Fraenkel, J. R. (1992). Hilda Taba's contributions to social studies education. *Social Education, 56*(3), 172–78.

Laney, J. D. (1999). A sample lesson in economics for primary students: How cooperative and mastery learning methods can enhance social studies teaching. *Social Studies, 90*(4), 152–158.

National Council for the Social Studies. (1994). *Expectations of excellence: Curriculum standards for social studies.* Washington, DC: Author.

Parker, W. C. (2008). *Social studies in elementary education* (12th ed.). Upper Saddle River, NJ: Pearson.

Taba, H. (1967). *Teacher's handbook for elementary social studies.* New York: Addison-Wesley.

Taba, H., Durkin, M. C., Fraenkel, F. R., & McNaughton, A. H. (1971). *A teacher's handbook to elementary social studies: An inductive approach* (2nd ed.). Reading, MA: Addison-Wesley. This foundational text addresses concept development and concept attainment models.

Web Sites

The following article available from the National Association for the Education of Young Children addresses teaching concepts to younger children:
http://journal.naeyc.org/btj/200509/mindes.asp

To assist with using the specific example provided in the Applications and Ideas section, students can search for concrete examples of citizenship in resources other than local newspapers or local newscasts. With teacher facilitation, students could consult web sites of both print and visual media sources, including major news organizations and YouTube.

Discovery Learning

INTRODUCTION

Discovery learning occurs when the teacher structures a classroom experience to help the students find answers through problem solving. The teacher is knowledgeable about a person designated by the state standards for this grade. Rather than giving students information in text or lecture format, the teacher allows students to discover the importance of the person through research, analysis, and interpretation. Students use the methods of the social science disciplines to determine the answers to the questions they pursue. Teachers ask students to act as historians by determining the perspective and bias of the writers of their sources. For example, students use teacher-made files of primary sources pertaining to the life of a local figure to create a biography of the figure for later use in another project. Older students can create their own collection of primary source information, while younger students can examine picture packets to determine particulars about their figure.

PROCEDURAL RECOMMENDATIONS

- Find a collection of the papers of the group or an individual being studied. Many universities and historical societies produce documentary editions of papers; most libraries also house them. The content and type of these papers vary. Typically, they include personal and professional correspondence, wills, business records, and public documents related to the person's life.

- Scan the index to find topics that relate to the objectives of future classroom study.

- Copy the relevant papers and chronologically put these in file folders for students to search. Libraries will have papers filed in this manner, and students need to get used to accessing information using this type of filing system. Give each student a copy of all the documents used. Librarians have converted a substantial amount of archival documents to electronic format. Teachers make hard copies of the relevant documents or save them on to computer files depending on classroom needs.

- When the primary sources are prepared, the teacher poses problems for students to explore. These problems or issues should link with social studies concepts or themes; encourage each student to choose a different problem to research based on the documents copied. The students are not to search all the papers of the person as they would in a library, but they do need to search through many topics to address their assigned person or group.

- While reminding students to focus on their chosen problem or issue, direct them to review the files to determine what they think the position of the person or group was on the specific issue under study. Students must cite information that they find in the documents as evidence.

- While the students work, ask them how they found their information and if there are ways they could find additional information. Also make sure they have found evidence to document their statements.

APPLICATIONS AND IDEAS

Elementary students use photocopies of World War II ration cards to create tickets for a series of transactions. For example, students use the ration cards when they make a purchase at the class store. To encourage problem solving, the teacher asks, "How should rationing cards be apportioned?" Students discuss who, if anyone, should be allowed more gas rationing stamps. In a related activity, students examine pictures from World War II to find other ways the war changed lifestyles. Students tell what they learned about life during the war from the pictures; they also describe shopping at that time and how it differs from shopping today. Students respond to questions about why we do not have rationing now, issues of war and peace today, and how modern nations can preserve peace.

Elementary students use the documents of Lewis Von Schweinitz (1927) to learn about his trip to visit pioneers. They design a mural of his trip using the descriptions of what he saw: trees, dense forests, and the smoke caused by burning the forest to clear the land for farming. The teacher helps students find other travel accounts from this time in history, and students check to see if any of the accounts mentioned clearing the land. They then present their mural to the class, showing the land at the time Lewis came and wrote about it. Students also are encouraged to respond to questions about how it would be possible to remove such large trees.

To study race relations, elementary-grade students use the documents of English members of the Society of Friends who came to the United States to do abolitionist missionary work. Students develop a T-chart titled "The State of Race Relations in 1853," labeling one side "Positive Characteristics" and the other side "Negative Characteristics." While students read the members' letters, they record evidence in the appropriate column. As the students work, the teacher asks them which pieces of evidence are informal or societal conventions and which are formal or institutionalized. The teacher also helps students find a copy of their state constitution, histories of race relations in their state, and journal articles and recent news clippings on the topic. Students then present an overhead transparency displaying their completed T-chart. Students also discuss present race relationships, why the U.S. Constitution changed, how the state constitution changed, whether prejudice was first formal or informal, and who works to stop racism.

Students use the documents of the Harmony Society to determine both how the Harmonist community members traded and how they supported themselves. Students create a research paper on this topic, using primary source material in an appropriate citation style. While the students work with these documents, the teacher asks them what role the community representative played for the members of the Harmony Society and how this role was different from their role of operating their store in town. After reading primary source materials and writing a first draft of their papers, students examine secondary sources about the life of the followers of George Rapp in the town of New Harmony, Indiana. Next, they read sections of their paper to the class. In large or small groups, students discuss how each member of the Harmony Society had enough provisions for the year, how everyone remained equal, and how the neighbor viewed the members of the Harmony Society.

ASSESSMENT

Abstract

Students determine the merits and draw backs of living in an intentional community. In the course of their study they question economic and social concepts such as community, scarcity, and need. They examine primary sources and prepare a presentation for the PTA that illustrates the advantages and concerns.

Prompt

The students use 15 documents photocopied from the typeset and translated papers of the Harmony Society. The students group the materials into ideas that they like about the society and things they dislike about the society. Next they put together arguments as to whether or not they would like to live in such a society. Finally, they must argue that people should accept or reject life in the Harmony Society and why. By the end of the first day make a list of reasons to join or not join. By the end of the second day make a list of reasons for citations that illustrate the good and bad points of the group. By the end of the third day make an argument to convince the audience members to join or not join the Harmony Society.

Directions

You will have the next three class periods to work on the following task before presenting it as part of the PTA meeting next week. You may work with your group of four at your cluster of desks or around the room. You will have access to a packet of photocopies, the internet, and books about communal societies and 1800–1850 in America from the library. Your group will come up with a list of ideas of ideas you like or dislike about the Harmony Society. Cite quotations from the primary sources to support your reasons. Then you will convert these ideas and reasons into a presentation that you and a partner can share with the PTA. You will want to cite examples from the primary source to illustrate your reasons and try to convince your audience that your position is correct. Look at the scoring rubric to determine if you have accomplished your task.

Procedure

The teacher will prepare by copying the rubric and the primary sources to distribute to students. The teacher will find appropriate web sites and books for the students about communal societies and 1800–1850 America. The teacher will go from group to group to listen to the students reasons and see the evidence they have found for why they would or would not like to live with members of the Harmony Society. At the end of the first day the teacher asks the students for a list of reasons to join or not join. At the end of the second day the teacher asks the students for a list of reasons for citations that illustrate the good and bad points of the group. At the end of the third day the teacher asks the students to convince the teacher to join or not join the Harmony Society.

Scoring Rubric

Benchmarks	1 Point	2 Points	3 Points	4 Points
V. Individuals, Groups, and Institutions	Students can list good and bad points about the Harmony Society	Students list one good and one bad point about the Harmony Society.	Students list at least two good and two bad points about the Harmony Society.	Students list at least two good and two bad points about the Harmony Society.
g. show how groups and institutions work to meet individual need and promote the common good, and identify example of where they fail to do so.	Students select quotations that support both good and bad points	Students select one quotation that supports each point that they make.	Students select at least two quotations that support each point that they make.	Students select at least two quotations that support each point that they make. Students use this information to make a persuasive presentation for one side or the other.

REFERENCES AND RESOURCES

A friendly mission: John Candler's letters from America 1853–1854 (Vol. 16, No. 1). Indianapolis, IN: Indiana Historical Society.

Arndt, K. J. R. (Ed.). (1975–1978). *Indiana decade of the Harmony Society 1814–1824* (Vols. 1–2). Indianapolis, IN: Indiana Historical Society.

Mealor, W. T., Jr., & Giannangelo, D. (2001). Geographic profiles: A technique for teaching spatial relationships. *Southern Social Studies Journal, 27* (1), 64–81.

Pope, M. (2000). The art of discovery. *Science Scope, 24* (3), 46–47.

Von Schweinitz, L. D. (1927). *The journey of Lewis David Von Schweinitz to Goshen, Bartholomew County in 1831* (A. Gerber, Trans., Vol. 8, No. 5). Indianapolis, IN: Indiana Historical Society.

Web Sites

Do History
http://www.dohistory.org

Jackdaws
http://www.jackdaw.com

Library of Congress
http://www.lcweb.loc.gov

The National Archives and Records Administration
http://www.archives.gov/education

University of Idaho
http://www.uiweb.uidaho.edu/special-collections/Other.Repositories.html

6

Inquiry Learning

INTRODUCTION

Inquiry projects are those learning experiences in which neither the teacher nor the students know how the learning activity will end or what answers they will find. Inquiry projects, in which the students select the topics to be studied, remain distinct from discovery projects, where the teacher selects the topics to be studied and has specific or correct answers targeted. Students examine issues or content of their choosing; often the questions that drive students to choose a particular issue contain some element of controversy. This strategy engages and excites students because they answer questions of their own design and selection. Inquiry empowers students to direct their own learning; they work with their teacher to develop academically rigorous projects that promote ownership of their social studies education.

PROCEDURAL RECOMMENDATIONS

- *Inquiry Steps:* There are several steps in the inquiry process, including raising doubt/concern, identifying the problem, formulating hypotheses, collecting data, evaluating and analyzing data, testing hypotheses, and beginning inquiry anew.

- *Raising Doubt/Concern:* Students have one or more experiences that provide information, create a dilemma, or stimulate a concern for them. Students raise an issue; it may be generated by an event or an observation about current news or society. Inquiry projects can be of a historical or a current nature. Teachers make inquiry applicable to their grade level by knowing their state standards and assessments and then designing field trips, inviting guest speakers, and creating other powerful experiences that capture the excitement of their students.

- *Identifying the Problem:* Students identify a problem based on their experience and state the problem. It must be precise and definable. Students formulate a question to be answered through further inquiry. Students come to their own conclusions about who discovered the New World or examine sources to decide whether conflict between Europeans and indigenous people was inevitable.

- *Formulating Hypotheses:* Students speculate as to why the problem exists. They determine questions based on this information that are of interest to them. With teacher facilitation, each student or group of students generates a guiding question for their exploration of the information, issue, or dilemma. It is important for students to determine a guiding question because it helps them focus their inquiry on a particular topic. After students become interested in a topic and determine what they want to explore and how they want to do it, they establish a guiding question to help themselves focus and to set limits to keep the project from getting so large that it is unmanageable. To differentiate instruction for younger students, look for illustrations, photographs, diagrams, drawings, tables, graphs, and charts they can use in exploring the beginning of the American Revolution. Older students use primary source documents to determine their own conclusions concerning who fired the first shots at Lexington.

- *Collecting Data:* Students identify sources and methods of gathering data such as interviews, surveys, document study, or news reports. Once there is agreement with regard to the questions generated, the students and the teacher search, access, and examine the necessary resources. Students use as many primary sources as possible, moving beyond traditional text resources. Information in inquiry projects comes from public and private records, interviews, surveys, news sources, field examinations, and a multitude of other sources. It is important to use a variety of resources. To make the collection of data manageable, the teacher collects the data and has it available in differential sets. Students with limited English or limited reading ability have one set of data that allows them easier access to information but still allows them the ability to participate and think deeply about the questions.

- *Evaluating and Analyzing Data:* Students analyze, synthesize, and evaluate all data before proposing any potential solutions. Students working on group inquiry projects must share decision making with their peers; decision trees can assist with both group and individual decision making. Teachers streamline this by having photocopies of blank decision trees in which students fill in the blanks (see Strategy 15).

- *Testing Hypotheses:* Students reflect on their findings and arrive at a meaningful product or answer that they share with a real audience. The product includes their initial guiding questions, the results of their research, and their proposed solutions. In creating a history of their school, younger students conduct oral history interviews of school personnel and create a book of quotations from the interviews while older students write a school history by looking at primary sources.

- *Beginning Inquiry Anew:* Students identify new questions and issues arising from their findings.

APPLICATIONS AND IDEAS

One group of students became interested in the gristmills located around their state after viewing a PowerPoint program produced by a state historical organization. The students voiced their interest in comments about the mills that they knew about or had visited; they asked many questions about how the mills worked. The teacher arranged a visit to a nearby mill during which students took photographs and interviewed the mill's fourth-generation owner. They learned details of the mill's original construction and discovered how it operated. During the interview, students learned how a small community had grown up around the mill and then vanished. After speaking to the mill owner about restoration, the students contacted the Department of Natural Resources, learned how the state regulates dams and obstructions on rivers and streams, and learned what was needed to restore the mill to working order. Students returned to the classroom, where they wrote articles about the past, present, and future of the mill. They used Microsoft Publisher templates to set up their articles and create captions for their photographs. They illustrated their articles with their photographs and created a PowerPoint presentation with scripted narration so they could speak to groups about the past, the present, and the future of the mill.

ASSESSMENT

- In a unit about Southern antebellum life, students look at photos of free Blacks. They look at plantation maps to determine spaces where enslaved persons lived and worked. Students might ask for more information about the enslaved people.

- Based on the experience of the students and their desire to learn more about enslaved persons, students ask what it was like to be enslaved, ask how it would feel, and wonder what it would be like to actually hear a former enslaved person speak.

- The following question might provide guidance for the students to pursue their study: "How did former enslaved persons describe their experiences in slavery through the Works Progress Administration (WPA) oral history project?" Students return to the guiding question to determine whether they are gathering information that is germane to their project or whether the information is taking them in a different direction. If they choose to go in a different direction, that is acceptable as long as they make a deliberate choice to do so rather than arbitrarily picking up bits of information and wandering around their topic. The guiding question is a guideline for reflection rather than an inflexible assessment standard.

- In evaluating the quality of information obtained from an Internet site, it is important to determine the credentials of the person or institution posting the Web site. Reputation is one of the best ways to determine if the site holds good information. A reputable historical society, museum, or university, such as the Iowa Historical Society, Old Sturbridge Village, or the University of Washington, have credibility due to their reputations in their respective fields. Each of these institutions is regularly reviewed by its peers. Peer review is another good way to determine if the information is reliable; rarely are items posted on the Internet peer reviewed. Perhaps a better way to determine the quality of the source is to see if there are other similar sources; while not foolproof, consensus is an excellent way to determine a quality Web site. Students look at transcripts of interviews with former enslaved persons, read published slave accounts, and listen to the reproduced WPA tapes.

- Students sort accounts into positive memories that may include family, worship, and community. They further sort negative memories that may include the categories of violence, fear, and hardship. Students examine the context of the data. Would there be any reason for the former enslaved persons not to disclose all of their memories? Would the fear of lynching, a White male interviewer, or the fact that this was a government project affect the content of the interviews?

- Students compile their research and create a readers' theater or a play to dramatize the interviews for members of the class.

- Based on what the students find, they may become interested in exploring the relationship between slavery and the presidency or what an enslaved person's experience on the Underground Railroad might be like.

4 Points	3 Points	2 Points	1 Point
Students engage in a topic and identify a concern they wish to explore.	Students engage in a topic and identify a concern they wish to explore.	Students engage in a topic and identify a concern they wish to explore.	Students engage in a topic and identify a concern they wish to explore.
Students develop and explore multiple guiding questions.	Students develop and explore multiple guiding questions.	Students develop and explore multiple guiding questions.	
Students gather multiple sources of evidence that they consider as they determine an answer to their problem.	Students gather multiple sources of evidence that they consider as they determine an answer to their problem.		
Students produce a product that communicates their findings to a real audience.			

REFERENCES AND RESOURCES

Edgington, W. D. (2001). Solving problems with twenty questions. *Social Education, 65*(6), 379–382.

Richburg, R. W., Nelson, B. J., & Tochterman, S. (2002). Gender inequity: A world geography lesson plan. *Social Studies, 93*(1), 23–30.

Trofanenko, B. M. (2008). More than a single best narrative: Collective history and the transformation of historical consciousness. *Curriculum Inquiry, 38*(5), 579–603.

VanSledright, B. (2002). *In search of America's past: Learning to read history in elementary school.* New York: Teachers College Press

Woelders, A. (2007). Using film to conduct historical inquiry with middle school students. *History Teacher, 40*(3), 363–396.

Web Sites

Ohio Department of Education
http://ims.ode.state.oh.us/ode/ims/rrt/research/Content/inquiry_based_learning_references.asp

Slavery and the presidency
http://www.understandingprejudice.org/slavery/

Teachnology
http://www.teach-nology.com/currenttrends/inquiry/curriculum/

Underground Railroad
http://www.nationalgeographic.com/railroad/

WPA tapes of former slaves
http://xroads.virginia.edu/~HYPER/WPA/wpahome.html

7
Questioning

INTRODUCTION

Benjamin Bloom (1956) identified six increasingly complex and abstract levels of educational goals and objectives, including: knowledge, comprehension, application, analysis, synthesis, and evaluation. The levels in this taxonomy are also often used to construct increasingly more complex questions. The six levels of questioning build on one another in that students must have knowledge before they have comprehension and comprehension prior to analysis. The top three levels—analysis, synthesis, and evaluation—form the basis for higher-level questioning or higher-level thinking. This is not to denigrate the importance of the lower levels of questioning, as these are foundational and provide the tools for building the higher-level questions. It is important for the teacher to move beyond the so-called lower-level questions and model for students a variety of questions. It is also possible that the teacher and students begin with a higher-level question that can best be explored by creating related lower-level questions to build a knowledge base. Aschner, Gallagher, Perry, and Afsar (1961) built upon the work of Bloom to identify five types of questions, including: cognitive-memory, convergent-thinking, divergent-thinking, evaluative-thinking, and guiding questions. As important as questioning skills are for teachers to model, it is even more important for students to demonstrate proficiencies in questioning at a variety of levels. Also note that this taxonomy was more recently revised by Anderson and Krathwohl (2001) to separate the knowledge and cognitive processes, creating a grid in which these two processes intersect, instead of a single linear progression. Both the original taxonomy and the revision are helpful in developing learning objectives and designing questions.

Teachers use questions for a variety of purposes in the elementary school classroom. Teachers use questions to arouse curiosity and to prompt students to improve. Teachers use questions to assess, to encourage participation, and to facilitate discussion. Teachers can use questions to focus the attention of the students, to guide student efforts in acquiring cognitive or social skills, and to promote thinking. Good questioning is essential in several of the other strategies in this text (See Strategies 5, 6, and 24)

PROCEDURAL RECOMMENDATIONS

- Students have a significant experience such as a field trip or a guest speaker.
- Students feel uncertainty and doubt; from this uncertainty, they identify a topic or issue that they wish to explore more.
- Students write their topic or issue in the center of a piece of paper within a circle.
- From there, they create a web by writing a list of ideas surrounding the circle to indicate what they would like to explore.

- Students place a circle around the each of the ideas and connect them to the center circle with a line.
- Students rework each idea into one of the levels of questioning until all of the ideas represent all six types of questions.
- Students draw a circle around the question and connect it to the idea with a line.
- Students can use the remaining paper to take notes on possible answers to their questions.

APPLICATIONS AND IDEAS

The students in Ms. Moon's classroom decide to find out about the Vietnam War. She asks a question to arouse curiosity: "Who has heard about the war in Vietnam?" To pursue this topic, they invite to their classroom a reporter who did network TV broadcasts from Southeast Asia during the Vietnam War before retiring to their community to be close to his grandchildren. The students work with a partner to write questions for their guest to answer during their interview with him.

- *Knowledge:* When did you arrive in Southeast Asia and when did you depart from there?
- *Comprehension:* So you served in Southeast Asia for ____ years?
- *Application:* Who or what did you consider to be the enemy?
- *Analysis:* What were the biggest differences between the urban and rural areas of Vietnam?
- *Synthesis:* How would you have used American troops in Vietnam if you had been in charge?
- *Evaluation:* What was the worst thing to happen to the people of Vietnam?

To assess the knowledge of the students, Ms. Moon asks for an example of each type of question by saying, "Who can share a knowledge question that you wrote?" When the students are finished working, she asks a question to guide student efforts in acquiring a social skill: "How many of you think that each student did an equal amount of work with your partner?" Most of the students raise their hands. To promote thinking she asks, "Which of your questions is your strongest thinking question?" After the students share their questions, she asks students to improve on their first attempts, "OK, you have heard some of the best questions from other people—are there any questions you wish to add to your list?" After students amend their lists, Ms. Moon facilitates discussion by asking, "Karen, what is one idea your group had?" After Karen responds, Ms. Moon turns the direction of the discussion to focus attention on a particular subject by asking, "How did the nature of the land of Vietnam shape the war effort?" The students respond about the physical features of Vietnam and its climate. She then encourages participation by telling students, "With a partner, list three things the United States did to adapt to fighting in Vietnam."

ASSESSMENT

This assessment is for question webbing.

4 Points	3 Points	2 Points	1 Point
Student identifies a topic.	Student identifies a topic.	Student identifies a topic.	Student identifies a topic.
Student generates ideas about the topic to explore.	Student generates ideas about the topic to explore.	Student generates ideas about the topic to explore.	
Student generates a question at each of the six levels of questioning.	Student generates a question at each of the six levels of questioning.		
Student evaluates the questions to determine if they are appropriate for each level of questioning.			

REFERENCES AND RESOURCES

Anderson, L. W., & Krathwohl, D. R., (Eds.). (2001). *A taxonomy for learning, teaching, and assessing: A revision of Bloom's taxonomy of educational objectives.* White Plains, NY: Addison Wesley Longman, Inc.

Aschner, M., Gallagher, J., Perry, J., Afsar, S., Jenne, W., & Farr, H.(1961). *System for classifying thought processes in the context of classroom verbal interaction.* Urbana, IL: University of Illinois.

Beck, I. L., & McKeown, M. G. (2002).Questioning the author: Making sense of social studies.*Educational Leadership, 60*(3), 44–47.

Bloom, B. S. (Ed.) (1956). *Taxonomy of educational objectives. The classification of educational goals.* White Plains, NY: Longman.

Bolgatz, J. (2005). Revolutionary talk: Elementary teacher and students discuss race in a social studies class. *Social Studies, 96*(6), 259–264.

Cooper, H., & Dilek, D. (2007). A comparative study on primary pupils' historical questioning processes in Turkey and England: Empathic, critical and creative thinking. *Educational*

Sciences: Theory and Practice, 7(2), 713–725.

Pappas, M. L. (2007). Learners as historians: Making history come alive through historical inquiry. *School Library Media Activities Monthly, 23*(10), 18–21.

Singer, A. J., Murphy, M. O., & Miletta, M. M. (2001). Asking the BIG questions: Teaching about the Great Irish Famine and world history. *Social Education, 65*(5), 286–291.

Web Sites

Bloom's Taxonomy
http://www.teachers.ash.org.au/researchskills/Dalton.htm

Center for Teaching Excellence
http://www.oir.uiuc.edu/Did/docs/QUESTION/quest1.htm

Document-Based Questions
http://nysut.org/standards/201-teachers-dbq.html

Newer Views of Learning
http://www.uwsp.edu/Education/lwilson/learning/quest2.htm

8

Primary Sources

INTRODUCTION

An important part of a historian's professional life is the examination and analysis of primary sources. The analysis of both primary and secondary sources contributes to a historian's interpretation of the past. While our intent is not to create mini-historians, a strong social studies curriculum includes an analysis of available and appropriate evidence in order to make informed decisions. Primary sources are one important category of evidence. Typically, primary sources are described as information in its original form. They have not been translated or interpreted by another. This information is first-hand and is created by those who participated in or witnessed an event. However, it is important to note that some historians consider primary sources to be sources created within the same historical time period. For example, an engraver's interpretation of an eyewitness's drawing of an event may be considered a primary source if completed in the same historical era (approximately 50 years). Primary sources include:

- First-person accounts (e.g., diaries, letters, eyewitnesses, meeting minutes, memoirs) in either text or audio
- Images (e.g., photographs, films/newscasts, posters)
- Documents (e.g., maps, treaties, birth records)
- Creative work of the time (e.g., art, music, literature)
- Physical/three-dimensional artifacts or objects (e.g., clothing, tools, toys, furniture, buildings produced during the time)
- Scientific data that has been collected but not interpreted

Primary sources can help students access moments of life from the past, revealing elements of social, political, economic, and/or cultural history. For example, younger students can compare toys they play with today with toys from the past that had similar functions. How are dolls from the past similar to dolls from the present? How are board games similar and different? In this example, a learning goal could focus on technological changes in the materials and abilities of the toys. A different learning goal could be to create a connection or bridge between the past and the present. Children, 100 or 150 years ago, were still children, playing with their toys and playing games with other children. Neither of these goals evaluate which toys are better; rather, the goals are about understanding the past through a comparison with the familiar and the present.

Older students can analyze techniques used to construct these same items and the way that the manufacture of consumer goods changed the way people lived (Falk & Dierking, 2000). Students can observe these changing ideas in the construction of toys, as in the previous example, or in hand tools.

Across time, hand tools that were first fashioned from wood later gave way to hand tools that were forged from metal and finally to hand tools that were created from molded polymers. Analyzing this progression over 150 to 200 years, or longer if artifacts are available, to determine the function of these artifacts and sorting them by chronological period could provide an interesting technological insight.

In addition to three-dimensional artifacts, the most common types of primary sources are public and private records. Public records are produced for a public audience. Think of the United States Constitution, the birth and death records of a community, and propaganda posters or leaflets. On the other hand, private records are not usually written to reach a public audience or to sway public opinion. Think of letters and diaries. Private records commonly reveal multiple conflicting accounts of events, but historians have long treasured primary sources of public and private figures as a way to access the past.

PROCEDURAL RECOMMENDATIONS

- Identify the learning objectives for the students.
- If the analysis of certain primary sources during one part of the lesson or unit will help students achieve these objectives, begin a search for appropriate primary sources. There are numerous places to find primary source materials. If you are looking to locate documents, photographs, recordings, and other two-dimensional sources related to the United States, consider the National Archives and Records Administration (www.nara.gov) and the Library of Congress (www.loc.gov). Their collections are extensive and cover local and national history. If the topic is very local—perhaps a study of how the local town or city was created—a local historical society or county records would be an appropriate place to search. If students are documenting more individual history—perhaps how members of the local community persevered through a natural disaster or what it was like to attend elementary school in the 1940s—it would be appropriate to talk with individuals who either have first-hand knowledge or have access to materials (which students could very carefully copy) that provide that first-hand knowledge. If the primary source material includes actually conducting interviews with individuals, consider oral histories, Strategy 39 in this book, as a guideline for you and your students. Three-dimensional artifacts are another wonderful source material. These may be harder to access and while replicas can be helpful, if a learning goal is technological development, mass-produced replicas utilizing newer materials will defeat that purpose. In that case, photographs of actual artifacts are more suitable, even though they do not provide something for the students to handle. However, if the goal is function, a replica might be suitable. In the search for artifacts, do not underestimate what is available to borrow from family and community members in barns, attics, basements, and storage units.
- At the appropriate place in the lesson or unit, introduce the primary source material the students are to analyze. Depending on learning objectives, students may examine the same or different materials. If the materials are from the Internet, determine if they are best accessed directly online (e.g., colorful, three-dimensional rotation, recording) or through a photocopy (e.g., for measurement). If the materials are borrowed, be sure to establish very clear procedures with students on the safe care and handling of other people's property.
- Primary source analysis typically occurs on three levels: literal, interpretive, and evaluative. See the sample Analysis Worksheets available on www.nara.gov for multiple examples of these levels of questions and prompts.
- The first level of analysis is *literal*. It is a literal description of the item. As difficult as it may be, and it is difficult, students should avoid any interpretation at this level. Focusing just on what they see may prevent an overinterpretation of the source. Consider questions or prompts such as: How big (or long) is it? What is it made of? Is there any writing on it? What does it say? What colors are used? What instruments do you hear? How many people/ items are in the picture? List them. Again, note that students are taking an inventory of the item; they are not interpreting or evaluating it—yet.

- The second level of analysis is *interpretive*. At this level, students begin to make inferences based on their literal examination. Appropriate questions include: Does it seem old or new? Why do you think that? Does it seem familiar or unfamiliar to you? Why? What do you think it might have been used for? Why do you think that? Who might have produced it and why? Who might it have been produced for and why? An important element here is that students are asked to back up their inferences with evidence they have gained from their examination of the primary source, as well as other available sources like their textbooks and prior learning experiences.

- The third level of analysis is *evaluative,* and it is the level that gets to why we have students examine primary sources. At this level, students are asked to determine what can be learned from the primary source. How does this primary source help us understand the larger topic under study, answer the historical question, and so on? What are some additional questions we want answered about the primary source or the topic under study that are still unanswered? What do we want to know about the creator of the primary source? These kinds of questions firmly place primary source analysis as one step in moving toward understanding. While some questions are answered, others are raised. It reinforces that primary source analysis is not the end goal of the lesson. Rather, it is a tool for understanding and a part of the process.

- Place students' conclusions into the lesson or unit, as appropriate.

APPLICATIONS AND IDEAS

Second-grade students can compare American colonial artifacts to objects in their homes by examining photographs of the artifacts listed below. Some artifacts have changed little across time, while others have changed radically or been replaced altogether. The students respond to this question: What can you find in your homes that replaced these artifacts?

Artifact Lineage	Historical Artifact Contemporary Object
Candlestick with a handle	Lamp
Plain pewter mug	Plastic cup
Chippendale corner cupboard with glass door	Kitchen cabinets
Queen Anne tea table	Kitchen table
Chinese filigree tea table	Coffee table
Broken-pediment secretary desk	Desk
Filigree bonnet-top chest-on-chest on frame	Bedroom dresser
Queen Anne side dining chair	Kitchen chair
Chippendale side dining chair with ball-and-claw legs	Dining room chair

After finding the comparable objects in their homes, the students determine the similarities and differences between these artifacts and the objects in their homes. This is an appropriate place to reinforce the idea of literal description of the items. Next, ask students to give reasons why they believe these artifacts have changed over time. Making inferences between the photographs provided and their home observations, and with teacher facilitation, students can note differences in materials and appearances even though, in many cases, the function has remained the same. A candlestick with a handle serves the same purpose as a lamp, yet they are technologically quite different. Desks—whether from a previous century, from a student's home, or at school—may have different appearances, but they all provide a place for a person to complete some work. In most cases, people write at their desks, even if their writing instruments (quill pen, pencil, computer) have changed. Students learn that technology changes the materials used in artifacts and that technology allows people to create new objects that meet their needs. Further, some items in their homes have no antecedents because people use technology to create new objects for amusement, communication, or convenience.

ASSESSMENT

An analytical scoring rubric is one way to distinguish which levels of analysis students are most adept at and which levels may need more instructional support in future lessons.

	Literal	Interpretive	Evaluative
3	A complete description is provided.	Reasonable inferences are noted and supported with evidence from the primary source.	Connections to the lesson and larger understanding of the topic are evident. Students pose additional relevant questions.
2	Most items/information from the primary source are noted.	Most of the inferences are reasonable and/or most are supported with evidence from the primary source.	Some connections to the lesson and larger understanding of the topic are evident. Limited additional questions are posed.
1	Some items/information from the primary source are noted.	Some of the inferences are reasonable and/or some are supported with evidence from the primary source.	Some connections to the lesson and larger understanding of the topic are evident OR limited additional questions are posed, but not both.
0	Nothing is listed.	No reasonable inferences are made.	No connections to the lesson or to future questions are made.

REFERENCES AND RESOURCES

Andrews, I. A. (1999). Significant treasures. *Canadian Social Studies, 33*(2), 61–62.

Barton, K. C. (2001). A picture's worth: Analyzing historical photographs in the elementary grades. *Social Education, 65*(5), 278–283.

Barton, K. C. (2005). Primary sources in history: Breaking through the myths. *Phi Delta Kappan, 18*(10), 745–753.

Bell, D., & Henning, M. B. (2007). DeKalb County, Illinois: A local history project for second graders. *Social Studies and the Young Learner, 19*(3), 7–11.

Fagan, B. (1998). Perhaps we may hear voices. Common ground: Archaeology & ethnography in the *Public Interest, 3*(1), 14–17.

Falk, J. H., & Dierking, L. D. (2000). *Learning from museums: Visitor experiences and the making of meaning.* Walnut Creek, CA: Altamira.

Gilliland-Swetland, A. J., Kafai, Y. B., & Landis, W. E. (2000). Application of Dublin core metadata in the description of digital primary sources in elementary school classrooms. *Journal of the American Society for Information Science, 51*(2), 193–201.

Hodysh, H. W. (2000). On the periphery of the tar sands: Documents in the classroom. *Canadian Social Studies, 35*(1). Retrieved April 24, 2006, from http://www.quasar.ualberta.ca/css/CSS_35_1/documentsYLin_the_classroom.htm

Kalish, C. (1998). Natural and artifactual kinds: Are children realists or relativists about categories? *Developmental Psychology, 34*, 376–391.

Labbo, L. D., & Field, S. L. (1999). Journey boxes: Telling the story of place, time, and culture with photographs, literature, and artifacts. *Social Studies, 90*(4), 177–182.

Libresco, A. S. (2000). History mystery: A documents-based lesson on women's rights. *Social Studies & the Young Learner, 13*(2), 1–4.

Mason, C. L., & Carter, A. (1999). The Garbers: Using digital history to recreate a 19th-century family. *Social Studies & the Young Learner, 12*(1), 11–14.

Mizell, L. (1998). Exploring primary sources: The ideal of liberty and the reality of slavery. *Social Education, 62*(6), 350–351.

Morris, R. V. (2006). Hitchcock versus Shaker chairs: Artifacts to teach about the rise and rejection of industrialism in the young Republic. *Gifted Child Today, 29*(1), 546–565.

Morris, R. V., Morgan-Fleming, B., & Janisch, C. (2001). The diary of Calvin Fletcher—Using primary sources in the elementary classroom. *Social Studies, 92*(4), 151–153.

Nelson, P. A. (2005). Preparing students for citizenship: Literature and primary sources. *Social Studies and the Young Learner, 17*(3), 21–29.

Rodriguez, H. M., Salinas, C., & Guberman, S. (2005). Creating opportunities for historical thinking with bilingual students. *Social Studies and the Young Learner, 18*(2), 9–13.

Web Sites

The Library of Congress (**www.loc.gov**) has an *American Memory* collection that is very useful for teachers.

The National Archives and Records Administration (**www.nara.gov**) provides an extensive digital archive of various primary sources, including documents, audio and video recordings, and photographs. In addition, NARA has a helpful section for educators, including various templates for primary source analysis.

PART II

Specific Social Studies Instructional Strategies to Advance Content Knowledge and Skills Development

The 42 strategies described in the following section are more detailed than those in the preceding part, as well as more specific to certain ages or learning objectives. Many reflect distinct social science disciplines, using the content, skills, and methods associated with those disciplines. We encourage teachers to integrate the social sciences when appropriate in order to encourage true social studies learning.

9

Archeological Digs

GRADE LEVELS	NCSS CURRICULUM STRANDS
✔ 3–5	I Culture
✔ 6–8	II Time Continuity, and Change
	IV Individual Development
	and Identity

INTRODUCTION

In an archeological dig, an anthropologist "reads" the remains of a group of people and their material culture to determine the life experience of that group. In a simulated archeological dig created by the teacher or older students for younger students, the younger students can formulate research questions by examining artifacts recovered from the site. They can reconstruct events that occurred on the site and make inferences about the quality of life these people experienced. Based on the evidence they recover, students can interpret the site. What items were next to one another? Are the items from the same or different eras? Why did some items deteriorate more than others? In working with a mock archeological site, students use evaluation by weighing evidence and placing it in context through documentation of the site. Without going into the field, students can determine the uses of evidence and learn how reference sources contribute to the narrative an archeologist creates to explain events. Students also get an opportunity to discredit a hypothesis if it is incongruent with evidence or if it remains unsupported by evidence.

PROCEDURAL RECOMMENDATIONS

- Select a site or span of time to interpret.
- Generate a possible story appropriate to the time or place.
- Determine the evidence needed to explain the story.
- Determine the sequence for disclosing bits of information.
- Use books on the history of architecture to find a floor plan and an exterior picture of the predetermined time or place. If a plan is unavailable, the teacher can draw one on graph paper based on an actual or virtual visit to the site. Save the picture for the conclusion of the dig.
- Select historically accurate artifacts for each part of the dig. If possible, purchase authentic artifacts to include in the site. If this is not possible, use photographs of artifacts.
- Find supporting explanatory information. Some artifacts are accompanied by descriptive tags or informative inserts. Other explanatory information can be found in works of art, encyclopedias, reference books, or on the Internet.

- Approach the dig from one of two perspectives: Begin the project as if archeologists have already removed all of the artifacts from the site, or create a mock site by burying artifacts in the site.
- If student work begins after the removal of artifacts from the site, place each bit of evidence or artifact in a folder and sequentially label the folders (i.e., in the order in which they would have been recovered or in which they should be examined).
- Have students photograph the site and describe the artifacts found. Timing is dependent on each site; usually students can photograph after examining one-quarter to one-third of the artifacts.
- Write directions for the students, including directions describing when they are to open the folders. Also, include an archeologist's report to be read after all of the folders have been opened so that students can see what the site might have looked like.
- Through effective questioning, help students recognize that the archeologist presents his or her best ideas only after considering all of the evidence that has been discovered and examined.
- If student work begins with the recovery of artifacts, students will need more detailed directions on how to prepare a site for artifact recovery; how to section off a site; how to recover artifacts without damaging them or the surrounding area; and how to clean, label, and store artifacts.
- Have students photograph the entire site, including the grid lines they created when they sectioned the site. Direct them to create notes regarding each artifact recovered.
- Interpret the photos.

APPLICATIONS AND IDEAS

Younger students can read artifacts and make comparisons to the present. Older students can support their inferences and document their hypotheses with evidence derived from primary sources. Upper elementary students were assigned an archeological dig at a site from the American Revolution. The artifacts recovered at the site were contained in a series of folders. The students examined the contents of each folder and then carried out the tasks as directed. Table 9.1 summarized the folder contents and directives.

The foundation, which indicated the arrangement of the rooms, and the picture of the house revealed it to be a Georgian-style house of colonial Virginia gentry. Both Loyalist and Patriot buttons found on the site established the groups of people present at the site, and coins established the time period. An archeologist also worked with records to determine the use of artifacts and looked at precedent from other historical sites from a similar time or place. In this simulation students also got to read records to determine how the artifacts they found fit into the context of the site and how they could connect the artifacts to the story of the site.

Students needed to re-create the story of what happened at this site based on the evidence from the artifacts recovered. The lead pencil indicated literacy, and the wine bottle impression revealed that there was foreign trade. The story the students re-created was defined by the archeology; for example, the arrangement of the rooms disclosed that people heated the rooms with fireplaces and cooled them with symmetrical paired openings that allowed breezes to pass through the house. The students could determine some facts but not others; for example, there was evidence that Loyalists and Patriots were both present in the house, but there was no evidence that they were both there at the same time or that they were in a battle at the site. Students needed to use their analysis skills to determine what was possible at the site and to determine what they did not have evidence to support.

Teachers can also create mini-archeological digs by using dishpans filled with sand to represent the different grid squares in an archeological site. The teacher salts the site with artifacts that would not have decomposed, such as glass, china, metal, bone, stone, horn, or shell. Students use trowels, paintbrushes, or dental picks to remove artifacts. The teacher can use permanent marker on the

TABLE 9.1 ARCHEOLOGICAL DIG		
1	Blueprints showing four rooms off a central hall; center stairway; fireplaces in every room; symmetrical arrangements of the floor plan including windows, fireplace, doors; front and back porches; evidence of columns	These are the foundations of a house. List five things they tell about the home.
2	Butler's Rangers button; musket ball; Royal Regiment of Artillery button	List one thing an archeologist can learn about its owner from each object. Find out more about these objects.
3	Picture, diagram, and text describing a Revolutionary War cartridge; illustration and description of the Butler's Rangers button; illustration and description of the Royal Regiment of Artillery button	List one new thing learned about each artifact from the documentation. How does this confirm or refute the list created in the last folder? Sift through dirt of the back right room.
4	George II coin; lead pencil	Find these objects. List one thing each object tells about its owner. Find out more about these objects.
5	Description of the King's shilling; photo and description of a lead pencil	List one new thing learned about each artifact from the documentation. How does this confirm or refute the list created in the last folder? Sift through dirt from the back left room.
6	Hand-forged spike; wine bottle impression; small porcelain cup	Find these objects. List one thing each object tells about its owner. Find out more about these objects.
7	Description of a wine seal; chart illustrating the types and dates of handmade nails	List one new thing learned about each artifact from the documentation. How does this confirm or refute the list created in the last folder? Sift through dirt from the front left room.
8	A hand-forged nail; Continental infantry button; American artillery button	Find these objects. List one thing each object tells about its owner. Find out more about these objects.
9	Illustration and description of an American artillery button; illustration and description of a Continental button	List one new thing learned about each artifact from the documentation. How does this confirm or refute the list created in the last folder? Draw how each room in the house might have looked.
10	A picture of a two-story Georgian-style colonial brick home	Based on all the evidence you have gathered, write a story to explain what might have occurred at the house.

bottom of the light-colored dishpans to indicate soil stains such as postholes, trenches, or trash pits. Dark soil stains indicate human activity: A stain for a posthole indicates a fence or structure, one for a trench indicates a possible wall or structure, and a trash pit is a great place to look for castoff rubbish. The teacher can also use permanent marker on the dishpans to indicate building materials such as brick, stone, or clay.

ASSESSMENT

Abstract:

Students use all of their experiences to create an archeological site report.

4 Points	3 Points	2 Points	1 Point
Student considers all of the evidence.	Student considers all of the evidence.	Student considers all of the evidence.	Student considers all of the evidence.
Student describes the evidence. Student interprets what the evidence means.	Student describes the evidence. Student interprets what the evidence means.	Student describes the evidence. Student interprets what the evidence means.	
Rationale if evidence is not used. Student exceeds the evidence	Rationale if evidence is not used. Student exceeds the evidence.		
Student cites other primary sources. Student cites other secondary sources			

REFERENCES AND RESOURCES

Black, M. S. (2001). Maturing gracefully? Curriculum standards for history and archaeology. *Social Studies, 92*(3), 103–108.

Hume, I. N. (2001). *A guide to the artifacts of colonial America.* Philadelphia: University of Pennsylvania Press.

Hume, I. N. (2005). *Civilized men: A James Towne tragedy.* Petersburg, VA: Dietz Press.

Morris, R. V. (2000). Teaching social studies with artifacts. *Social Studies, 91*(1), 32–37.

Panchyk, R. (2001). *Archaeology for kids: Uncovering the mysteries of our past—25 activities.* Chicago: Independent Publishers Group.

Yell, M. M. (2001). Uncovering Pompeii: Examining evidence. *Social Education, 65*(1), 60–67.

Web Sites

Anasazi Heritage Center
http://www.blm.gov/co/st/en/fo/ahc/teach/loankits.html

Chicago History Museum
http://www.chicagohistory.org/static_media/pdf/historyHands/ CHM-TipsforAssemblingYourArtifactKit.pdf

Colorado Historical Society
http://www.coloradohistory.org/programs/school_prgms/edu_kits.htm

Personalizing the Past
http://www.historykits.com/

Society for American Archeology
http://www.saa.org/Public/resources/artkits.html

10

Architecture and Landscape Design Significance

GRADE LEVELS	NCSS CURRICULUM STRANDS
✔ 3–5	I Culture
✔ 6–8	II Time Continuity, and Change
	III People, Places, and Environments
	IV Individual Development and Identity

INTRODUCTION

When a family has children, the residence starts to change. First, there is the emergence of a sandbox, swing, and slide, and perhaps a fence. Next, there will be a variety of toys in the garage, the grass under trees will get thin, and maybe some sports equipment such as a basketball hoop will be set up. When the children are older, perhaps there will be a swimming pool, a volleyball net, a backstop for baseball, or a soccer goal. As the family and their needs change, they will make dynamic changes in the way the land around their house is used. Each of these changes resulted when the members of the family determined priorities for their lives and made choices about how they were going to live as a family and how they would live in the house. As the members of a family realize that they have different interests and abilities, they work to change the environment in which they live.

Human–environment interaction is one of the five themes of geography, as is movement of ideas and goods. Students use their observations of geography to help them interpret how people organize the space around them. Students see how people change the land to meet their needs and how geography is shaped by those who live there. They see how new ideas come into the family, and the family members acquire new things to help them act out these ideas of what constitutes the good life, or they replace old things that no longer help them enact their idea of a good life. As they observe geographic construction, students notice the changes that are occurring around them and the changes that have occurred across time. The shapes and arrangements of buildings, the establishment of public spaces, and the definition of private space are all socially constructed.

PROCEDURAL RECOMMENDATIONS

- Upper elementary students work in groups of four to determine how a city street has changed across time.
- Find the repositories of local historical photo collections in the community by checking the library, historical society, and museum.
- Look for streetscapes and images of neighborhoods.
- Identify the structures that still exist in the historical photos.
- Find multiple images of the same structure to show change across time.
- Find some images of buildings that should have been saved that are now gone.
- Look for maps, especially Sandborn Insurance maps, plat maps, and lithographs called bird's-eye views for context and community perspectives.
- Scan the photos into .jpeg files.
- Organize the images in Microsoft PowerPoint by chronology, by moving from east to west down a main street, by regions, neighborhoods, or other themes.
- Photograph existing structures and street views comparable with the historical photos.
- Once imported to PowerPoint, put these images on a split screen in order to compare the past with the present.
- Identify each slide with a caption.
- Older students can present this information to younger students.

APPLICATIONS AND IDEAS

People modify their environment to meet their needs via the following means: farming, ranching, mining, mineral acquisition, water distribution, industry, commerce, transportation, or residential uses. All of these activities dramatically change the land, but some uses are more permanent than others. Looking at old photos, it is amazing how large structures could be present just 100 years ago and vanish without a trace and how large towns could shrink to small towns over a generation. Comparisons of contemporary and historical maps show the incredible twentieth-century growth of cities. Some uses of the land remain fairly consistent; for example, the site of Jericho has been continually occupied for several thousands of years. Other changes occur quickly across a generation or less as shown in the book *The Little House* (Burton, 1978); gas stations changed from service centers, to mini-marts, to fast-food restaurants; some even went out of business.

Whether these shifts are observed or prolonged, people change the landscape to meet their needs, and students can see these changes from collections of local photos showing the location in time and comparing the historical image to the present. One group of students created a slide program, titled *Connersville: Then and Now,* in which they gathered and scanned historical photographs from their community and their local historical society. They went to the same site and took digital photos of the site 20, 50, 75, or 100 years later; using PowerPoint, they displayed these images on split screens to contrast the changes over time. Some of the sites had not changed at all, while others had changed dramatically. Students identified the changes and the continuity in their community as they interpreted the photographic evidence of multiple views of the same location.

Students can create drawings of the arrangement of plantation outbuildings after examining materials featuring actual American colonial landscapes. Encouraging students to create architectural drawings helps them see how people in colonial America integrated both the art and science of the Enlightenment into their lives. Upper elementary students examine pictures of the gardens of colonial Virginia to determine what people valued when they planted the gardens. One picture shows a symmetrical garden with a brick-path central axis edged in boxwood, planted with ground cover, and surrounded by fruit trees. A second picture shows a dependency, such as a springhouse or privy, in a similar garden; a third illustration features the plans of Carter's Grove plantation house, gardens, and grounds. A fourth picture shows the grounds, outbuildings, drives, and gardens of Mount Vernon.

In their garden drawings, younger students can show the use of decorative or produce-bearing plants. The students work in small groups to discuss their ideas and compare gardens from that era to those of the present. What overarching goals or principles guided the people who laid out these gardens? How did people use their gardens for recreation, entertainment, or communication of status? Through effective questioning, the teacher draws student attention to the symmetrical arrangement of the gardens and their well-ordered paths. They note the interaction between the garden and the dependencies as well as the similarities or differences between gardens designed for show and those designed for produce. They learn how the dependencies have a utilitarian purpose yet also fit into the layout of the plantation.

Upper grade elementary students examine how the dependencies, outbuildings where work is conducted, form part of the working landscape around the plantation house. Using laminated tour maps, students examine the grounds, dependencies, and gardens of four different plantations: Gunston Hall, Monticello, Mount Vernon, and Poplar Forest. Monticello and Poplar Forest were both designed by Thomas Jefferson. Using an erasable marker, students label the job performed in each dependency; they check their work by consulting the answer key on the back of each map. Students evaluate the importance of each job by its proximity to the house or state reasons why an outbuilding would be located at a greater distance from the house. Students can evaluate what the location of the dependencies tells about the way people thought about work.

4 Points	3 Points	2 Points	1 Point
Consider at least two primary and two secondary sources.	Consider at least two primary and two secondary sources.	Consider at least two primary and two secondary sources.	Consider at least two primary and two secondary sources.
Define who is working and living in each of these buildings. What does the task or building require, and what smells, inconveniences, or dangers are involved in the work?	Define who is working and living in each of these buildings. What does the task or building require, and what smells, inconveniences, or dangers are involved in the work?	Define who is working and living in each of these buildings. What does the task or building require, and what smells, inconveniences, or dangers are involved in the work?	
How do jobs and living arrangements change according to region: Chesapeake Bay, Louisiana, Northern states, and South Carolina? How does the placement of the slaves' dwellings change from the eighteenth to the nineteenth century? How is it affected by the number of slaves the owner has?	How do jobs and living arrangements change according to region: Chesapeake Bay, Louisiana, Northern states, and South Carolina? How does the placement of the slaves' dwellings change from the eighteenth to the nineteenth century? How is it affected by the number of slaves the owner has?		
Student selects a position regarding the question and supports it with evidence.			

Students create their own maps of gardens and outbuildings using drawing paper and colored pencils. Students write a description of their property, giving a rationale for the placement of their outbuildings. In their location of outbuildings, they can take into consideration historical accuracy and function as well as noise, sights, and odors. In their drawings, older students can include their reasons for placing features at specific locations and describe the interaction between aesthetics and function. They justify their arrangement in terms of the Enlightenment ideals of symmetry, balance, and order.

ASSESSMENT

The scoring guide above works well with the activity in which students draw a map with gardens and outbuildings. A similar scoring guide could be developed based on the questions posed in this assessment task.

Middle school students extend their studies of landscape by examining other primary and secondary sources in order to write an essay about slave life in dependencies. The students are asked to address the following question: Does the fact that the slaves' quarters are not very far from the main house indicate that the owner did not feel the need to be so far removed from the African slaves, or does it mean he wanted them near enough to keep an eye on them? Can it be an act of responsible management or a lack of trust?

REFERENCES AND RESOURCES

Alibrandi, M., Beal, C., Thompson, A., & Wilson, A. (2000). Reconstructing a school's past using oral histories and GIS mapping. *Social Education, 64*(3), 134–140.

Burton, V. L. (1978). *The little house*. Boston: Houghton Mifflin.

Domosh, M. (2000). Cultural patterns and processes in advanced placement human geography. *Journal of Geography, 99*(3–4), 111–119.

Gokay, M. (2004). Door to the future, understanding portals of ancient Seljuk colleges. *International Journal of Art and Design Education, 23*(1), 63–72.

Morris, R. V. (2000). The history walk: Integrated multi-age learning. *Gifted Child Today, 23*(4), 22–27, 53.

Morris, R. V., & Obenchain, K. M. (2001). Social studies standard on a university campus. *Journal of the Illinois Council for the Social Studies, 61*, 13–26.

Web Sites

Amon Carter Museum
http://www.birdseyeviews.org/

Farm and Home Publishers
http://www.farmandhomepublishers.com/county_plat_maps.php

Live Search Maps
http://maps.live.com/

Rockford Map Publishers
http://www.rockfordmap.com/

Sanborn Maps
http://sanborn.umi.com/

11

Case Studies

GRADE LEVELS	NCSS CURRICULUM STRANDS
✔ 3–5	Any (Depending on Topic)
✔ 6–8	

INTRODUCTION

Case studies are general narrative descriptions of situations and incidents (Kowalski, Weaver, & Henson, 1994). They are particularly useful in social studies because they encourage students to explore multiple perspectives, analyze issues, and make decisions, all of which promote higher-level and critical thinking (Wright, 2002). Case studies in social studies provide details of an actual or fictional event, familiar or unfamiliar, either historical or current, that is then analyzed to determine the central problem and propose alternative solutions. Case studies dispel any myths that the social studies curriculum is a march through time or that things just happen. Students are able to see how people do and did make decisions as well as the availability of alternatives. The links to the social studies curriculum are almost limitless. Younger students can examine concrete and familiar issues such as a school recycling program or a hypothetical theft in the classroom. Picture books also provide the content with which to create a case. Older students can analyze Supreme Court cases; school, local, state, and national policy issues; or moral cases. Note that the use of the term *case* does not necessarily imply a legal case. Legal cases may be examined and studied (see the Strategy 34 in this text); but legal cases are just one source of information for a case study. Case studies can be created by the teacher or purchased commercially.

PROCEDURAL RECOMMENDATIONS

- Determine whether all students will examine the same case or work on separate cases. If they are to work on separate cases, be sure that the cases are related to a central theme or issue. Older students could look at specific legal cases. For example, students studying juvenile rights might compare the essential issues and opinions of *New Jersey v. TLO* (due process) (http://www.law.umkc.edu/faculty/projects/ftrials/conlaw/tlo.html) or *Bethel School District v. Fraser* (freedom of expression) (http://www.law.umkc.edu/faculty/projects/ftrials/firstamendment/bethel.html) in order to understand the complexity of their own rights and responsibilities as citizens. Intermediate students could examine the case for a school recycling program or the arguments for and against a salad bar in the cafeteria. Younger students could examine one specific case as presented through a picture book. They might examine the character Goldilocks to determine the appropriateness of her entering the three bears' home without their permission.

- Provide students the background information on the case. This information may be presented in writing, with visual information (e.g., Web sites, video, photographs), or through a brief lecture. The background information includes the social studies concepts, topics, or themes that tie to the lesson objectives, as well as the essential facts and evidence in the case.

- Have each student or small group develop a case record. This should include a narrative description of the incident, event, or situation and information the students consider essential. Illustrations within a book or created by the teacher help younger students or struggling readers. The case should also introduce and fully describe the dilemma or problem. The case should provide enough information so that different reasonable positions, as well as a solid rationale backing each of the positions, is evident. Have students note the positions of each of the individuals or groups introduced in the case as they work to understand each person's or group's point of view, relationship to the case, and expertise. Have students note how the issue presented in the case relates to the topics under study in class.

- If necessary and appropriate, encourage students to seek outside information to better understand the case. If they are examining a Supreme Court case, it might help to examine other court decisions. Similarly, if they are examining local environmental issues, it might be helpful to explore how other communities solved similar problems.

- Introduce the challenge and the role students are to play in recommending a solution. Students can study the case by themselves or in very small groups. Have them identify with a particular individual presented in the case, asking, for example, "If you were Luis, what would be the main issues of interest? Describe what solution you would propose." This step also encourages students to put themselves into others' shoes. One student's personal position may be different from Luis's position on the case. However, by asking a student to represent Luis's position, the student must first understand Luis and then try to understand what would be of interest to Luis.

- Develop and propose alternative solutions. Students should analyze these solutions for positive and negative consequences. It might be helpful to use the decision tree/decision-making grid presented in Strategy 15. If possible, ask students to decide on one best resolution to the problem.

- If students are working in small groups, have them prepare a brief presentation that outlines their best solution. After all students have presented their solutions, ask the small groups to review their solutions and determine if they would make any changes based on the new information presented.

APPLICATIONS AND IDEAS

Whether creating a case study or choosing an existing one, teachers should keep in mind the characteristics of quality cases. The following checklist, adapted from Kowalski and colleagues (1994), can be used to evaluate case materials.

Quality Case Study Checklist

1. Disinformation (i.e., extraneous details that require students to sort through relevant and irrelevant information) should be present in the case.
2. The problem presented should be complex, and there should not be an easy or obvious solution. The problem should, however, be solvable, even if the students recognize that the best resolution may not satisfy everyone.

3. The problem presented should be real and important to the students. Students rarely become engaged in a case that does not *hook* them. Cases involving juvenile or school issues have a natural appeal.

4. The case and its central problem should relate to the social studies topic under study. Examining the case should require students to further explore the content, skills, and affective goals of the social studies curriculum. For example, if the class is studying the concept of equality under the law, Supreme Court cases such as *Plessy v. Ferguson*, and B*rown v. Board of Education of Topeka, Kansas* would provide additional content and context for learning the concept.

5. The high-quality case should have multiple foci. One central issue should be accompanied by several related issues or concepts. For the example listed in item 4, racism, local control of schools, and economics are related issues.

ASSESSMENT

A holistic scoring rubric, similar to the one described in Strategy 34, could be adapted for use with this strategy.

REFERENCES AND RESOURCES

Carlson, J. A., & Schodt, D. W. (1995). Beyond the lecture: Case teaching and the learning of economic theory. *Journal of Economic Education, 26*(1), 17–28.

Horton, P. (2000). A model for teaching secondary history: The case of Fort Pillow. *History Teacher, 33*(2), 175–183.

Kowalski, T. J., Weaver, R. A., & Henson, K. T. (1994). Case studies of beginning teachers. New York: Longman.

Long, G. P. (1994). Constitutional rights of juveniles and students: Lessons on sixteen Supreme Court cases. Bloomington, IN: Social Studies Development Center, ERIC Clearinghouse for Social Studies/Social Science Education. The issues and cases in this text relate directly to juvenile issues, including freedom of expression (school newspapers) and search and seizure (purses and lockers).

Misco, T. (2009). Teaching the Holocaust through case study. *Social Studies, 100*(1), 14–22.

Van Scotter, R., White, W. E., Hartoonian, H. M., et al. (2007). A gateway to social studies through topical history. *Social Studies, 98*(6), 231–235.

Wright, I. (2002). Challenging students with the tools of critical thinking. *Social Studies, 93*(6), 257–261.

Web Sites

http://www.channelonenetwork.com/teacher/articles/2007/01/02/1_voice/assembly.pdf
This site has a legal case study about students' rights in schools.

12

Cemetery Studies

GRADE LEVELS	NCSS CURRICULUM STRANDS
✔ 3–5	I Culture
✔ 6–8	II Time, Continuity, and Change
	III People, Places, and Environment
	IV Individual Development and Identity

INTRODUCTION

In many communities, buildings and resources that illustrate a history of a community have disappeared over time or are difficult to access. However, cemeteries remain, and they are often well cared for resources that hold many parts of a community's history. A cemetery study is only useful if it is contained within a lesson or unit of study in which information from a cemetery will advance student learning. They are particularly well suited to inquiries (see Strategy 6) of community history. Cemeteries are themselves a primary source (see Strategy 8), as well as being full of other primary sources. For example, cemeteries illustrate a variety of patterns related to the population trends of a community. This may include disease, wars, migration, conflicts, religious and other group affiliations, and the influence of technology. Evidence of patterns are found in birth dates, death dates, fraternal groups, military service, families, racial segregation, or socioeconomic status. Students examine the layouts, headstones, and inscriptions in a cemetery to gather information. They then map these patterns for display when they return to the classroom. The display is one way to graphically display the information (data) the students have gathered. For example, if the cemetery includes a large plot dedicated to World War II casualties, but only a few headstones indicate Iraq War or World War I casualties, students explore reasons for this discrepancy. In the past, students made rubbings of tombstones in order to create a visual record of the resources. However, the fragility of many tombstones makes the creation of rubbings inadvisable, and in some cases, illegal. The availability of digital cameras provides an easy substitution when it is necessary to examine specific monuments and stones back in the classroom.

PROCEDURAL RECOMMENDATIONS

- Have students brainstorm questions related to the topic of study for which they want to find answers when they are in the cemetery. These questions could involve patterns in dates, social or political groups, or families. Students write these questions on notebook paper to take with them into the field.

Before leaving for the cemetery, address the following five step:

- Direct students to check local ordinances related to cemeteries and discuss with them appropriate behavior in cemeteries. Remind the students that while they are in the cemetery to conduct some research, others in the cemetery are probably there because of the loss of a loved one. Even if there are no graveside services, people may be visiting graves of loved ones. If another party is using the cemetery, it is best to stay a significant distance away from that party. Voices carry in the park-like expanse of the burial ground. However, most of the time school groups have cemeteries to themselves. Also, care needs to be exercised to make sure monuments are not inadvertently damaged. Students should refrain from stepping on flat stones and leaning or resting on raised stones because they may move slightly or topple off their base. Any items such as flags, stuffed animals, small toys, flowers, or wreaths left by the markers in a cemetery need to stay there.

- Arrange for students to receive basic instruction in using a digital camera; also instruct them in how to create a tombstone rubbing. Students will use both of these tools to gather data. If possible, obtain permission from the community or church for doing tombstone rubbings. Again, be very aware that tombstone rubbings may not be possible. Photographs and field notes are an appropriate and adequate substitute.

- Obtain a map of the cemetery that, at minimum, indicates roads, buildings, and major monuments. Some maps may also have the dates when certain sections were added; family plots (often an indicator of socioeconomic status); sections for war veterans; and areas of racial, religious, or ethnic segregation. Maps may be obtained from the local cemetery sexton or through contacting city or county officials. If the cemetery is affiliated with a house of worship, common in many rural communities, it is appropriate to contact the church or synagogue leaders. While the map itself is an excellent primary source and will probably provide the answers to some of the students' questions, it may also create new questions.

- Examine the map before going to the cemetery to establish a focused plan for data collection. This is an essential step and will help to keep students from wandering around without a clear idea of what they are supposed to do and where they are supposed to be. Consider what sections should be visited and why. Who will visit which sections, and what will they specifically be looking for? Each student or team of students working together should have a map of the section of the cemetery they will be working in. Also, divide the map into a manageable—sized grid, with numbers along one axis and letters on the other axis.

- Before leaving, make sure each student/team has all of the necessary equipment. At minimum, this should include question(s) to be answered, a digital camera, paper and writing instruments, a map of the area to be examined that can be written on, a tape measure, and materials for tombstone rubbings–if allowed and necessary.

- In the cemetery, have students look for the answers to their questions; they should document evidence they believe answers their questions. This evidence should be documented through taking digital photographs of the evidence, plotting the location where the evidence was gathered, and noting how they think the information may be helpful in their study. Note the sample data collection chart below in the assessment section.

If, and only if, rubbings are allowed, use the following procedures:

- Making a tombstone or metal plaque rubbing requires a large piece of blank light-colored paper and either a partner to stabilize the paper and keep it from moving or a quantity of masking tape to secure the paper to the stone.

- It is best to go to the cemetery after the dew has burned off in the morning and when it is has not recently rained because water will soak through the paper and prevent the tape from sticking.
- Use a dark-colored crayon (or a light-colored crayon on dark paper). Remove the paper from around the crayon, and rub the flat side of the crayon across the surface of the paper using a circular motion.
- Deeply incised or raised lettering works best, but some folk art on tombstones can also be copied in this manner.
- Be careful not to get any crayon wax on the tombstone or to leave any tape or paper behind.
- Back in the classroom, have students share their evidence with the class concerning the patterns they found and tell the class how they think they will answers their questions. Students can then compare the evidence they collected and assist one another in answering their questions.

APPLICATIONS AND IDEAS

One group of third-grade students took pictures of seven tombstones in the parish cemetery of Bruton Church in Williamsburg, Virginia. They searched the graveyard for monuments with legible inscriptions from the eighteenth and nineteenth centuries. Students had to read the inscriptions and place the photos in chronological order; they created a time line from their work that they could sort first by birth date and then by death date. By recording distribution patterns on their map, students determined that legible stone locations did not have a recognizable pattern. Students collected multiple photos, maps, and tombstone rubbings to share with other students in the class.

Another group of third-grade students took a series of 10 photos of raised monuments. Each stone monument stood over 20 inches off the ground; they were a variety of shapes—ovals, rectangles, and spires. The students asked their peers to examine the monuments for common elements and to speculate why the colonial parishioners used the practice of elevated monuments. By looking at the patterns they produced on their maps, students discovered that the elevated monuments were located closer to the church. Students then formed hypotheses about why this was so.

ASSESSMENT

Consider the following data collection chart as one part of an assessment task. Students' abilities to gather, record, and evaluate data are essential social studies skills. The ability of students to translate these data into reasonable conclusions/answers to their questions is an indicator of informed decision-making.

Item #	Item	Documentation	Description/ Identifying Characteristics	Map Location	Evidence Useful for Which Questions
1	Child's gravestone	Photograph #1, measurements recorded in notebook	Name is Earl Howell; wings at the top of stone	G4	Death occurred during flu outbreak —may be related.
2	Stone statue	Photograph #2, measurements recorded in notebook, drawing of location relative to nearby gravestones	Shape of an angel (wings) holding two children; has a date of 1885 on the base; statue was added in 1900	G4	There are a lot of kids' graves in the area; maybe kids who died of flu are here.

Based on the data I/we have collected, I/we believe that the answer to [insert relevant question] is [insert answer]. I/We believe this for the following reasons: [insert relevant evidence]. For example, using the edited data chart above, a student may conclude: Based on the data I collected, I believe the that the answer to why so many kids died in the middle 1880s is that there was a flu in the area that killed a lot of people, including kids.

REFERENCES AND RESOURCES

Capelle, J., & Smith, M. (1998). Using cemetery data to teach population biology and local history. *American Biology Teacher, 60,* 690–693.

Kincade, L. (1996). Resurrecting history in the high school classroom. *Social Studies Review, 35*(3), 10–11.

Smith, S. (1998). Making German-American connections through culture projects. *Unterrichtspraxis/Teaching German, 31*(1), 55–58.

Web Sites

This article
http://archaeology.about.com/od/mortuarystudies/a/evergreen.htm
on About.com includes an interview with a teacher about a multiyear cemetery project involving a large number of students. It is an example of how this strategy can expand into something much more than a lesson.

The Association for Gravestone Studies
http://www.gravestonestudies.org/publications.htm
is a good resource for teachers. It provides links to publications and other resources helpful for those working in cemeteries. Most of the information will not be accessible to students.

The Massachusetts Studies Project provides an excellent list of tips for working in cemeteries. The link is
http://www.msp.umb.edu/LocHistoryTemplates/MSPCemeteries.html

The PDF file found at
http://www.oregon.gov/OPRD/HCD/OCHC/docs/Workshops/ Cemetery_Lesson_Sources.pdf
from the State of Oregon provides links to specific lesson plans for cemetery studies.

A Web site chronicling the history of Rochester, New York, also includes a page dedicated to typical symbols found on Victorian-era tombstones. The page may be found at
http://www.vintageviews.org/vv-tl/pages/Cem_Symbolism.htm

To introduce cemetery vocabulary, as well as the variety of markers and monuments found in a cemetery, visit
http://www.tngenweb.org/darkside/typology.html.
This site, *Sickness and Death in the Old South,* has a variety of information; the vocabulary link above may be the most helpful for this strategy.

13

Community Maps

GRADE LEVELS	NCSS CURRICULUM STRANDS
✔ K–2	II Time, Continuity, and Change
✔ 3–5	III People, Places, and Environments
✔ 6–8	VI Power, Authority, and Governance
	VII Production, Distribution, and Consumption

INTRODUCTION

Strategy 1 presented multiple conceptions of a community, including a geographic community. Even within this conception, students belong to multiple communities, including the classroom and school communities, perhaps a neighborhood community, and certainly a town, city, and global community. This strategy, which introduces making community maps, works best with the conception of a neighborhood community. Of course, not every student lives in the traditionally defined neighborhood. Some students live on farms or ranches, several miles from the nearest neighbor. And they may attend a school surrounded by farmland or ranchland. Other students live in large apartment buildings or in apartment complexes; the building or complex may be a community. In these settings, students may ride a bus to and from school daily, which does not introduce them to the neighborhood around their school. These multiple kinds of a geographic or physical community do not take away from the opportunity for students to create community maps, indicating the streets and other important markers with labels. This strategy is useful for teaching and reinforcing map skills, including the components of a map (e.g., legend, scale, compass rose) and how to use the information or data contained on a map. It may be modified for younger students; they find their way to school and back home again by mapping all the streets between the two sites. Children can begin by mapping their playground, their school, or their room at home. They can use three-dimensional wooden blocks to represent many of these things before they are developmentally ready for two-dimensional paper representation. Students of all ages can use school milk cartons and shoe boxes to represent housing, schools, factories, shopping centers, service providers, and social organizations. Intermediate students can plan a community or reflect on the decisions city planners made for their community regarding land usage. Older students can begin to think about zoning, city planning, and balancing the needs of different people in the community. This strategy encourages students to examine and evaluate land usage, laws that protect the community and citizens, and ways members of the community help people.

PROCEDURAL RECOMMENDATIONS

- Ask parents and older siblings to help younger students look for and discuss the meaning of street signs, lights, and pavement marks as they travel through the community. Have students bring shoe boxes and cardboard to school.

- Have students build a small model of the school using a small box covered with paper. Depending on the level of the students, scale may be introduced at this point. For example, most schools are bigger than most individual homes. With prompting, students could choose boxes to approximate the size of these buildings, noting the difference. However, if scale is introduced, students may also compare the sizes of their homes. While students do live in different dwellings of different sizes, a discussion of this difference may not be part of the instructional plan.

- Using a map, help students locate where they live. Provide assistance as they create the roads that get them from their home to school: Use large sections of cardboard or large sheets of paper for the map's surface and represent the streets, including two-way and one-way streets, with masking tape. Label streets with permanent marker. This map will look quite different in a densely populated urban environment, a small town or city, and a rural community. If a city is densely populated, consider choosing one district or section to map. Conversely, if a rural setting is so large that a community map is impractical, consider using a map of a local town with which students are familiar.

- Have each student write his or her address on a model of his or her home and then locate his or her residence on the appropriate street. In situations where students are mapping a specific district or a town where students do not live, instead of labeling one's own home, students may choose to write the address of, for example, a community business, park, or school and then locate and place it on the map.

- In class, have students make a list of all the places they go after school and on weekends. As a homework assignment, have students ask their parents to list all the places their parents go during the day. Request that families discuss with young students the purposes of the buildings they visit frequently. This could include the post office, school, employment locations, malls, grocery stores, dog parks, and courthouse or other government buildings.

- Referring to these lists, have students create shopping, service, factory, and office districts on their maps. Encourage students to reflect on the relationships among these areas and determine the best arrangement for all the buildings in the community. That is, how easy is it for people to get to the places they travel to each day or week? Are certain kinds of buildings near one another? For example, are doctor's offices near the hospital? Should some buildings be near one another, while it may not be necessary for other kinds of buildings/businesses to be near one another?

- As a corollary activity, have students evaluate signs that give information; they can determine when signs are distracting and when they provide useful information.

APPLICATIONS AND IDEAS

Students in a second-grade class used construction paper to "pave" the streets on their maps and to cover boxes for homes, businesses, government buildings, and factories. They created a grid of streets replicating those in their community. Students created advertising media for their businesses so that they could find out what other businesses sold. As students carried out their tasks, teachers posed questions such as the following:

- How will we plan our city so that people can easily find things?
- How can the post office and the delivery people know where we live?

- Why do we have stop signs in some areas and not in others?
- What happens if we have too many or too few stop signs?
- Where should we put our houses, shopping centers, and factories?
- What might happen if they are too close or too far away from our homes?
- Where should we put the bus station, the train station, and the airport? Why?
- What is outside our city?

Extending the conversation into an examination of public policy, students converted half of their classroom floor into an area in which to experiment with local public policy in relation to traffic laws and ordinances on land usage. They determined which policies and laws helped which people the most and which, if any, should be abolished.

Assessment

In order to assess student-created community maps, consider a performance checklist, similar to the checklist for readers' theater, Strategy 41. Be certain to list criteria that are consistent with the lesson's objectives and that are observable for individuals and/or groups.

References and Resources

Benson, J. S. (2000). Centerville/Centerville: An exercise in mental mapping. Teacher's notebook. *Journal of Geography, 99*(1), 32–35.

Ekiss, G. O., Trapido-Lurie, B., Phillips, J., et al. (2007). The world in spatial terms: Mapmaking and map reading. *Social Studies and the Young Learner, 20*(2), 7–9.

Fertig, G., & Silverman, R. (2007). Walking and talking geography: A small-world approach. *Social Studies and the Young Learner, 20*(2), 15–18.

Fisher, C., & Binns, T. (Eds.). (2000). Issues in geography teaching. London and New York: Routledge/Falmer.

Green-Milberg, P. (1999). Geography and field work: An exercise for the elementary school. *Canadian Social Studies, 33*(3), 70–72.

Hinshaw, C. (1998). It's a flat world. *Social Studies & the Young Learner, 11*(1), 30–31.

Keiper, T. A. (1999). GIS for elementary students: An inquiry into a new approach to learning geography. *Journal of Geography, 98*(2), 47–59.

Kirman, J. M. (1996). Urban map tag: An elementary geography game. *Journal of Geography, 95*(5), 211–212.

McKay, R. (1998). Colouring maps does not geographic education make. *Canadian Social Studies, 32*(3), 74.

Milson, A. (1998). Mental mapping: Today my home, tomorrow the world! (Pull-Out 1). *Social Studies & the Young Learner, 11*(1), 1–2.

Morris, R. V. (1999). Ice and sand: Linking the sandbox to geographic features in elementary social studies. *Social Studies & the Young Learner, 11*(4), 6–10.

Sobel, D. (1998). Mapmaking with children: *Sense of place education for the elementary years.* Portsmouth, NH: Heinemann.

Taketa, R. (1996). Using field sketch mapping to teach basic mapping concepts in elementary school geography. *Journal of Geography, 95*, 126–130.

Thompson, G. (1999). "I thought the world was flat, like the maps showed it!" Building geographic understanding with elementary students. Elementary teaching ideas. *Social Education, 63*(5), 269–271.

Web Site

http://www.ncge.org/i4a/pages/index.cfm?pageid=1 is the Web site for the National Council for Geographic Education; it contains a variety of resources and links for teaching geography.

14

Custom Boxes

GRADE LEVELS	NCSS CURRICULUM STRANDS
✔ K–2	I Culture
✔ 3–5	III People, Places, and Environments
✔ 6–8	IX Global Connections

INTRODUCTION

The interactive custom box visually presents information that helps teach a particular social studies concept or skill. The teacher or a student fills a shoe box or slightly larger container with artifacts that represent a specific time, place, or group of people. These artifacts could include newspapers, photos, postcards, dolls, toys, nonperishable food, religious items, or household tools. For the box to be truly interactive, it must be more than just a three-dimensional encyclopedia; children must physically and intellectually work with the information contained in it (Lee & Ashby, 2001). Students review the artifacts to develop concepts and make generalizations about the contents of the box. The teacher can model the process students are to follow before assigning independent work. Students can carry out tasks independently, in pairs, or in small groups; they benefit from an examination of a variety of custom boxes. Younger students might use a custom box to learn about the daily life of a pioneer as they explore artifacts used on an early farm. Older students can use artifacts to determine the different religions practiced in colonial Pennsylvania and then investigate how laws influenced the diversity of religious beliefs.

PROCEDURAL RECOMMENDATIONS

- Select a topic related to your learning objectives.
- Obtain a small cardboard or shoe box that is easy to store and durable enough to withstand substantial handling. Inexpensive plastic boxes can be purchased at discount stores.
- Determine what tasks students will carry out with the contents of the box. Be sure these tasks are appropriate to help achieve your instructional objectives.

- Display clear, brief, and age-appropriate directions for the students on or in the custom box. Record directions on a digital recorder for primary students who need oral directions.
- Think about the presentation of the box. Boxes that have surprises in them engage students. For example, a box about trains might contain a small tape of train sounds; another might contain a paper foldout of the *Titanic* sliding into an iceberg.
- Place small reproductions of artifacts in the box for the students to puzzle over and explore.
- Graphically present information on controversial issues. Each side can be illustrated with opposing flaps, pull tabs, or information wheels.
- Put maps, graphs, charts, and illustrations that support the topic in the box.
- Place some sort of text in the box that students can read to obtain more information.

APPLICATIONS AND IDEAS

For example, to illustrate the local economy of Ireland, a custom box might contain a block of peat, which is a locally produced heat source, and some linen, which is a national export produced from locally grown flax. Some items could be included to represent both the tradition and the culture of Ireland, such as a replica of the Blarney Stone; a Celtic cross, which is representative of the majority religion; a tape recording of Celtic folk music; and a tin whistle with music as an example of a folk instrument. A hat badge from an American Civil War army unit called the Irish Brigade reminds students of the historical impact of mass migration to America. Modern Ireland is represented through national and international news from a Dublin newspaper, photographic views of Ireland today, and maps. Students also can add elements of controversy to the custom box to encourage discussion.

Questions that may be asked related to a custom box on Ireland include:

- To what time period does the box refer?
- Which side or what part of the box is the most appealing to students? Why?
- To what location does the box refer?
- How does the box represent a group or region?
- Does the box perpetuate any stereotypes or myths? Which ones and how?
- What is the danger of just sampling the culture?
- What can the box not tell?
- What controversial issue is raised by the content of the box?

Custom boxes might be used for simulations of international festivals where students display their work. In class, students share more formally what tasks they carried out to complete the assignment, where they obtained information, and how they arrived at a final product. Teachers might trade boxes with their colleagues in other states or nations and have the students attempt to determine where the box originated.

Assessment Task

Custom Box Scoring Rubric

_____ (3 points possible) *Artifacts* – The box contains at least two artifacts that relate information about the topic selected.

    3 – Three or more artifacts

    2 – Two or more artifacts

    1 – One or more artifacts

_____ (3 points possible) *Controversial Issue* – The box contains at least two artifacts that relate information about an issue that caused people to take sides about the specific topic. Students earn points for explaining controversial issues.

    3 – Explain both sides of two controversial issues

    2 – Explain both sides of one controversial issue

    1 – Explain one side of a controversial issue

_____ (3 points possible) *Map, Graph, or Chart* – Two sides of the box feature a map, graph, or chart that relates information about your specific topic. Students earn points for including graphic information that supports the culture or time period selected.

    3 – Three or more maps, graphs, or charts

    2 – Two maps, graphs, or charts

    1 – One map, graph, or chart

_____ (3 points possible) *Illustration* – Two sides of the box feature at least one illustration. This is a drawing, a photograph, or a photocopy. Students earn points for conclusions that identified, explained, or exemplified the culture or time period selected.

    3 – Three or more illustrations

    2 – Two illustrations

    1 – One illustration

_____ (3 points possible) *Narrative* – One side of the box features accurate information presented in narrative form.

    3 – Student writing using three or more sources

    2 – Student writing using one source

    1 – Photocopy

_____ (15 points possible) Total Points

REFERENCES AND RESOURCES

Glennon, R. C., Hickey, M. G., Gecsei, K., & Klein, S. (2007). A school-wide effort for learning history via a time capsule. *Social Education, 71*(5), 261–266, 271.

Lee, P., & Ashby, R. (2001). Empathy, perspective taking, and rational understanding. In O. L. Davis, Jr., E. A. Yeager, & S. J. Foster (Eds.), *Historical empathy and perspective taking in the social studies* (pp. 21–50). Lanham, MD: Rowman & Littlefield.

Morris, R. V. (2000). Teaching social studies with artifacts. *Social Studies, 91*(1), 32–37.

Morris, R. V. (2001). How teachers can conduct historical reenactments in their own schools. *Childhood Education, 77*(4), 196–203.

Wasta, S. (2001). Changing attitudes through art, literature, and artifacts: A China experience. *Social Studies, 92*(1), 4–9.

Web Sites

AZ Trading Post
http://www.aztradingpost.com/artifacts.html

Ethnic Arts and Facts
http://www.ethnicartsandfacts.com/node/2

Folk Art
http://www.folkart.com/servlet/StoreFront

Ohio History Teacher
http://www.ohiohistoryteachers.org/02/03/ms1d.shtml

Pictures of Record, Inc.
http://www.picturesofrecord.com/stone%20tools.htm

Decision Trees and Decision Grids

GRADE LEVELS	NCSS CURRICULUM STRANDS
✔ 3–5	II Time, Continuity, and Change
✔ 6–8	VII Production, Distribution, and Consumption

INTRODUCTION

Decision trees and decision grids are a very specific type of graphic organizer (see Strategy 24). They are often used in an economics curriculum. Although each looks a bit different, they all serve the same purpose. They provide a concrete visual of the central problem and the decisions that need to be made when limited resources (e.g., money, time, product) meet unlimited wants. When students use these graphic organizers, they are able to clearly illustrate all of the reasons why a certain decision should be made. This clarity is achieved by examining and discussing all of the criteria considered in making an informed decision as well as all of the alternatives available. Trees and grids also allow students to examine broader policy decisions from both historical and current perspectives.

Decision trees and decision grids work best in relation to topics involving decision making. For example, in a unit on personal economics, students might be asked to make a decision on what to do with a gift of money. In an immigration unit, students might be asked to examine the criteria on which a nineteenth-century Chinese family bases its decision to immigrate to the United States.

PROCEDURAL RECOMMENDATIONS

- Once a decision has been isolated for study, direct students to consider all of the issues involved in making the decision. In the immigration example, these issues might include family concerns, economic opportunities, and health. Students determine these criteria by studying primary and secondary sources. Diaries and letters in which the writer ponders difficult decisions provide clues about the issues weighed by individuals in similar situations. Secondary sources that provide a social and historical context are also examined.
- Have students determine reasonable alternatives. They begin by brainstorming all of the ways in which the problem can be solved or the decision might be made. In the immigration

example, one alternative would be not to immigrate; another would be to immigrate to a country other than the United States. Again, examining relevant sources assists students in determining reasonable alternatives.

- Have students create a grid or a table listing the alternatives across the top, with each alternative in its own box or cell. List the criteria down the left side of the table, with each criterion in its own box or cell. It does not matter which category is listed across the top and which is listed down the side; just be sure that alternatives are listed with alternatives and criteria are listed with criteria. The size of the table depends on the alternatives and criteria identified. If there are three criteria and six alternatives, then a three-square by six-square grid or table is needed.

- Input each criterion and alternative.

- Have students match each criterion with each alternative and decide if the result is good (+) or bad (−). In the immigration example, students may first examine the criterion of family and the alternative of immigrating to the United States. After reflecting on what they have learned from relevant resources, students may decide that immigrating would have negative consequences, as it would cause the extended family to separate.

- After students examine all criteria and alternatives, consider all evidence, and determine which decisions carry positive and which carry negative consequences, have them look holistically at each alternative. Which is predominantly positive? This should be the best alternative. Have students refer to their resources again. Does the decision they reached parallel that made by families in the nineteenth century?

- In an alternative approach, have students rank in order the criteria across the alternatives. Instead of assigning a + or −, students assign the best alternative a high number (6 if there are six alternatives, 4 if there are four alternatives, etc.); they assign the worst alternative a 1. Direct students to calculate the alternative with the highest value; this should be the best decision. Teachers should be aware that ties often occur with the +/− system. After additional research and reflection, students can repeat the process with just the items that tied, or they can try the numerical approach. In addition, rarely are the criteria considered absolutely equal in importance. Major decisions are affected by human emotion and desire. In the immigration example, the criterion of family may be much more important than that of economic opportunity. On the other hand, an individual with no family ties to his or her homeland may place more weight on economic opportunity. Students might determine that certain criteria carry a double weight. That is, a + would translate to a ++ ; a score of 4 would translate to 8. Finally, sometimes a decision is made that seems to defy all analyses of criteria and alternatives. Such a decision requires more intense research and discussion to determine why the decision was made.

Decision trees are slightly different from decision grids. A decision tree template is featured in Figure 15.1. Decision trees begin with a problem or issue as the root or trunk of the tree. In economic theory, the placement of the problem may be at the top, side, or bottom of the page. To help students connect to the tree metaphor, place the problem at the bottom of the page, where they would typically draw the trunk or root system of a tree. Students then add alternative solutions to the problem as primary branches, with consequences of choosing each alternative as secondary branches. Tertiary branches can serve as the positive and/or negative ramifications of each consequence. The decision is noted at the top of the tree. As with the decision grid, decision trees encourage a thoughtful analysis of the solutions to a problem or issue by identifying, examining, and evaluating multiple alternatives. For the teacher wishing to incorporate an economic perspective, decision trees and decision grids lend themselves to discussions of basic economic problems and concepts.

FIGURE 15.1   Decision Tree Template

APPLICATIONS AND IDEAS

Decision grids follow a fairly standard format. There can be as many criteria and alternatives as the particular decision requires. For intermediate students unfamiliar with using a decision grid, a four-by-four grid is certainly sufficient.

Table 15.1 features a grid that examines the disposition of a birthday gift of $100. There are many different ways to spend the $100, and in this case, the student is trying to make the best decision. The criteria for making the decision are listed on the left, and the alternatives are listed across the top. In this case, each criterion is of equal value; no one criterion carries more weight than another. Each cell in the grid includes a positive or negative notation, representing the positive or negative of the alternative for each criterion.

In the example in Table 15.1, buying a new skateboard has four signs. That seems to be the best alternative for spending the $100. The personal decision a student makes may not be the one an adult such as a parent or teacher would make; nevertheless, this student's decision was carefully weighed. Other students, when given the same $100, might have different alternatives and different criteria. This is also true in historical and current events. When given the same opportunity to make a decision, different people (e.g., leaders) make different decisions based on the evidence, alternatives, and criteria they weight.

TABLE 15.1	EXAMPLE OF A DECISION GRID			
WHAT SHOULD I DO WITH $100?				
ALTERNATIVES ➡ CRITERIA ⬇	SAVE FOR COLLEGE	BUY THE NEWEST VIDEO GAME	DONATE ONE-HALF TO CHARITY AND SAVE THE REST FOR COLLEGE	BUY A NEW SKATEBOARD
Mom and Dad say okay	+ Mom and Dad say it's my money	+	+	+ I can do what I want with it
Fun for me now	– Not so much fun now	+ Lots of fun now	– Might feel good, but not very much fun	+ Lots of fun now
Good for me later	+ Will help pay for college	– Probably not; there are new games all of the time; something better might come along	+ Saving for college is good; donating may or may not make a long-term difference	+ Skateboarding is good exercise; I could compete and make more money; it could keep me healthy—if I don't fall and get hurt
Share with my friends	– I don't get to do anything with friends in this option	+ We would have fun playing the new games together	– No opportunity to share with friends	+ I could skate with my friends

ASSESSMENT

An analytical scoring rubric would work well with decision grids and decision trees.

	Criteria	Alternatives	Evaluation
3	All reasonable criteria for making a decision are listed.	All reasonable alternatives are listed.	Student supports decision with evidence from decision tree/grid.
2	Most reasonable criteria for making a decision are listed.	Most reasonable alternatives are listed.	Student uses some evidence to support decision made.
1	Very few reasonable criteria for making a decision are listed.	Very few reasonable alternatives are listed.	Student uses very little evidence to support decision made.

REFERENCES AND RESOURCES

Agency for Instructional Technology, Canadian Foundation for Economic Education, & Joint Council on Economic Education. (1989). *Econ and me: Teacher's guide.* Bloomington, IN: Agency for Instructional Technology. This teacher's guide provides a decision tree template. It accompanies a video series on elementary economics instruction; a decision-making lesson is included in the video.

National Council on Economic Education. (1997). *Voluntary national content standards.* New York: Author. Note that many materials produced by the National Council on Economic Education (NCEE) (known as the Joint Council on Economic Education) use various forms of decision trees and decision grids in economics lessons.

Schug, M. C. (2007). Why did the colonists fight when they were safe, prosperous, and free? *Social Education, 71*(2), 61–65.

Vargha, L. D. (2004). Buyer beware! Economics activities for middle school students. *Social Studies, 95*(1), 27–31

Web Sites

The NCEE Web site includes many excellent teaching strategies and materials as well as additional links to other helpful resources.

In particular, the *EconEd Link* at
http://www.econedlink.org
provides access to numerous lesson plans, some of which utilize a decision-making model.

For a sample U.S. history lesson, check out
http://www.econedlink.org lessons/index.php?lesson=EM581&page=teacher.
This lesson addresses the U.S. Civil War.

The site
http://www.ackland.org/education/k12/grant_website/LPFactandOpinion.html
has a lesson plan that utilizes a decision tree in American history and art. Teachers will need to adapt this to fit their own learning objectives.

The lesson found at
http://www.slaveryinamerica.org/history/hs_lp_burialgrounds.htm
utilizes a decision tree in middle school history and African slave history in the United States.

The PBS-supported interdisciplinary unit plan
http://www.pbs.org/opb/conquistadors/teachers/pdf/unit4.pdf
includes one lesson that utilizes a decision tree.

16

Digital Storytelling

GRADE LEVELS	NCSS CURRICULUM STRANDS
✔ 3–5	II Time, Continuity, and Change
✔ 6–8	III People, Places, and Environments
	IV Individuals, Groups, and Institutions

INTRODUCTION

Students can make their own audiovisual materials when none exist, or as a way to demonstrate their learning. This is especially important for state and local history, but it is also necessary when there is not a market for a publisher to create materials on more obscure topics the students may become interested in exploring. This activity requires that students generate research questions, gather data, and interrogate the data before preparing it for dissemination. This strategy promotes the development of sequencing skills. Students sequence events as they generate a script and select illustrations. Students organize and produce information to share with an audience. Students in many classes give oral reports. An abundance of computer software is available to assist students in creating their slide shows. Students use a digital camera to make a Microsoft PowerPoint presentation. The PowerPoint slide show oral report asks students to incorporate all of the research skills they have learned from examining primary sources (see Strategy 8) in addition to creating a visual component to the presentation.

Students produce a real product for a real audience using this strategy. Younger students might tell a story by creating and narrating a script and illustrating it with still shots. They might import just a few images showing the same location at different times in history. Older students can build multiple-screen presentations that blend video recordings, maps, historical images, and contemporary images. They might work in groups to convey their position about an issue, illustrate both sides of the issue, or encourage the audience to take a stand about the issue. They can then share their work with peers, parents, and community groups such as local historical societies.

PROCEDURAL RECOMMENDATIONS

- Have students form small groups of approximately four students each.
- Assist students in selecting a social studies topic to explore, possibly from a field trip or current event. Connect the topic to something that is already a part of the social studies curriculum.

- Have the groups brainstorm and select the content they wish to interpret from an experience, story, primary source, interview, or combination of these.

- Prompt students to select the approach they wish to take with their audience. Will their production include only their point of view? Will it show multiple sides of an issue? Who is the intended audience? Will the production let the audience members decide at the end what position they will take?

- Direct each student to independently write a narrative with an introduction, body, and conclusion that is congruent with the content and central theme of the proposed product.

- While creating the narrative, encourage students to use primary source material and establish historical context by including quotations from famous persons of the era as well as common people with dissenting opinions.

- Have group members share their individually produced narratives with their group members. Allow time for groups to select the segments of these narratives that they believe can best be combined into a master script. Students will also need time to edit. This includes working on transitions, reading for consistent language and terminology, as well as other issues.

- Direct groups to decide on the junctures in their master script where they will illustrate their narrative with images. Students may select the interval for illustration as every 2 to 10 seconds or every specified number of lines of text. Students might choose simply to illustrate the most interesting action events with images.

- Have students generate a master script that includes both the text of the production and the points at which illustrations will occur.

- Have each student in the group gather illustrations. Encourage students to use photos of sites and artwork, and refer them to fashion plates, historical clothing books, and patterns for historically authentic characters. Books showing tools, houses, and antiques can also help the students.

- Students import photographs from the digital camera into presentation software such as PowerPoint.

- Students can photograph bookplates or other artwork. Encourage original artwork, because illustrating their own artwork adds another layer of understanding for some students. Crayon, marker, colored chalk, oil pastels, charcoal, gauche, collage, and mixed media on white or manila paper may all be used for illustration.

- Direct students to prepare a storyboard to serve as a pictorial representation of each illustration. Create the storyboard first in erasable pencil with simple drawings. The storyboard should include a numbered drawing for each image. One drawing represents one frame. Each illustration should be accompanied by a brief explanation.

- Have students practice reading their portion of the script aloud and then take turns reading into the microphone. Encourage students to speak with clarity, expression, and appropriate volume. Digitize the voice and import it into your program.

- Assist students in locating and recording appropriate period music for use during the opening, background, or credits.

- Set the presentation for automatic advance.

- The teacher may wish to invite parents for the slide show premiere.

APPLICATIONS AND IDEAS

An elementary class developed a PowerPoint slide show on the Civil War Battle of Antietam using five types of slides to illustrate their program. They used modern slides of the preserved battlefield including landscapes. Students also used details from the battlefield site, including murals in the visitor's center; base reliefs on monuments; statues placed on the battlefield; a cannon; and period structures such as houses, barns, and outbuildings. They used slides of historical reenactors in battle. They downloaded and scanned slides from books of actual Civil War photographs and period drawings. They also downloaded and scanned maps and contemporary artwork of the battle. In their narration, students used quotations to tell their story, including humorous anecdotes that illustrated the life of the common soldier. In their script they told of leadership in combat and related the story of the battle as it unfolded. Students also interpreted the information they presented and told why this battle was important.

In another example, elementary students who attended a school named after a local pioneer wanted to share the life story of this person with other students in their school. The class took a field trip to the cemetery to see the final resting place of the pioneer and her family. The elementary students then used records donated by the local chapter of the Daughters of the American Revolution to learn about this pioneer. They selected interesting events from the woman's life to create a script. They then selected high-interest scenes to illustrate with crayon on manila paper. They debated about which scenes were the most important to illustrate and what material to include. They produced and narrated a project and shared it with many different classes in the school. After the classroom debut, both the local chapter of the Daughters of the American Revolution and the state Junior Historical Society invited the students to present their work.

Another class of older students formed nine groups to learn about the Sumerians, Babylonians, Hittites, Phoenicians, Hebrews, Assyrians, Chaldeans, Lydians, and Persians. Each member of each group researched the assigned civilization and examined its government, religion, division of labor, class structure, system of writing, and contribution to the world. Each group member recorded important information; as a group, students decided what information to include in their production. Each group submitted a completed project, including narration and music. In addition, each student turned in his or her notes and three bibliography cards listing his or her sources. The title page included a descriptive title for the project, the names of all group members, and a list of illustrations. The presentations were each five to seven minutes in length.

ASSESSMENT

An upper elementary class became interested in a horse farm located near an interstate highway. On a previous field trip, these urban students had seen Percheron draft horses pulling mechanical equipment used for preparing fields, planting, and harvesting that piqued their interest in historical farming practices. Working with their teacher, the students called the farmer and arranged to visit the farm. They interviewed the farmer, took pictures as he described his horses, handled equipment, learned details about how it worked, and found out how horsepower operated it. Later in the day, students photographed the farmer gathering corn into shocks; back in the classroom, students transformed their notes into a story to accompany their digital images. They then sorted and placed the images in order and finally created a digital narration to accompany the program. After rehearsing several times, the students presented their PowerPoint slide program to the state social studies council as a sample of exemplary student work.

4 Points	3 Points	2 Points	1 Points
Students created a series of images that illustrated a demonstration of late-nineteenth-century technology.	Students created a series of images that illustrated a demonstration of late-nineteenth-century technology.	Students created a series of images that illustrated a demonstration of late-nineteenth-century technology.	Students created a series of images that illustrated a demonstration of late-nineteenth-century technology.
Students created a story to accompany their images that described history, geography, and economics.	Students created a story to accompany their images that described history, geography, and economics.	Students created a story to accompany their images that described history, geography, and economics.	
Students compared the advantages and disadvantages of farming like this.	Students compared the advantages and disadvantages of farming like this.		
Students evaluated why there were few farms like this left near the city.			

REFERENCES AND RESOURCES

Escobar, D. (2001). *Creating history documentaries: A step-by-step guide to video projects in the classroom.* Waco, TX: Prufrock Press.

Green, T. (2001). Tech talk for social studies teachers: Virtual expeditions. *Social Studies, 92*(4), 177–179.

Grosvenor, I., & Lawn, M. (2004). Days out of school: Secondary education, citizenship and public space in 1950s England. *History of Education, 33*(4), 377–389.

Postigo, Y., & Pozo, J. I. (2004). On the road to graphicacy: The learning of graphical representation systems. *Educational Psychology, 24*(5), 623–644.

VanSledright, B. A. (2002). Fifth graders investigating history in the classroom: Results from a researcher-practitioner design experiment. *Elementary School Journal, 103*(2), 131–160.

Web Sites

Brainy Betty
http://www.brainybetty.com

Digital History
www.digitalhistory.uh.edu/images.cfm

Free Digital Photos
http://www.freedigitalphotos.net/

New York Public Library
http://digitalgallery.nypl.org/nypldigital/index.cfm

Templateswise
www.templateswise.com

17

Discerning Qualifications

GRADE LEVELS	NCSS CURRICULUM STRANDS
✔ 3–5	III People, Places, and Environments
✔ 6–8	IV Individual Development and Identity
	V Individuals, Groups, and Institutions
	VI Power, Authority, and Governance

INTRODUCTION

Through the strategy of reflective choice, students look at the criteria for a specific job or task, scrutinize applicants for that job, and determine the rank order of the candidates in order to best fill that task. Students see only applications, letters, or personnel files without the photo or name of each applicant; they then work with a list of each applicant's accomplishments up to the time of the selection. The nature of the task requires that the individual students first evaluate the candidates and sort them into a ranked order before talking with their peers to rationalize why they ordered them thusly. Prejudices and biases are discovered as students list the reasons for selecting or rejecting certain candidates. Students discern qualities that they deem important through a decision-making process.

Students work with real problems from the past; in each of these situations students determine what they think and then make decisions. They consider the point of view of the person making the decision, which is often made with limited information; they then need to weigh the evidence. They also need to evaluate whether the choice is good for the individual, the group, or society.

Students can consider many types of jobs including the following: who should be selected to write the Declaration of Independence, who should be elected President after looking at four or more parties, who should be the first man in space from the first seven astronauts, who should take leadership of the civil rights movement, which immigrants should be invited to settle in Spanish Texas, who should assume leadership for women's suffrage, and who should be given overall command of the D-Day invasion of Normandy. In each of these examples, many conflicting claims and highly qualified people are available from which to choose.

PROCEDURAL RECOMMENDATIONS

- To construct this type of situation, a problem with multiple characters is needed. For example, "Who should represent the commonwealth of Virginia at the Constitutional Convention?" For this situation, all of the members of the delegation are included as possible representatives, as are some other groups of people. English generals, Loyalists, women, and enslaved persons are included so that every person on the list would not have automatically signed the Constitution. By thus selecting the characters from which the students can choose, students are allowed an opportunity to discuss who could not have been selected at that time, who left the commonwealth during the Revolution, and how the people of Virginia split over the controversial issue. Students see factions and minority opinions and give voice to other points of view rather than just reflecting the majority.

- Many times students see decisions as being very obvious choices when viewed in retrospect, when in reality the decision was anything but obvious at the time. In this case, which of the delegates chose not to sign?

- After the potential representatives to the Constitutional Convention are selected, a limited and equitable amount of information is given about each character. This is to help the younger students get to the facts and not be overwhelmed with information; older students can use more elaborate and complex information.

- The information about the character is limited to what was available at the time they were selected for the convention. Sometimes information such as place of birth, age, past failures, and economic or social standing will affect the student's ranking preference. In this case discussion of those issues can expose bias, myths, and stereotypes. For example, students frequently reject Benjamin Franklin as a member to the Constitutional Convention due to his age, ill health, and tendency to sleep during proceedings. Students need to consider other characteristics, such as his reputation or ability to be conciliatory, that are not apparent at first glance.

- Next, students get the opportunity to justify their rankings with a peer and with the entire class before getting to research and find out more about the characters.

- In the debriefing, ask students to consider: What did they learn from this procedure? How does it apply to their lives today?

APPLICATIONS AND IDEAS

Students receive a packet of papers with identities in addition to a situation such as the following: In the opening days of the Civil War, President Lincoln has to select leaders for the army. Whom would he choose? The person must have the correct qualifications: He must have graduated from West Point, and he must have had experience in the military. Rank these applicants from 1 to 9, with 1 being the highest.

Applicant #1 [Pierre Gustave Toutant Beauregard]

- Was the son of a prominent French Creole family
- Attended private schools
- Graduated second in his class at West Point
- Was an engineer on General Winfield Scott's staff during the Mexican War
- Was named Superintendent of West Point

Applicant #2 [Albert Sidney Johnson]

- Attended Transylvania College and then graduated with honors from West Point
- Served in the Black Hawk War

- Was appointed the senior Texas brigadier general and the next year served as the Texas Secretary of War
- Served as a colonel in the Mexican War and was sent to discuss surrender terms with the Mexicans
- Led an expedition to Utah and headed the army operation on the Pacific Coast

Applicant #3 [Joseph Eggleston Johnston]

- Graduated from West Point thirteenth in his class
- Served in the Seminole War
- Resigned from the army to become a civil engineer
- Saved a party of government surveyors from an Indian attack
- Was a brigadier general and part of the prestigious topographical engineers

Applicant #4 [Robert Edward Lee]

- Came from a good family and was the son of a Revolutionary War hero
- Attended West Point, graduating second in his class
- Served as General Winfield Scott's chief engineer during the Mexican War
- Was Superintendent of West Point
- Worked for the Corps of Engineers and then served in the cavalry

Applicant #5 [George Brinton Mcclellan]

- Was educated in private schools and the University of Pennsylvania and graduated second in his class at West Point
- Worked on General Scott's staff in the Mexican War
- Served as an engineering instructor at West Point, undertook western military and construction projects, and went to Europe to study armies and war
- Resigned from the army and became the chief engineer of the Illinois Central Railroad
- Became the president of the Ohio and Mississippi Railroad in 2 years

Applicant #6 [George Gordon Meade]

- Was born in Spain
- Attended West Point, graduating nineteenth in his class
- Resigned from the army after serving the minimum one-year tour of duty to become an engineer and surveyor
- Rejoined the topographical engineers as a surveyor
- Served in the Mexican War

Applicant #7 [Philip Henry Sheridan]

- Was born to Irish immigrant parents
- Entered West Point when he was 17 by lying about his age
- Was suspended for a full year after attacking a cadet officer with a bayonet
- Graduated near the bottom of his class after 5 years
- Fought Indians in the NorthWest, in what is now Oregon

Applicant #8 [William Tecumseh Sherman]

- Was one of 11 children and his father died when he was young
- Graduated sixth in his class from West Point
- Was assigned to staff duties in California during the Mexican War
- Became a banker, but his bank failed; lost the only case he brought to court as a lawyer
- Served as a superintendent of a military academy

Applicant #9 [George Henry Thomas]

- Studied law and served as a deputy court clerk
- Graduated twelfth in his class from West Point
- Went to Florida to fight the Seminole Indians
- Earned commendation at Monterey and Buena Vista during the Mexican War
- Taught artillery and cavalry at West Point

After students finish rating the candidates, they turn to a classmate and justify why they gave some applicants high marks and others low marks. Then the teacher asks the class members if they saw any patterns in making the selections they made. Where do the class members agree and where do they disagree? Next, the teacher passes out a list of names to go with the applicants.

Applicant #1: Pierre Gustave Toutant Beauregard
Applicant #2: Albert Sidney Johnson
Applicant #3: Joseph Eggleston Johnston
Applicant #4: Robert Edward Lee
Applicant #5: George Brinton McClellan
Applicant #6: George Gordon Meade
Applicant #7: Philip Henry Sheridan
Applicant #8: William Tecumseh Sherman
Applicant #9: George Henry Thomas

Students need to pool their knowledge about these applicants to determine who each candidate was and whether or not he would be a good Union army commander for President Lincoln. Do the students see any patterns? Next, students divide the list of names and go to the computers to determine what had happened to the applicants by the end of the Civil War. Students also discover how each applicant chose on which side of the Civil War he would fight.

ASSESSMENT

For a more current example, use this strategy to explore local government. Ask students what qualifications the mayor of their town needs. With a partner, students brainstorm a list of qualities they want the mayor to possess. Next, students prioritize the order of the criteria. They then compare their list of criteria with their peers. Each person provides a justification for the order of their qualifications based on what they think would be good for a community. They make a list of qualities where they disagree and compare these lists with those of the class. Ask students what might happen if a mayor did not possess these skills.

4 Points	3 Points	2 Points	1 Point
Students create a list of qualities for their mayor.	Students create a list of qualities for their mayor.	Students create a list of qualities for their mayor.	Students create a list of qualities for their mayor.
Students prioritize their lists of qualities.	Students prioritize their lists of qualities.	Students prioritize their lists of qualities.	
Students provide a justification for their order of qualifications.	Students provide a justification for their order of qualifications.		
Students determine what might happen if a mayor lacked each quality.			

REFERENCES AND RESOURCES

Allen, R. F. (2000). Civic education and the decision-making process. *Social Studies, 91*(1), 5–8.

Chilcoat, G. W., & Ligon, J. A. (2000). Issues-centered instruction in the elementary social studies classroom. *Theory & Research in Social Education, 28*(2), 220–272.

Dyson, R. (2004). The Civil War on the Internet: A selection of the best Web sources for educators and students. *Social Studies, 95*(5), 211.

Rubin, B. C., & Giarelli, J. M. (Eds.). (2007). *Civic education for diverse citizens in global times: Rethinking theory and practice.* Mahwah, NJ: Erlbaum.

Wilen, W. W. (2004). Refuting misconceptions about classroom discussion. *Social Studies, 95*(1), 33.

Web Sites

America's History in the Making
http://www.learner.org/courses/amerhistory/interactives/

Educating for Democracy
http://www.cms-ca.org/CMS%20white%20paper%20final.pdf

National Center for History in the Schools
http://nchs.ucla.edu/standards/

Thinking Skills: Northwest Regional Educational Laboratory
http://www.nwrel.org/index.html

18

Field Trips of Distinction

GRADE LEVELS	NCSS CURRICULUM STRANDS
✔ K–2	II Time, Continuity, and Change
✔ 3–5	III People, Places, and Environments
✔ 6–8	IV Individual Development and Identity
	V Individuals, Groups, and Institutions
	VI Power, Authority, and Governance
	X Civic Ideals and Practices

INTRODUCTION

Students enjoy field trips; they learn from both the sites they visit and the knowledgeable people who staff the sites. All of the learning that students accrue in their field experiences becomes useful when they return to their classroom and complete projects based on those experiences (Field, 2001). By preparing questions before taking a field trip, younger students are better able to use the experience to obtain valuable research data. In order to help them demonstrate their knowledge, older students can gather data from the field and combine it with the research they did in preparation for the trip; when students return from their field trip, they need to document their experience. Younger travelers narrate class stories for their teacher to record, while older students record their peripatetic adventures in journals. Students can focus on how the site is interpreted, note if they see any discrepancies with the interpretation of the site, and then evaluate the site to determine what changes need to be made before they return.

As much as the adventurous educator would like to try, the world is too large to take a group of students everywhere to see everything of merit. When time and distance conspire to make the field trip within the school day impossible to manage, then, and only then, is a virtual field trip necessary. Some sites can be viewed vicariously using a computer screen; on the pseudo–field trip, students and teachers can see digital images of the site ranging from snapshots to complex 360-degree views or elaborate computer models of the site. Regardless of the media used, the virtual field trip will allow students to get content information from the site; it will also allow students to see views of the site, and there will be historical photographs and artwork connected with the site. The virtual field trip nearly always proceeds in a linear fashion to explore the site.

Procedural Recommendations

- Plan the field trip a year in advance, basing your site selection on a particular purpose, theme, or instructional objective. Talk to teachers who have led successful field trips to determine school policies.

- Teachers can provide leadership in helping students and parents raise money to defray the costs of an expensive field trip. However, they should not allow fund-raising to consume much of their time. A strong sense of curricular responsibilities should guide time management.

- Determine how all the sites visited will relate to one another. Plan activities to meet the instructional objectives. Arrange for students to do something besides just listening to presentations at the site. One might have them simply take notes or draw a quick sketch to take back to the classroom.

- Obtain administrative approval for the trip, and make arrangements for transportation.

- Make a reservation for the group at each site. The site may have pre-visit activities. Make sure the agents in charge of the site know why the students are coming and what they need to accomplish. Plan well in advance to ensure that students do nothing on site that they could have done just as well at school and that the tour is both meaningful and challenging. Ask the docent to introduce specific controversial issues and ideas during the tour or program.

- Send information to parents about when the trip will occur; what the students need to bring; plus the costs, hours, food arrangements, overnight accommodations, and itinerary.

- Make sure all field trip procedures set forth by the administration are known and followed. Make arrangements to call an administrator if there is a delay in the return trip. Carry a first-aid kit and establish procedures for emergency room visits. If extra staff personnel are involved on the trip, have them drive an extra car to follow the bus in case of student illness.

- During the trip enforce school-sanctioned disciplinary measures. Tell students how to thank docents either orally or by applause. Establish cleanup procedures for the bus, dining rooms, cabins or dormitories, and community areas such as hotel lobbies.

- Note the names of outstanding docents for special thanks, and request them for subsequent field trips.

- After returning from the trip, have students write thank-you notes to all adults who helped with the experience. Evaluate the sites visited. Ask if the trip was a worthwhile investment of time, effort, and finances.

If students choose to explore the virtual field trip, they will need some assignment to go with this exploration. Here is a model that could help students interact with the chosen Web site.

- What is the name of this group of people mentioned on the Web site? Why do we remember them?

- What point of view does this Web site communicate (e.g., celebration, curiosity, remembrance, patriotism, patronization)?

- What else was happening in the world when the events of this Web site occurred? Find this group on the globe, and determine how far students are from the site.

- Evaluate the ideas that are presented. Are they good for society? Are they sustainable?

- How does this Web site connect students to other people in other places in time?

- What is a common theme between students and this group (such as equality, freedom, justice, liberty, literacy, oppression, or poverty)?

- Does this Web site highlight any controversial issues? What are the two or more sides that this site explores? With which side do students more nearly agree? Why?

APPLICATIONS AND IDEAS

On a family field trip each first-grade student took one parent to Washington, D.C., for three days. Each parent was responsible for his or her child and stayed in a room with the child at night. During the day, the parents traveled with the children as a group, participated in tours and activities that were developmentally appropriate, built on the strengths of the site, and helped the children work with their peers. Together they visited monuments, spent time in the Smithsonian Institution, and saw famous buildings. This cross-generational experience helped to broaden the world for the students, gave them positive experiences with their parents, and provided them with the safety and security they needed to travel. It helped the teacher meet social studies goals and promoted positive social interactions between peers.

In reinforcing the curricular connections of a field trip to Washington, D.C., students may be asked to recall some of their experiences, apply, and evaluate that knowledge. The suggested ideas that follow work with most elementary-aged students. Primary students should be able to name five people who made a contribution to the development of the nation and two of those contributions. Primary students need to pick one person as the most important and tell why they think he or she made the most important contribution. At the end of the trip, primary students should make a chart of their nominees for V.I.A.—very important American—to hang in their room and tell why their nominee deserves this recognition.

Middle-grade elementary students should be able to name three sites they visited and how those sites contribute to the process of democracy. Middle-grade elementary students should evaluate what would happen if this process did not occur. At the end of the trip, middle-grade elementary students can create a cartoon with five frames showing what their community would be like if government did not work.

Many students have an opportunity to go to Washington, D.C., as an extension of their middle school U.S. history curriculum. The members of one group might prepare for their field experience by training to become tour guides at the individual sites they will visit. They select their site by lottery and then obtain information about it from at least three books, the Internet, teacher-created files, and flyers. Each student develops an 8-minute presentation that addresses two questions: (1) Why is this structure important? (2) What happens here? Next, students select a controversy related to the site; in their presentation of the controversy, they summarize the arguments for both sides but remain impartial. They use color pictures to highlight their presentations and generate an outline of their script. They rehearse their presentations, keeping track of the time each one consumes. On the day of their presentations, they distribute a descriptive tri-fold travel brochure that they created using Microsoft Publisher.

The group's teacher is aware congressional representatives often meet their constituents on the Capitol steps for a "meet-and-greet" session and a photo opportunity. The teacher also knows that students need strong preparation for this session: They need to know about the personal background of their senator or representative as well as his or her legislative experience, committee memberships, political affiliation, and political background. The teacher assists students in discovering what bills are coming out of or going into committee and in finding out about the bills to be voted on by the full Congress. He or she helps students prepare specific questions to ask their senator or representative about these bills, what he or she does during a typical day, how he or she raises funds, what issues will come up in the next election, or how he or she stands on various issues.

A field trip to Washington, D.C., also includes visits to many important historic sites. During these visits, students share their travel brochures and other information about the particular site they researched, thus adding to the store of information presented by tour guides and site authorities. Students also collect flyers, leaflets, handouts, ticket stubs, postcards, and photos during the trip. All of these items give the students data and artifacts they can use when they return to the classroom.

After the field trip, students use all the material they gathered as well as additional resources on the Internet to create a class scrapbook about Washington, D.C. They write an introduction for the scrapbook in which they discuss the purpose of the field trip. They describe the cost of this opportunity: What did they give up to go on this trip? They also discuss the rights and responsibilities of group membership: How were they entrusted with responsibilities on this excursion? Next, they evaluate their role in group planning before departure: How were they involved in decision making? In the next section of the scrapbook, students use one page to describe each site they visited; each page must have a picture with an accompanying caption. In addition, students evaluate the importance of the sites, give reasons for their opinions, and describe their responses to the sites. The final section of the scrapbook is the conclusion. In this section students evaluate the trip. They identify the sites they consider most valuable or interesting and tell how the trip might be improved. Next, students report on what they learned from participating in the trip. Finally, they explain how they have changed because of the trip.

For a virtual field trip another class decided to examine a common theme, *Pyramids Around the World*, by going to Web sites anywhere in the world where they could find information. They started in Egypt, of course, but they also moved to other sites in Africa, Iraq in Asia, Mexico, and Cahokia in North America, and finally Peru in South America. They found pyramids, ziggurats, and truncated pyramids. Using this knowledge, they constructed a wall mural of the world with each site labeled and a picture of the pyramidal structure affixed to it. Beneath each site, students wrote why they thought people built a pyramid at the site. By looking at a common shape, the students examined politics, religion, commerce, agriculture, and social structure in many different parts of the world.

ASSESSMENT TASK

Upper elementary students need to tell how each branch of government affects life in their community and evaluate whether government jobs could be done by other persons or groups in their community. At the end of the trip to Washington, D. C., upper elementary students could design a chart showing the job the other person or group could do for government. The students check to see if they have all of these items in their project:

_____ How does this branch of government affect life in your community?

_____ Could the job be done by other people in your community?

_____ Who is the person or group?

_____ What job could this person or group do?

_____ What advantages would there be if this person or group did the job for government?

_____ What disadvantages would there be if this or another person or group did the job for government?

REFERENCES AND RESOURCES

Field, S. L. (2001). Perspectives and elementary social studies: Practice and promise. In O. L. Davis, Jr., E. A. Yeager, & S. J. Foster (Eds.), *Historical empathy and perspective taking in the social studies* (pp. 115–138). Lanham, MD: Rowman & Littlefield.

Morris, R. V. (2005). The Clio Club: An extracurricular model for elementary social studies enrichment. *Gifted Child Today, 28*(1), 40–48.

Morris, R. V. (2004). *The Atterbury files*: An extracurricular inquiry project illustrating local history. *Gifted Child Today, 27*(3), 28–35.

Morris, R. V., & McNeely, J. (2002). Eighth grade study-travel trip to Washington, DC. *Social Science Docket, 2*(1), 3–9.

Stone, R. (2002). *Best practices for high school classrooms: What award-winning secondary teachers do.* Thousand Oaks, CA: Corwin Press.

Urdanivia-English, C. (2001). Whose history? Social studies in an elementary English class for speakers of other languages. *Social Studies, 92*(5), 193–197.

Web Sites

Ball State University Electronic Field Trips
http://www.bsu.edu/eft/home/00front.htm

Cahokia Mounds
http://www.cahokiamounds.com/

Colonial Williamsburg
http://www.history.org/visit/TourtheTown/

Conner Prairie
www.connerprairie.org/discover_learn/distancelearning

Inca
www.inkanatura.com/coastchiclayotrujillotucumepyramids.asp

Mesopotamia
http://www.mesopotamia.co.uk/ziggurats/home_set.html

Monticello
http://explorer.monticello.org/

Mysterious Places
www.mysteriousplaces.com/mayan/TourEntrance.html

Nova Egypt
www.pbs.org/wgbh/nova/pyramid

White House PBS
http://www.pbs.org/wnet/whitehouse/virtual.html

19

Flannel Boards

GRADE LEVELS	NCSS CURRICULUM STRANDS
✔ K–2	II Time, Continuity, and Change

INTRODUCTION

Telling social studies stories on a flannel board helps young students connect with characters through the use of a manipulative. As they learn the story and its imbedded concepts, students have a visual connection to the events recounted. For students examining the American Revolutionary era, the story of Samuel Adams comes to life as they look at his experiences, how he changed, and what issues he faced. Students understand and interpret historical narratives through characters and places (Yeager & Foster, 2001). For younger students, the teacher can prepare flannel board stories to illustrate important social studies concepts, people, or events. Older students can make their own flannel board manipulatives to illustrate stories they share with their peers.

PROCEDURAL RECOMMENDATIONS

* Purchase or make a flannel board. You will need a piece of flocked cloth or flannel large enough to completely cover a piece of masonite, plywood, or cardboard and fold over to the back. After trimming off excess fabric, use glue to attach the flannel to the back of the board. Keep the flannel stretched tightly across the front.

* Choose a trade book that addresses lesson objectives and that has a strong sense of chronology, an essential understanding in the discipline of history. With a clear chronology, students can explore the concepts of change and continuity as well as cause and effect. For example, picture books by Jean Fritz contain a clear, strong line of chronology and are used in the second-grade classroom example below.

* Select photos of the main characters in the story to scan and print on glossy paper. Textbooks, picture books, magazines, coloring books, and even original student art are good sources. Cut out these pictures, mount them on heavy card stock or tagboard, and glue flannel, sandpaper, emery cloth, or Velcro to the back of each item.

* Tell the story, introducing, moving, and removing characters as needed. At junctures you determine in advance, pause and have students predict what happens next. Also have students evaluate the actions of the characters.

- Have students use the characters to retell the story to evaluate comprehension.
- Orally present a different story about the same character(s) or event(s) to the students. Again, have students predict what happens next and evaluate the actions of the characters.
- Have students use the flannel board characters to retell the story.
- Have students compare the two stories, discussing the different interpretations.

APPLICATIONS AND IDEAS

Students in a fourth-grade classroom examined the life of Abraham Lincoln. First, they formed partnerships and selected an aspect of his life they wanted to study. Some students wanted to explore Lincoln's family and childhood; others were interested in his political career or his presidency; still others wanted to examine his role in the Civil War and his personal and political relationships. They selected pictures they wished to scan, mount as directed earlier, and retell what they had read about Lincoln by manipulating the characters on the flannel board. As they told their story, students pointed out a compelling issue. They showed how Lincoln made a decision and explained the positive and negative aspects of that decision. The teacher had students discuss the question "Would citizens elect Abraham Lincoln to the presidency in the twenty-first century?" In a second-graded classroom, the teacher read Jean Fritz's *Why Don't You Get a Horse, Sam Adams?* Students created flannel board characters and then told the story to one another. Later, students heard another story by Jean Fritz about John Hancock. Once again, they told the story to their peers using flannel board figures. The students then compared these two figures who lived at the same time and in the same place and who worked for the same cause. While students retold the stories, the teacher asked questions to measure their comprehension. She asked students to judge whether these two figures would be effective political leaders today.

Teachers choosing to assess student comprehension of the story used a performance rubric similar to the one in Table 19.1. After the teacher initially told and discussed the story, students retold and interpreted the story.

ASSESSMENT

TABLE 19.1 FLANNEL BOARD COMPREHENSION PERFORMANCE CHECKLIST

Essential Element	Observed	Not Observed	Comments
Correctly identified key characters.			
Correctly sequenced events.			
Orally, in writing, or visually demonstrated understanding of key concepts.			
Upon questioning, made reasonable predictions of subsequent actions in the story.			
Upon questioning, made reasonable and developmentally appropriate evaluations of character behaviors.			

REFERENCES AND RESOURCES

Banks, D., & Gallagher, D. (1993). Teaching as a sensory activity: Making the Maya come to life. *Social Studies & the Young Learner, 5*(4), 11–12.

Baumgartner, B. (1981). The beginnings of an investigation into folktales told in Pennsylvania. *Social Studies Journal, 11,* 45–49.

Fritz, J. (1996). *Why don't you get a horse, Sam Adams?* New York: Putnam.

Henegar, S. (1998a). Storytelling and history. *Social Studies Review, 37*(2), 68–71.

Henegar, S. (1998b). Storytelling and history. Part 2. *Social Studies Review, 38*(1), 80–83.

Lindquist, T. (1996). Social studies now. Use simple puppets to connect core subjects. *Instructor,106*(1), 91–92.

Marmor, M. (1995). The Holocaust: A personal encounter. *Canadian Social Studies, 29,* 150–153.

Millstone, D. H. (1995). *An elementary odyssey: Teaching ancient civilization through story.* Portsmouth, NH: Heinemann.

More, R. (1987). Storytelling as a teaching tool. *Social Studies Journal, 16,* 25–26.

Spagnoli, C. (1995a). Storytelling: A bridge to Korea. *Social Studies, 86,* 221–226.

Spagnoli, C. (1995b). These tricks belong in your classroom: Telling Asian trickster tales. *Social Studies & the Young Learner, 8*(2), 15–17.

Totten, S. (1994). Telling the Holocaust story to children (Pull-Out 2). *Social Studies & the Young Learner, 7*(2), 5–8.

Yeager, E. A., & Foster, S. J. (2001). The role of empathy in the development of historical understanding. In O. L. Davis, Jr., E. A. Yeager, & S. J. Foster (Eds.), *Historical empathy and perspective taking in the social studies* (pp. 13–19). Lanham, MD: Rowman & Littlefield.

Web Sites

The University of North Carolina has a Web site that includes lesson plans for teachers. This lesson plan (**http://www.learnnc.org/lp/pages/2858**) utilizes a flannel board to reach language arts objectives.

Based on a 1999 article from *Teaching Exceptional Children*, this website (**http://www.teachervision.fen.com/china/resource/2971.html**) has a fully developed lesson that works for a wide variety of learners.

20

Folk Culture

GRADE LEVELS	NCSS CURRICULUM STRANDS
✔ K–2	I Culture
✔ 3–5	III People, Places, And Environments
✔ 6–8	V Individuals, Groups, And Institutions

INTRODUCTION

Students can make connections to local history through folk culture. It can be a recent tradition brought to the area or an ancient tradition that has existed in the area for hundreds of years. A sample of folk art created by indigenous people is listed by region in the following table:

Region	Folk Art	Origin
Midwest	Carved wooden decoys	Chippewa
Northwest	Ribbon work	Miami
Northwest	Carved/masks	Tlingit
Southeast	Baskets	Cherokee
Southwest	Weaving	Navajo

Many different people brought folk craft traditions with them to the United States; through the use of folk art, students can examine how ethnic groups adopted media to reflect their national heritage and bring beauty into their lives. For example, German settlers brought Franktur, a decorative calligraphy, and Scherenschnitte, a form of paper cutting, to North America. Students can describe what makes these art forms particularly good examples of German culture and then draw conclusions about what their culture valued. Students evaluate where different ideas about design and media come from and whether the ideas transfer from place to place. Students need to consider questions of authenticity, representation, and voice when they copy work traditionally done by other groups of people.

History books often overlook the contributions of women to culture; and, often devalue domestic folk craft. Students can explore women's domestic lives by looking at their handiwork. Mothers taught handiwork skills to their daughters across multiple generations: tatting and lace making, quilting, candle wicking, crocheting, embroidery, crewel, and cross-stitching. Many examples of folk art are available for students to bring to class; in addition, resource people are readily available to demonstrate these crafts. Students can learn how these items provided entertainment, demonstrated accomplishment, and performed a particular function. They can learn how people provided for their families and added beauty to their lives at the same time.

When teachers use folk songs in the classroom, students experience music shared by many people across time and location. Students engage in listening, comparing the musical experience to their other experiences, evaluating the connections to themselves, forming questions, and seeking new meaning from the musical experience. In the last decade, accessibility to world music has rapidly expanded, thus giving global audiences new performance experiences (Binns, 2000). Song lyrics are often political and present a specific message. In addition to expanding listeners' horizons, the music can give a voice to oppressed people, thus helping students develop new appreciation for diverse perspectives. Through the Internet, both fringe groups and international groups have a venue for their music. Students now have a buffet of styles, messages, and aesthetics from which to listen.

Younger students might listen to folk music about transportation and then compare the lyrics of several songs. Music can lead them to empathize with people in similar circumstances or to share common understandings of events and relationships. They might analyze the problems encountered by travelers or determine that the songs selected reveal a particular point of view, event, or place—or perhaps celebrate a universal emotion. Students can compare transportation songs from Australia, Canada, India, Kenya, and Scotland. All of these countries have an English tradition, so little interpreting will be needed to determine the significance of the words. Recent immigrants and those students learning English can contribute folk songs representing their heritage, culture, and/or nation from which they immigrated. Looking across songs from different places and languages for common themes, attends to both academic and social goals.

Older students can listen to folk music about labor and then determine what the songs disclose about people and the issues relevant to labor history. They can also explore labor-related problems in a democracy and explain how, in modern Western society, the laborer can be both indispensable and expendable. Students' musical experiences help them interpret and understand the world around them when they compare tunes from Ghana, Ireland, Israel, Jamaica, Singapore, and the United States. They can determine whether labor is thought of differently in other countries. They can also determine whether similar or different labor problems exist in those countries.

Procedural Recommendations

- Gather information about a variety of crafts and folk art forms. Be sure the information collected is appropriate to the developmental levels of the learners.
- Have students research the people who practice the craft or folk art by using the Internet or materials from the school, classroom, or community library. Students can also research the history of the craft or art form.
- Locate people in the community who practice this craft or art form, and invite them to class to explain and demonstrate their work.
- Have students generate questions to ask the presenters and take notes during the presentations. Consult Strategy 25 to help prepare students for a guest speaker. As a follow-up, have students write about what they learned in a newspaper article format.
- Arrange for students to practice the art. Display their finished pieces in the classroom, a school hallway, or an area in the community.

- Have students write an addition to their newspaper article about their work by drawing on what they learned from their research and from the classroom demonstrations.

- When incorporating folk music, type the lyrics from selected songs sharing a particular theme into a PowerPoint presentation or prepare an overhead transparency so students can see the lyrics projected on a screen and can sing along. If you prefer, print the song lyrics on paper so students can have individual song sheets.

- Prepare to sing lyrics for the students to model the melody. You might also use audio files, compact discs, or recorded clips of music to augment your presentation.

- Have students examine the first of the selected songs to determine from the lyrics how the songwriter felt in regard to the issue about which he or she wrote. Ask recall questions about the lyrics. Invite students to share any background information they may have about the song.

- Ask students to predict what the next song tells about the singer. Present the song and encourage students to sing along. Then have students find evidence from the song to support or refute their predictions.

- Continue this process until all the songs have been presented. Have students tell about the theme or themes that seem to connect each of the songs presented.

- Next, present the same tune with two different sets of lyrics. These may be from different regions or represent different perspectives. Have students identify these perspectives and hypothesize why the writers wrote two versions of the same song.

APPLICATIONS AND IDEAS

Students sing and analyze the lyrics of four songs to determine how people felt during the Civil War, identify shared concerns, and track historical or cultural events. They sing *John Brown's Body* and respond to the following questions: What did John Brown do, and what was his calling? Why do you know this tune? Students then compare the lyrics of *John Brown's Body* to those of *The Battle Hymn of the Republic* and describe how Julia Ward Howe changed the words. The teacher asks the students to predict what the next song, *Just Before the Battle, Mother*, tells about soldiers who served during the Civil War. They search the song's lyrics to find evidence in support of their predictions. After singing the next song, *All Quiet Along the Potomac*, the students compare its lyrics to those of *Just Before the Battle, Mother*. They determine similarities in the two songs. Next, students sing the same tune, *Battle Cry of Freedom*, with two sets of lyrics, one from the South and the other from the North. They determine which set of lyrics represented the Southern and which represented the Northern point of view. They also hypothesize why two versions of the same song were written.

A first-person historical presentation of a Southern soldier features songs expressing Southern sentiments. Table 20.1 lists suggested songs and corresponding questions for discussion. The soldier begins his presentation with a song that the Northern soldiers sang as they marched through the South and tells what that song meant to him as well as to those who heard it in the South. Next, the

TABLE 20.1 THE CIVIL WAR: A SOUTHERN PERSPECTIVE	
SONG	QUESTION FOR DISCUSSION
"Marching Through Georgia"	What was the Northern perspective of the Civil War?
"Yellow Rose of Texas"	Who was Hood, and what happened to him in Tennessee?
"Oh, I'm a Good Old Rebel"	Why would the soldier refuse a pardon?
"Hard Times Come Again No More"	Why was this song so popular across the nation?

TABLE 20.2   LABOR IN THE UNITED STATES

SONG	PROBING QUESTION
"No More, My Lord"	Why would enslaved African-Americans sing this song while they were cutting down trees and clearing brush for cotton?
"Leave Her, Johnny, Leave Her"	Why would American sailors sing this song when pulling into port?
"Look for the Union Label"	How did the Ladies' International Garment Workers' Union attempt to change popular opinion in the mid-twentieth century?

soldier sings about what happened to his army. Then he sings about his feelings after the war with regard to the issues of the lost cause, failed rebellion, need to regain citizenship, voting, and reconstruction of the nation. Finally, he relates how his last song captures the national sentiment to be done with the war and to put it aside forever.

In another classroom, students explore the theme of labor in the United States through song. Some labor songs express frustration with working conditions; many songs advocate hope or social change. Table 20.2 lists songs students study with corresponding discussion questions. Students learn that while enslaved African-Americans had no choice in their employment conditions, they could offer a song of hope and implied protest as they worked. Students also learn that because sailors were no longer bound to a ship once they finished their voyage and had access to land, they could afford the risk of satire through their music as they readied a ship to enter the final port. Finally, students learn through music that the International Ladies' Garment Workers' Union attempted to convince the public to buy American-made clothing with a national advertising campaign. The catchy tune, lyrics, and visual image of women standing together for economic security and political power were persuasive, although the song did not substantially change consumer spending habits.

Accounts of European Americans captured by Native Americans are powerful stories and captivating in their own right, but when musicians set these stories to music, they become even more enticing. Students listen to the story of George Ash in Kevin Stonerock's *Indian Man* and Cynthia Ann Parker in Andy Wilkinson's *White Women's Clothes*. Both songs tell about European Americans who were captured in their youth, were assimilated into a Native American tribe, and later in life were torn between the two cultures. Both songs also explore societal expectations for those who were captured and how those expectations conflicted with the individual's desires. Students consider the role of gender in allowing the main character in each song to make a decision regarding his or her future life.

ASSESSMENT

Students might attempt to re-create a variety of folk art forms using similar methods and materials. Younger students might use the somber black and vibrant red and blue colors of the Amish when they create paper quilt blocks in the style of Amish quilt patterns. Orally, students would need to explain the following information about their quilt block in the following checklist:

_____ Who makes this type of quilt?

_____ Why do they make this type of quilt?

_____ Where do these people live?

_____ What is the social function called when people gather to make quilts?

_____ What contributions do women make to their family when they make quilts?

_____ How are these quilts used to help others?

REFERENCES AND RESOURCES

Binns, T. (2000). Learning about development: An "entitlement" for all. In C. Fisher & T. Binns (Eds.), *Issues in geography teaching* (pp. 190–204). New York: Routledge/Falmer.

Delacruz, E. M. (1999). Take a walk on the wild side with folk artist Jack Barker. *Art Education, 49*(2), 46–52.

Kellman, J. (1996). Women's handwork: Stories of similarity and diversity. *Art Education, 49*(2), 33–39.

Morris, R. V., & Obenchain, K. M. (2001, Summer). Three methods for teaching the social studies to students through the arts (Electronic version). *Canadian Social Studies, 35*(4).

Zachlod, M. (2000). Integrating anthropology in elementary social studies. *Social Studies Review, 39*(2), 38–41.

Web Sites

American Folk Art Museum
http://www.folkartmuseum.org/

Andy Winkinson Online
http://www.andywilkinson.net/

Folk Music of England, Scotland, Ireland, Wales, and America
http://www.contemplator.com/folk.html

Kevin Stonerock's Living History
http://www.kevinstonerock.com/Livinghistory.html

Shelburn Museum
http://www.shelburnemuseum.org/

21

Games

GRADE LEVELS	NCSS CURRICULUM STRANDS
✔ 3–5	II. Time, Continuity, and Change
✔ 6–8	III. People, Places, and Environment
	IV. Individual Development and Identity
	VI. Power, Authority, and Governance

Introduction

Teachers and students can use the popular formats of games to highlight well-known individuals, places, or events. Such formats provide novelty and excitement and are effective in encouraging students to connect new learning to their previous experience. Typically game shows assess only trivial knowledge or factual recall information, but game modifications allow students to review material or to demonstrate mastery of material. Students adapt games to explore decision making. Younger students need teacher assistance in setting up and playing the game; older students set up the rules and play the game with minimal teacher supervision.

While competition motivates some students effectively, other students are apathetic about it; and the corrosive effects of designating winners and losers in the classroom is contrary to the goals of civic education. The new games movement of the 1970s provided many non-competitive games as an alternative to games where there are defined winners and losers; it also provided for the restructuring of games to remove the loser and winner labels. The dawn of video games provides social studies teachers with an effective way to skirt the winner and loser dilemma because students play against a computer. However, student exposure to game violence is a concern in many places around the country. In considering which games to select, consider the issue of representations of graphic violence.

Procedural Recommendations

* Determine which game format best supports the content to be addressed. Remember, while the strategy may help to engage the learners, the goal of using games is to facilitate the learning.

- Determine appropriate adaptations. Most of these games reinforce prior learning of facts. Typically, they do not work well with analysis, synthesis, or evaluative thinking. Consider this information and the classroom setting when making the appropriate adaptations. For example, if using a *Jeopardy* format, write the clues as fill-in-the-blank, multiple-choice, or true–false questions and have students answer the questions. This is different from the typical *Jeopardy* structure, which requires the players to answer in the form of a question. Write the questions on 3" × 5" cards. Older students can generate their own questions.

- Arrange teams or use grouping procedures that are effective in your classroom. Heterogeneous groups are recommended.

- Review the game procedures and rules of play with the students, including how long teams may collaborate before they must issue a response. The game show landscape changes monthly; students may be more or less familiar with different game shows. Providing students with an example of the game show that is the inspiration for the classroom game show will assist students in making that connection. This may be something simple like a 5- to 10-minute video clip of the show.

- Establish ground rules for behavior during and at the conclusion of play.

- Determine which team goes first.

- Arrange for scorekeeping.

APPLICATIONS AND IDEAS

Students in one classroom might collaborate to produce a *This Is Your Life* program about a prominent historical figure. In a unit of study on the American Revolutionary War era, students select an individual they would like to study. With teacher facilitation and through additional study, the class determines who, from the era, would know about this person. These contemporaries may be professional colleagues, family members, individuals who agree and disagree with the work of the individual, and so on. These contemporaries serve as the guests who are brought onstage to talk about their relationship with that individual.

In this program, the audience meets John Adams, the featured figure. They also meet Richard Henry Lee, Abigail Adams, John Hancock, John Quincy Adams, and Samuel Adams—all figures from Adams's life. Once the contemporaries are chosen, students are assigned roles. In a large class, two students are assigned one person. Students research the featured individual as well as their person, paying particular attention to when and where their lives intersected and the historical, political, economic, and social context of their relationship. Of particular interest are primary source documents, in this case letters that contain references to one another or transcripts of conversations between the two. During the show, students play each of the roles, discussing the events of Adams's life, including his accomplishments in Revolutionary Boston and during his presidency. The teacher weaves together the stories told by the guests in a chronology of Adams's life. Students demonstrate content mastery in their presentations and in their conversations with one another.

In another classroom, students who model their presentation on the television show *Survivor* demonstrate a series of skills such as operating a voting machine, mediating a dispute between two students, or planning a protest. The members of each team then draw fate cards to see who leaves the island because he or she inhaled second-hand smoke, lived downstream from a dioxin spill, or did not wear a seat belt. Notice how the students use human-created environmental hazards rather than the corrosive social pressure of voting their peers off the island.

If the goal is decision making using *Who Wants to Be a Millionaire?*, create economic or historical scenarios in which students choose from alternatives, explaining and supporting their choices. When students play *Who Wants to Be a Millionaire?*, they examine values. In court case scenarios, they make a choice between two opposing values such as privacy and free speech. At the next level, students appeal and win more or keep what they have; students go to the next level by looking at case law or legal precedent. This activity encourages students to think seriously about the type of society in which they want to live. They make studied decisions, risking judicial review of those decisions.

ASSESSMENT

The following scoring guide is suitable for the *This Is Your Life* scenario.

4 Points	3 Points	2 Points	1 Points
The student defines how his or her person relates to the time period.	The student defines how his or her person relates to the time period.	The student defines how his or her person relates to the time period.	The student defines how his or her person relates to the time period.
The student defines a crucial decision his or her character had to make with the main character.	The student defines a crucial decision his or her character had to make with the main character.	The student defines a crucial decision his or her character had to make with the main character.	
The student defines how his or her character could solve a problem with the main character.	The student defines how his or her character could solve a problem with the main character.		
The student exhibits attributes that indicate historical empathy.			

REFERENCES AND RESOURCES

Akkerman, S., Admiraal, W., & Huizenga, J. (2009). Storification in history education: A mobile game in and about medieval Amsterdam. *Computers & Education, 52*(2), 449–459.

Allison, J. (2008). History educators and the challenge of immersive pasts: A critical review of virtual reality "tools" and history pedagogy. *Learning, Media and Technology, 33*(4), 343–352.

Erwin, E. J., & Morton, N. (2008). Exposure to media violence and young children with and without disabilities: Powerful opportunities for family-professional partnerships. *Early Childhood Education Journal, 36*(2), 105–112.

Gentile, D. A., & Gentile, J. R. (2008). Violent video games as exemplary teachers: A conceptual analysis. *Journal of Youth and Adolescence, 37*(2), 127–141.

Tuzun, H., Yilmaz-Soylu, M., Karakus, T., Inal, Y., & Kizilkaya, G. (2009). The effects of computer games on primary school students' achievement and motivation in geography learning. *Computers & Education, 52*(1), 68–77.

Web Sites

Axis and Allies
www.wizards.com/default.asp?x=ah/aa/welcome

National Geographic Society Underground Railroad
http://www.nationalgeographic.com/railroad/

Oregon Trail
http://oregontrail.org/

P. T. Barnum Museum
http://www.lostmuseum.cuny.edu/office.php

Where in the World Is Carmen San Diego?
http://www.abandonia.com/en/games/13/Where+in+the+World+is+Carmen+Sandiego.html

22

Genealogies

GRADE LEVELS	NCSS CURRICULUM STRANDS
✔ 3–5	II Time, Continuity, and Change
✔ 6–8	III People, Places, and Environments
	IV Individual Development and Identity

INTRODUCTION

Rather than using symbols of trees, students can chart their family history by generation levels in order to identify who was alive at what particular time and to examine how that person connected to state, national, and world events. A generational level shows siblings, cousins, and stepsiblings in parity rather than in linear relationships, thus helping students value a variety of different family configurations represented in classrooms. Generational levels can help students understand that everyone comes from somewhere and that groups of people connect with one another. Younger students might make connections to where people in their family lived by mapping their location and migration patterns. By using this tool, older students can see how their family connected with historical migration patterns.

Students might also use this strategy to explore prominent families in American political history, including the Adams and Kennedy families of Massachusetts, the Bushes of Texas, the Tafts of Ohio, and the Lees of Virginia. These families have long traditions of public service and political stewardship across multiple generations. It also is beneficial for students to research families that are less well known but that have also contributed to the political, social, economic, or cultural history of the United States over many generations.

PROCEDURAL RECOMMENDATIONS

- Provide a model family featuring a famous political family in the United States. Ask students what the family indicates about the commitment of some families to public service.
- Demonstrate how to construct generational levels using members of your own family.

- Invite students to bring information about their family to class and make a generational-level chart. As an alternative, have students ask school staff members if they can use their family's information to make generational charts, or have students select notable families from recent or distant history to place on the chart.

- Direct students to match each generational level to four different historical events that each person on the chart experienced—one local, one state, one national, and one international.

- Have students create a card file, using a program such as Inspiration, that features each member of the family, a brief biography of him or her, a picture of him or her, documentation about his or her life, and a description of how he or she relates to the rest of the family. "Hot Buttons" on each card link the family member to others at different levels.

- Provide students, without access to Inspiration, another variation of this activity. Have these students collect written and visual artifacts from each generation. These might include letters, postcards, telephone directory listings, birth announcements, and photographs. Have students place each artifact in a separate envelope or folder. These artifacts become clues, requiring students to organize information about the people selected.

APPLICATIONS AND IDEAS

An upper elementary school class examines the story of the Harrison family. Each time students open an envelope, they are given a clue describing another generation of the family. They arrange these people in order, from the earliest family members to the most recent, and place any supporting documentation near their name. When they finish, they consult the answer key in the last envelope. The content of each envelope is described in Table 22.1

Harrison Family Answer Key

    I. Brief biography of Benjamin Harrison I

   II. Brief biography of Benjamin Harrison II

  III. Brief biography of Benjamin Harrison III

       A. Berkeley flyer

          1. Postcard of a Berkeley bedroom

   IV. Brief biography of Benjamin Harrison IV

    V. Postcard of Benjamin Harrison V

   VI. Postcard of William Henry Harrison

       A. Grouseland flyer

          1. Picture of Grouseland's main hall

  VII. John Scott Harrison picture

       A. Brief biography of John Scott Harrison

 VIII. Brief biography of Benjamin Harrison

       A. Description of Benjamin Harrison; his first wife, Caroline Scott; and his second wife, Mary Dimmick

       B. Postcard of the Benjamin Harrison home

       C. Benjamin Harrison home flyer

          1. Picture of the Harrisons' Victorian parlor

   IX. Family tree of the Harrison family

TABLE 22.1   THE HARRISON FAMILY

ENVELOPE #	DOCUMENT	EVIDENCE
1	Description of Benjamin Harrison; his first wife, Caroline Scott; and his second wife, Mary Dimmick	Describes the nuclear family of President Benjamin Harrison
2	Brief biography of Benjamin Harrison III	Makes the connection between Benjamin Harrison II and Benjamin Harrison IV
3	Brief biography of Benjamin Harrison	Makes the connection between the President and his ancestors
4	Berkeley flyer	Describes the Harrison ancestral home and the Harrisons who lived there
5	Postcard of the Benjamin Harrison Home	Illustrates the Victorian presidential home in the Midwest
6	Postcard of Benjamin Harrison V	Illustrates a conservative revolutionary
7	Benjamin Harrison home flyer	Describes the Victorian President and his family in the Midwest
8	Brief biography of John Scott Harrison	Describes the only man to be both the son and the father of a president
9	Grouseland flyer	Describes the family of William Henry Harrison
10	Brief biography of Benjamin Harrison II	Makes the connection between Benjamin Harrison I and Benjamin Harrison III
11	Picture of Grouseland's main hall	Illustrates the Federal home of William Henry Harrison
12	Postcard of a Berkeley bedroom	Illustrates the Georgian home of the Harrison family
13	John Scott Harrison picture	Illustrates the father and son of two presidents
14	Brief biography of Benjamin Harrison IV	Makes the connection between Benjamin Harrison III and Benjamin Harrison V
15	Picture of the Harrison's Victorian parlor	Illustrates the social context within the time period
16	Postcard of William Henry Harrison	Illustrates the President of the United States
17	Brief biography of Benjamin Harrison I	Begins the Harrison family dynasty in Virginia that will emerge as colonial gentry
18	Family tree of the Harrison family	Shows the members of the Harrison family

ASSESSMENT

When tracing one's own family's geneology, and using blank outline maps of the world and the nation, show how the member of a family migrated to different places and how and when this person settled in the area in which he or she now resides. Compare the personal migration story to major migration patterns in U.S. or world history. Have students research the migration patterns of members of their family or of the family they selected for their generational chart.

4 Points	3 Points	2 Points	1 Point
Identify the family's country of origin.	Identify the family's country of origin.	Identify the family's country of origin.	Identify the family's country of origin.
How does the family movement to the United States support or contradict immigration patterns?	How does the family movement to the United States support or contradict immigration patterns?	How does the family movement to the United States support or contradict immigration patterns?	
Identify the family's movement within the United States, listing starting and ending states.	Identify the family's movement within the United States, listing starting and ending states.		
How do the family's movements within the United States support or contradict the national migration trends?			

REFERENCES AND RESOURCES

Barton, K. C. (2001). A picture's worth: Analyzing historical photographs in the elementary grades. *Social Education, 65*(5), 278–283.

Levstik, L. S., & Barton, K. C. *Doing history: Investigating with children in elementary and middle schools* (3rd ed.). Mahwah, NJ: Erlbaum.

Putnam, E. (2002). Using personal family documents in document-based instruction. *Social Science Docket, 2*(1), 27–28.

Singer, J. Y., & Singer, A. J. (2004). Creating a museum of family artifacts. *Social Studies and the Young Learner, 17*(1), 5–10.

Wade, R., Gardner, D., Doro, P., & Arendt, S. (2007). Bridging the years: An intergenerational history project. *Social Studies and the Young Learner, 19*(3), 24–28.

Web Sites

Ancestry.Com
http://www.ancestry.com/

Cyndi's List of Genealogy Sites on the Internet
http://www.cyndislist.com/

Family Search
http://www.familysearch.org/eng/default.asp

The National Archives
http://www.archives.gov/genealogy/

U. S. Census Bureau
http://www.census.gov/genealogy/www/

23

Globes

GRADE LEVELS	NCSS CURRICULUM STRANDS
✔ 3–5	III People, Places, and Environments
	IX Global Connections

INTRODUCTION

Globes have the advantage over maps in their ability to show the size and shape of an area exactly as they appear on the earth's surface. Primary students can use a globe to help track the migration of families to the United States. Using their fingers on the surface of the globe, they trace families that came across the Bering Straits and from Europe, Africa, Asia, and Central America. Students can ask questions about why families came to America. They need to look at forces that were pushing families out of their homelands and forces that were attracting families to America. Students evaluate which would have been hardest: leaving home, making the trip to America, or starting a new life in America?

Students can create their own globes by blowing up a balloon, covering it with papier-mâché, painting it blue, cutting out paper continents, and labeling the oceans. Elementary students find the interrelationships between the continents challenging when they must move from the two-dimensional surface of a map to the three-dimensional surface of a sphere. Using their finished globes, students can study continents, oceans, directions, latitude, longitude, poles, and climate zones as well as the relationships between places and the people who inhabit them. Because they create their own models, students do not depend on the interpretation of others. Younger students might focus on the ratio of water to land, and older students might develop a color-coded globe key.

PROCEDURAL RECOMMENDATIONS

- To illustrate the fact that three-fourths of the earth is comprised of water, have students form a circle and toss an inflatable globe from person to person, noting how often they catch the globe where oceans are marked.
- Cover the floor with a large drop cloth. Cover work surfaces with newspaper.
- Mix cellulose wallpaper paste in a large bucket with twice the amount of water suggested in the directions. Stir this mixture; let it set for 15 to 20 minutes.

- Have each student blow up a balloon and attach his or her name to the knot end.

- Direct students to tear newspapers into strips, dip each strip into the wallpaper paste, remove any extra paste, and cover their balloon in one coat of newspaper. After allowing the coat to dry overnight, have the students repeat the process until the balloon is coated with six layers. Use paper towels on the last layer for a smoother finish.

- Provide overhead transparencies for students to use in creating continents. Have students trace the continents onto the transparencies and then transfer the image to white or colored paper. Have them neatly print the name of each continent in ink. Students can prepare their continents by using different map projections including the Robinson projection, which is considered by many experts to be the most accurate in terms of landmass distribution.

- Have students create labels for the oceans.

- When the globes are dry, have students use blue tempera paint to cover the surface. Then have them use liquid school glue to adhere the paper continents to the earth's surface. Make small cuts in the continents from the edges toward the center and add more glue for more secure adhesion. Check each student's globe for accuracy before the glue hardens; relationships between continents on a sphere compared to a wall or book map will be difficult for some students to discern.

- Finally, have students attach ocean labels to their globe.

- As an alternative, students can create a globe by using yarn soaked in liquid starch to wrap around the surface of a balloon. When the starch dries and the students pop the balloon, a stiff yarn shell remains. Students can glue continents onto the globe's surface. These globes are more fragile than those made of papier-mâché but are much faster to construct and to dry. This is also an easier globe-making method for younger students. Students get the same practice in looking for the relationships between landmasses and water.

APPLICATIONS AND IDEAS

Some elementary students ask why they had to cut their continents to get them to fit on the globe. The teacher uses those questions to extend the original globe-making lesson. The teacher cuts old red rubber playground balls that have gone flat over time into hemispheres. Each student receives a hemisphere with directions to flatten it on his or her desk. As hard as they try, the elementary students cannot get the hemispheres to flatten out. Several enterprising students do figure out they can try to stretch the ball. At that teachable moment, everyone gets to talk about what happens to the brand name on the sides of the old playground balls when they stretch, and the youngsters come to understand why Greenland and Antarctica look larger than South America on some maps. For older students, the teacher can introduce the distortions created by different map projections.

With the finished globes, the elementary students are able to play Simon Says. Each student stands at his or her desk with his or her globe. The teacher gives directions: "Simon says, move to Africa," and the students all move their fingers to Africa. Because they are standing next to their desks, the teacher can quickly see who needs more help and who is doing well. Students are able to locate the continents, oceans, poles, circles, tropics, hemispheres, and the equator. If they move to the north, south, east, or west from a continent, the teacher asks them to name the next feature: "Simon says, What ocean is west of Africa?" and students move their fingers in that direction. If Simon issues a directive without using his name (e.g., "Move to the Indian Ocean"), students who move are out and must sit down, but they continue to follow along on the globe. When the fifth "out" sits down, the first "out" can stand up again. The game is challenging, but every student is still participating.

Elementary students have a globe in front of them, and the teacher has a DVD of geographic features projected on the front wall. The students quickly spin the globe to the place where they locate the mystery feature: It can be a sea, peninsula, bay, coastline, river, mountain range, or island. It can also be a political feature such as a nation or a state. Finally, it can be a monumental feature such as the Eiffel Tower, the pyramids in Egypt, the Great Wall of China, Taos Pueblo, or the Vatican. Students learn the geographic themes of both places and locations from working with the globe.

ASSESSMENT

Elementary students trace the triangle trades with their fingers: to New England for rum, to Africa for enslaved persons, to the West Indies for molasses, and back to port. In another trade triangle, students trace New England wheat, lumber, horses, and fish to the West Indies for bills of exchange, to Europe for manufactured goods, and back again to port. Then on a blank map they draw and label their transactions. With every transaction, the captain of the ship makes a profit. These questions continue to be debated by students as they explore and question what it means to be entangled with the slave trade.

4 Points	3 Points	2 Points	1 Point
Identifies the products transported on each side of the triangle in both triangles of trade.	Identifies the products transported on each side of the triangle in both triangles of trade.	Identifies the products transported on each side of the triangle in both triangles of trade.	Identifies the products transported on each side of the triangle in both triangles of trade.
If you sold molasses for rum as part of the triangle trade, would you be involved in the slave trade? If you first conducted business on one triangle trade route, then the other, and then back to the first, would you consider yourself the captain of a slave ship or a businessman?	If you sold molasses for rum as part of the triangle trade, would you be involved in the slave trade? If you first conducted business on one triangle trade route, then the other, and then back to the first, would you consider yourself the captain of a slave ship or a businessman?	If you sold molasses for rum as part of the triangle trade, would you be involved in the slave trade? If you first conducted business on one triangle trade route, then the other, and then back to the first, would you consider yourself the captain of a slave ship or a businessman?	
If, as a ship's captain, you did not earn money from the triangle trade, how would you get the money you needed to feed your family? There were other ways a ship captain could make money but not as quickly.	If, as a ship's captain, you did not earn money from the triangle trade, how would you get the money you needed to feed your family? There were other ways a ship captain could make money but not as quickly.		
Is there an ethical difference between the people who sailed the ships to transport the slaves and the people who bought the slaves to work on their land?			

REFERENCES AND RESOURCES

Beck, P. (2002). *GlobaLinks: Resources for world studies, grades K–8*. Worthington, OH: Linworth.

Kirkwood, T. F. (2001). Our global age requires global education: Clarifying definitional ambiguities. *Social Studies, 92*(1), 10–15.

Levstik, L. (2001). This issue: Rethinking social studies. *Theory into Practice, 40*(1), 2–5.

Quashigah, A. Y., & Wilson, A. H. (2001). A cross-national conversation about teaching from a global perspective: Issues of culture and power. *Theory into Practice, 40*(1), 55–64.

Risinger, F. (2001). Teaching economics and the globalization debate on the World Wide Web. *Social Education, 65*(6), 363–365.

Yost, M. G. (2001). Passport to the millennium. *Teaching History: A Journal of Methods, 26*(2), 98–101.

Web Sites

European Space Agency
http://earth.esa.int/earthimages/

Flash Earth
http://www.flashearth.com/

Geology
http://geology.com/satellite/

Google Maps
http://maps.google.com/

Terra Server–USA
http://terraserver-usa.com/

24

Graphic Organizers

GRADE LEVEL	NCSS CURRICULUM STRANDS
✔ K–2	Any (Depending on Topic)
✔ 3–5	
✔ 6–8	

INTRODUCTION

Graphic organizers allow students of all ages to organize information in visual ways. For some students, this visual representation is a way to make meaning of what they are reading or hearing. It allows them to see connections not always evident in a traditional narrative. Young students use graphic organizers to assist their understanding of categories and classification. Students moving into middle school experience developmental changes. Intellectually, they move from concrete thinking to abstract thinking (Van Hoose, Strahan, & L'Esperance, 2001). Students in these grades also interact with more complex historical, political, social, and economic information. Students facing these more challenging tasks use a variety of graphic organizers to assist in the organization of data for analysis and interpretation. Graphic organizers take on a variety of forms, including flow charts, graphs, tables, Venn diagrams, and concept maps.

PROCEDURAL RECOMMENDATIONS

- Graphic organizers work well with many but not all topics. When students compare data, look for relationships, or find cause and effect in the data, they are using graphic organizers.
- If students are unfamiliar with or unaccustomed to using graphic organizers, provide an introduction by constructing a basic sample task that uses graphic organizers. If the assignment examines relationships among individuals, the sample may require an examination of the relationships among the branches of the U.S. government. Provide a blank flow chart (see Figure 24.1), and begin by identifying the three branches. Have students label each branch on the flow chart. Ask what additional information is pertinent, and add this information (e.g., specific departments, officials, responsibilities) under each branch.

FIGURE 24.1　A Flow Chart

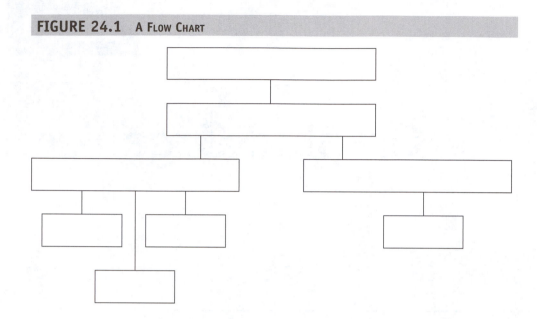

- Ask students to characterize the relationships among the branches and determine an appropriate way to visually illustrate these relationships. Can they depict the relationships on the flow chart? Do they need an additional diagram?

- If the assignment requires students to compare characteristics, a sample task might ask students to compare the belief systems of the world's major religions. Provide a Venn diagram (see Figure 24.2), and explain that each circle represents a religion. Where the two circles overlap, students list characteristics or beliefs those two religions share. Students list characteristics or beliefs exclusive to each religion in the parts of the circles that do not overlap.

- If students are looking at issues that examine cause and effect, a fishbone organizer (Figure 24.3) may be appropriate. Students list the issue or the effect (e.g., failure of the Articles of Confederation) along the spine. A "bone" is constructed of the causes. In the case of the failure of the Articles of Confederation, students may list "no central treasury" as one of the bones.

FIGURE 24.2　A Venn Diagram

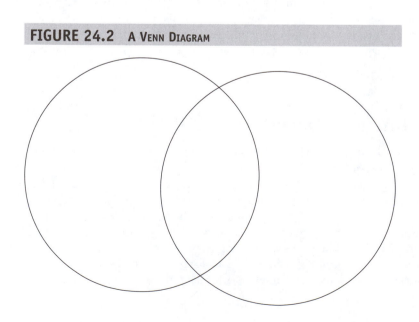

FIGURE 24.3 A FISHBONE ORGANIZER

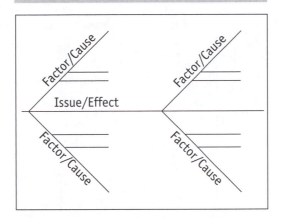

- After students understand the purpose of graphic organizers and the variety that are available to assist in organizing information, incorporate them into lessons.
- For struggling learners, the teacher can modify a graphic organizer in a few ways. (1) Provide a graphic organizer that is partially completed in order to further model the strategy. (2) Provide a blank graphic organizer to the student. Also provide the appropriate answers (either words or pictures) cut out and ready to tape or glue in place on the graphic organizer.
- As students become more familiar with using graphic organizers, challenge them to develop their own graphic organizers to display and explain the information with which they are working. See Figures 24.4 and 24.5 for additional graphic organizers.

FIGURE 24.4 A CONCEPT MAP OR CONCEPT WEB

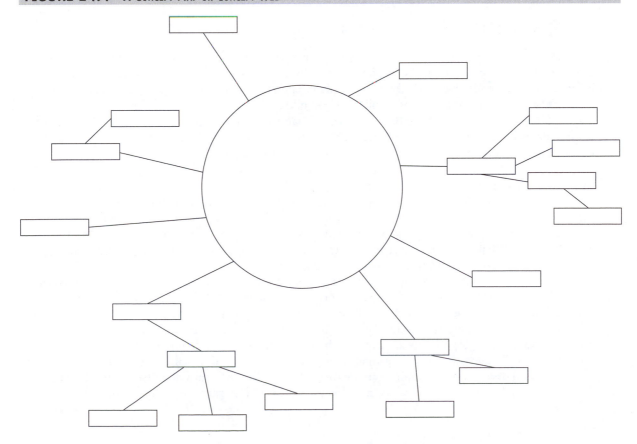

FIGURE 24.5 A KWL CHART

What do we **K**now?	What do we **W**ant to know?	What have we **L**earned?

APPLICATIONS AND IDEAS

KWL (what we Know, what we Want to know, what we Learned) charts are commonly used by teachers in numerous ways. In the example that follows, students use the KWL chart to track their learning about Rosa Parks. At the beginning of a cooperative biography project (see Parker, 2008), students (individually) and the class (collectively) build a KWL chart based on their current knowledge of Mrs. Parks. On the board (under "What do I Know"), the teacher writes the students' comments, noting that they know she was African American and from the South. While the teacher writes this information, students are also asked to create their own chart.

Once students have shared what they know, the teacher presents some new information about Mrs. Parks, including her early involvement with the National Association for the Advancement of Colored People (NAACP), the discrimination faced by her brother after World War II, and her experiences at the Highlander Folk School. Synthesizing this new information along with their prior knowledge, students suggest several questions that they want to answer. All of these questions are written in the "What Do I Want to Know" section of the chart. In addition, students note specific questions that interest them on their individual KWL charts.

Students are assigned to bring the answers to their questions and the source of the information to the next class. At the next class, the new information is shared and recorded on the individual and collective KWL charts (see Figure 24.6). Based on the new information and with facilitation from the teacher, students raise new questions. They begin a new search, that information is shared and processed, and the stages are repeated again. Throughout this process, students are able to see how their understanding evolves: New information is gained, misperceptions and misinformation are addressed, and deeper understandings are developed. The class then moves on to additional stages of the cooperative biography (such as synthesizing information, or writing and illustrating). At the

FIGURE 24.6   KWL ON ROSA PARKS

What do I **K**now?	What do I **W**ant to Know?	What have I **L**earned?
She was African American.		
She was tired and wouldn't stand up on a bus.	Why was she told to move?	She wasn't tired. There were segregation laws in Alabama in the 1950s.
She was from the South.		
She was involved in civil rights.	How involved was she in the NAACP?	She was the secretary.
She was old.	How old was she?	She was 42 when she was arrested.
	What is the Highlander Folk School?	It provided training in activism.
	How many siblings did she have?	Sylvester was her only sibling.
	Was she married? Kids?	She married Raymond Parks and had no children.

conclusion of the project, students are asked to retrieve their personal KWL charts and do two things. First, they are asked to note what they have learned under the "What Have I Learned" portion of the chart. This provides a wonderful opportunity for students to stop and think about all that they have learned over the duration of the project. Second, students are asked to extend the "What Do I Want to Know" section with new questions they have about Rosa Parks. While the project has ended, this exercise acknowledges that not every question has been answered and that answering some questions creates new ones.

ASSESSMENT

Rather than thinking about evaluating graphic organizers, consider them an assessment task. The teacher can use a student-created Venn diagram to determine if students are able to distinguish between distinct and shared characteristics when comparing two items or stories. A KWL chart can be used by both students and teacher for assessment. The "K" serves as a diagnostic assessment of what students are bringing to the lesson. The teacher can then decide on some content to cover quickly, while other content, perhaps not mentioned or misunderstood by students, will get more attention. At the end of a lesson, the "L" is a wonderful self-assessment for students.

REFERENCES AND RESOURCES

Dye, G. A. (2000). Graphic organizers to the rescue! Helping students link—and remember—information. *Teaching Exceptional Children, 32*(3), 72–76.

Egan, M. (1999). Reflections on effective use of graphic organizers. *Journal of Adolescent & Adult Literacy, 42*(8), 641–645.

Ekhami, L. (1998). Graphic organizers: Outlets for your thoughts. *School Library Media Activities Monthly, 14*(5), 29–33.

Gallavan, N., & Kottler, E. (2007). Eight types of graphic organizers for empowering social studies students and teachers. *Social Studies, 98*(3), 117–123.

Irwin-DeVitis, L., & Pease, D. (1995). Using graphic organizers for learning and assessment in middle level classrooms. *Middle School Journal, 26*(5), 57–64.

Lindquist, T. (1997). Social studies now! A graphic organizer to help kids manage facts. *Instructor (Primary), 107*(4), 72.

McTighe, J. (1992). Graphic organizers: Collaborative links to better thinking. In N. Davidson & T. Worsham (Eds.), *Enhancing thinking through cooperative* learning (pp. 182–197). New York: Teachers College Press.

Parker, W. C. (2008). *Social studies in elementary education* (13th ed.). Upper Saddle River, NJ: Pearson Education.

Van Hoose, J., Strahan, D., & L'Esperance, M. (2001). *Promoting harmony: Young adolescent development and school practices.* Columbus, OH: National Middle School Association.

Web Sites

Inspiration is a software package that assists students in categorizing and classifying ideas and information. It provides several different graphic organizer templates, including concept maps and outlines.
http://www.strategictransitions.com/

The Literacy Matters Web site
(http://www.literacymatters.org/content/study/organizers.htm) has several links for graphic organizers.

The Saskatoon Public Schools Web site has a great site explaining and providing examples of graphic organizers. Check out
http://olc.spsd.sk.ca/DE/PD/instr/strats/graphicorganizers/index.html

Guest Speakers

GRADE LEVELS	NCSS CURRICULUM STRANDS
✔ K–2	I Culture
✔ 3–5	II Time, Continuity, and Change
✔ 6–8	IV Individual Development and Identity
	V Individuals, Groups, and Institutions
	VI Power, Authority, and Governance
	IX Global Connections
	X Civic Ideals and Practices

INTRODUCTION

Guest speakers, who are eyewitnesses to historical and current events, encourage students to obtain data from a primary source (See Strategy 8). Guest speakers are often the *hook* into a unit of study or part of a culminating event that ties the unit together. Guest speakers can also inspire students to improve their research skills. Data obtained from a guest speaker may enrich or sometimes challenge data obtained from other primary sources, such as other guest speakers or first-person accounts. Information presented by guest speakers leads to an awareness of multiple perspectives, a key skill in understanding concepts in history and social studies. Guest speakers also challenge secondary and tertiary sources such as the popular media, the Internet, and texts, thus encouraging students to evaluate their sources of information. Guest speakers also encourage students to employ multiple sources when conducting research.

PROCEDURAL RECOMMENDATIONS

- Many topics under study in social studies classrooms include varying interpretations of events or outcomes. When considering such a topic for study, consider the availability of guest speakers who can enrich the study. These may be eyewitnesses to events or scholars who have extensively studied the event or topic.

- Guest speakers are almost exclusively available on a local basis; some of the following organizations may provide speakers: immigrant associations, local colleges/universities, service clubs, travel clubs, and veterans' organizations.

- Ask parents in a survey at the beginning of the year if they would like to speak or if they have contacts who would like to speak.

- Include learning objectives that encourage students to examine multiple perspectives and develop research skills.

- Examine the basic text or information to which students will have easy access. Search for examples that give only one or two perspectives of the event or for examples that lack detail or explanation. For example, an account of the American Revolutionary War era may contain only the pro-independence perspective. To fully understand the era, it is important also to understand the perspective of colonists who remained loyal to England.

- Once the areas lacking detail or perspective are identified, begin a search for individuals in the community who could add information and perspective. Eyewitnesses, university scholars, historical reenactors, and frequent travelers are all potential guest speakers. Contact the local historical society, state humanities committee, area colleges and universities, or veterans' associations for assistance.

- Determine the most appropriate time in the unit to include guest speakers. Consider the purpose of the visit. Will the guest speaker provide the anticipatory set for the unit, or will he or she challenge traditional views? Allocate an appropriate amount of time for the guest speaker to work with the students.

- Prepare both the speaker and the students for the visit.

- Determine what kinds of interactions the speaker and the students will share. Will the speaker present formally? Will students be encouraged to ask questions throughout the presentation or only at the end? Is a question-and-answer session without a formal presentation a better alternative? Will the speaker bring artifacts? Can the artifacts be handled by the students?

- Provide the speaker with the goals or objectives of the lesson. It may also be helpful to provide the speaker with a copy of the text or resources used by the students. If the speaker is not familiar with a young audience, give him or her some tips on working with your students.

- Remind students of respectful behaviors. Help students prepare questions for the guest. Select one or two students to serve as hosts—they can greet the guest at the office, escort him or her to and from the classroom, and assist with any materials the guest brings.

- After the guest speaker leaves, debrief with the students. What new information was presented? How is that similar to or different from what has been studied? To learn more, what other sources (texts, primary sources, guest speakers) could be consulted? You might use a KWL (what we Know, what we Want to know, what we Learned) chart before and after the guest speaker's visit (see Strategy 24, Figure 24.5). After the speaker leaves, students can examine the "Know" and "Want to Know" portions of the chart to determine what they have "Learned" and what new questions they have. These new questions become the basis for research.

- Have the students send a thank-you note to the speaker.

APPLICATIONS AND IDEAS

Students in Mr. Chang's primary class are excited and anxious about their first days of school. Mr. Chang has been working with the students to see their classroom and school as a civic community, a place where people have specific roles and responsibilities. In class Mr. Chang has talked about his responsibilities as the teacher: teaching the students, treating them justly, and keeping them safe from harm. Students also have brainstormed their responsibilities as citizens of the classroom community. They identified being good listeners, taking care of the physical classroom, asking questions when they do not understand, and helping one another learn are some of these responsibilities.

Mr. Chang wants to expand his students' understanding of community, citizenship, and rights and responsibilities from the classroom community to the school community. He and the students create a list of people who might provide some insight into the school community, including the principal, a secretary, the school nurse, a fifth grader, a custodian, a librarian, and a lunchroom employee. The students and Mr. Chang work to provide as much variety as possible and talk with as many people as possible. With help, the class develops a list of questions to ask each potential visitor. Because the lesson is about community and citizenship, all of the questions focus on whether this person believes the school is a community and, if so, what his or her rights and responsibilities are within the community. Questions include where in the school the potential guest works and what he or she does. (A school map helps with this part.)

Mr. Chang individually approaches each person to ask if he or she would be willing to briefly speak to his class. They all agree, and he provides them with the list of questions. He asks each person to speak for approximately 5 minutes and to answer questions for another 15 minutes. He also asks each one if he or she needs assistance with any materials he or she would like to distribute to the class. One speaker is scheduled to attend class each day for seven days. It will be the first activity of the day after attendance.

It is now time to prepare the class for the guest speakers. Mr. Chang shares the schedule with the students, using pictures on the calendar so students will know who is attending. He asks for two or three volunteers to serve as hosts for each speaker. The hosts will escort the speaker to his or her seat, provide a glass of water, hand out any materials, and introduce the speaker. Mr. Chang talks with his students about how to be attentive listeners, when to ask questions, and how to carry out specific host responsibilities.

As each speaker visits, students become more comfortable. Mr. Chang facilitates the question-and-answer sessions to reflect his curriculum goals of community and citizenship by asking questions in addition to the ones already given to the speakers. For example, the librarian is asked how books and reading contribute to the development of a citizen. The principal is asked to describe the school as a community.

After all of the speakers have presented, Mr. Chang writes two student-dictated records summarizing the visits. The first describes how their classroom is a community and explains the role of each student in the classroom community. The second describes how their school is a community and explains the roles of their guest speakers in the school community.

ASSESSMENT

For students studying the concept of community, the following assessment rubric would work. Note that it includes not only information gained from the guest speaker, but from other lessons and a broader discussion of community. For very young students, this may be completed by the teacher through a brief, informal interview with each student.

4 Points	3 Points	2 Points	1 Point
Student identifies how his or her classroom is a community.	Student identifies how his or her classroom is a community.	Student identifies how his or her classroom is a community.	Student identifies how his or her classroom is a community.
Student explains the role of each student in the classroom community.	Student explains the role of each student in the classroom community.	Student explains the role of each student in the classroom community.	
Student explains how the school is a community.	Student explains how the school is a community.		
Student explains the role of the guest speaker in the school community.			

REFERENCES AND RESOURCES

Billings, N. C. (2006). Bringing globalization into the classroom. *Journal of Family and Consumer Sciences, 98*(3), 48–50.

Kubota, R. (2001). Learning diversity from world Englishes. *Social Studies, 92*(2), 69–72.

Poling, L. G. (2000). The real world: Community speakers in the classroom. *Social Education, 64*(4, Suppl.), M8–M10.

Web Sites

American Association of Museums
http://www.aam-us.org/

American Association of State and Local History
http://www.aaslh.org/

American Legion
http://www.legion.org/homepage.php

Peace Corps
http://www.peacecorps.gov/

State Humanities Councils
http://www.h-net.org/~local/emails.html

Historical Characters

GRADE LEVELS	NCSS CURRICULUM STRANDSRER
✔ 3–5	I Culture
✔ 6–8	II Time, Continuity, and Change

INTRODUCTION

Guest speakers have already been discussed in this text as an effective social studies strategy. Unfortunately, guest speakers from distant times and places are not available to share their experiences with students. One way to bring these distant figures into the classroom is to have students create a persona or represent a real person in order to interpret a time or place for which a real guest speaker is not available. The student tells his or her story in the first person and encourages others to ask questions of the character, although younger students may be more comfortable presenting just a monologue. Students might dress in period clothing and supplement their presentations with artifacts, primary sources, or audiovisuals. This strategy allows the performing student to explore another person's life from that person's perspective. It further allows observing students to interact with and question a character that they cannot reach in real life. It is an effective strategy for teachers themselves to use when presenting information about a particular historical figure.

PROCEDURAL RECOMMENDATIONS

- Establish objectives for the lesson or unit, identifying those figures whom the students will study. Have students choose a character who will enhance their own and their peers' understanding of the central concepts of the unit.

- Assist students in gathering multiple and varied resources regarding the chosen character. Resources include biographies, autobiographies, letters, diaries, and newspaper clippings that tell about the life and accomplishments of the character.

- Have students collect additional information regarding the time period in which the character lived. This social, political, and economic history will provide information regarding occupations, the roles of men and women, inventions, dress, the political climate, major industries, the standard of living, and other important issues of the time. This information is crucial to placing the character on the continuum of history and in the context of the character's world. For example, a student who chooses to portray Cesar Chavez should be aware of the labor movement of the mid-twentieth century and should access information about the time period, the western agricultural environment, the authentic voices of those whom Chavez was representing, and contemporaries working for similar causes.

- After the students have gathered and examined information, have them construct a concept map or other graphic organizer to arrange their presentation.

- For each item on their concept map, have students use note cards to record important facts, incidents, and perspectives. For example, one item on the Chavez concept map might be "Pesticides." Note cards could include information such as the types and effects of pesticides Chavez protested against and subsequent legislation regarding pesticides and agricultural worker safety. (See References and Resources in this strategy for materials on Cesar Chavez.)

- Allow ample time for students to prepare their presentation. Advise them to present their information in a series of stories that tell the life of their figure. The use of stories works better than simple memorization: If a student attempts to memorize a script, forgetting a specific line creates frustration. Creating stories from facts allows students to weave in conversational elements.

- Once students have generated a series of narratives, have them polish their presentation by effectively weaving their stories together. Direct them to look for chronological links, links between individuals in the stories, or links between important events.

- Consider props and costumes only after the preceding steps are completed. Students can become distracted by the search for costumes and props and neglect the academic and scholarly preparation of information on their character. In addition, the search for historically accurate props and costumes is easier once the student is familiar with his or her character and that figure's time period. Props and costumes do not need to be elaborate: a hat, quill pen, food item, shawl, or book suffices for many characters. Accuracy is key for props and costumes. While it may be impossible to find authentic paper and writing instruments of the eighteenth century, a wirebound notebook and ballpoint pen are too far removed. Instead, students could age paper using tea and prepare a pencil by removing the eraser, shortening it, and distressing its appearance.

- Note that first-person historical presentations can be of whatever length is appropriate for students' ages and the amount of time available for individual presentations.

- There is an important caveat and complex issue to consider here. It is important for students to study individuals from a variety of backgrounds who have made diverse contributions to society. However, there is legitimate concern when portraying someone from another race, ethnicity, or sex. From complex issues of cultural appropriation to students relying on caricatures, students' understandings of a person's time and place in history may get lost in these other issues. On the other hand, in a homogeneous classroom, it is limiting to only study individuals who represent the students' race, ethnicity, and/or sex. There are no easy answers; think carefully about the objectives you have for your students' learning.

APPLICATIONS AND IDEAS

In Kathy's sixth-grade optional Leadership course, students chose individuals from history that they believed exemplified the leadership characteristics they had been studying, including integrity, good communication, flexible, and clear vision, among others. Because the focus of the course was on leadership, not a particular time or place in history, students were encouraged to consider individuals from around the world and throughout history. However, to avoid students spending too much time on the search and therefore limiting their time for research and preparation, Kathy spoke with the fourth- and fifth-grade teachers to find out what individuals had been studied in previous years. Then Kathy and the school librarian pulled several children's biographies for student use. They worked to include biographies at several different reading levels, of both women and men representing different ethnicities, and from around the world. Although doing so was difficult, they worked to include some examples from outside the political world. This included individuals who were leaders in the scientific and cultural worlds. This preparation was not intended to limit student options. Rather, it was to assist those who were struggling to identify someone and to reinforce the leadership characteristics that the class had been studying. Students were allowed to choose someone from the provided list or suggest someone else. Kathy and one of her students, Stephen, had a discussion about John Chapman (aka Johnny Appleseed). Stephen remembered reading about Johnny Appleseed in fourth grade. The story interested him because of his family's orchard business. But he was struggling to determine whether John Chapman was a leader or just someone who wanted to help people moving west by planting fruit trees. Recognizing this as a good opportunity to look beyond political leaders, Kathy encouraged Stephen to read some more before deciding for sure. Eventually, Stephen decides that Chapman was a leader, just not in a traditional way. On the day of the class presentation, Stephen chose to use just an apple as his prop, and he focused his five-minute presentation on two things. First, he mentioned the biggest tall tales associated with Chapman, telling his classmates that these were just stories and not true. Second, he briefly talked about how Chapman had a clear vision and good communication (two leadership characteristics that had been studied). In addition to presenting their historical characters to their class, the students created a Speaker's Bureau that they made available to the other teachers in the school.

ASSESSMENT

Evaluating oral reports and presentations can be a challenge. The sample performance scoring guide in Table 26.1 attends to the performance nature of the first-person historical presentation while including elements of content. It also provides an opportunity for the student to participate in assessment. The performance scoring guide should be adapted for different ages and abilities.

TABLE 26.1 PERFORMANCE SCORING GUIDE FOR HISTORICAL CHARACTERS PRESENTATION

CRITERIA	POINTS POSSIBLE	TEACHER EVALUATION	STUDENT EVALUATION
Biographical details: The presentation includes accurate and concise information about the character's life. Include: • Important childhood and adolescent experiences • Important influences (e.g., family, teachers, mentors) • Important events as adult (e.g., school, marriage, career) • Other important details and events that influenced the person	20		
Contribution/relevance: The presentation addresses the importance and contributions of the character and his or her relevance to the unit under study. Include: • What is the individual most famous for? • Perception of individual during his or her lifetime • Perception of the individual throughout history	20		
Accuracy: The presentation—including content, props, and audiovisuals—is accurate. Include: • Props and audiovisuals are accurate • Annotated bibliography of all sources	10 20		
Poise and presentation: The student is poised and well-prepared during the presentation. There is little or no reliance on notes.	15		
Character development: The presentation is in character. The student is believable as the character, speaking in first person, avoiding contemporary slang.	15		
Totals	**100**		

REFERENCES AND RESOURCES

Cedeno, M. E. (1993). *Caesar Chavez: Labor leader. Hispanic heritage.* Brookfield, CT: Millbrook Press.

Cockcroft, J. D. (1995). *Latinos in the making of the United States: The Hispanic experience in the Americas.* New York: Franklin Watts.

Cruz, B. C., & Murthy, S. A. (2006). Breathing life into history: Using role-playing to engage students. *Social Studies and the Young Learner, 19*(1), 4–8.

Davis, C., & De Angelis, T. (Eds.). (1990). *Labor studies curriculum for teachers.* Minneapolis: Labor Education Service, Industrial Relations Center, University of Minnesota.

Drake, F., & Corbin, D. (1993). Making history come alive: Dramatization in the classroom. *Teaching History: A Journal of Methods, 18*(2), 59–67.

Jimenez, C. M. (1992). *The Mexican American heritage: With writing exercises.* Berkeley, CA: TQS Publications.

Morris, R. V. (2002). Presidents' Day in second trade with first-person presentations. *Gifted Child Today, 25*(4), 26–29.

Pinchot, J. (1973). *The Mexican Americans in America.* Minneapolis, MN: Learner Co.

Tchudi, S. (1998). *The young Chautauqua handbook: A guide for students, parents, teachers, and community leaders.* Reno, NV: Nevada Humanities Committee.

Web Sites

Social Education devotes its April/May issue every year to children's literature. Autobiographies, biographies, and books about social history are prevalent. Scholastic publishes a series of biographies of famous Americans written for intermediate-grade students. Check out the Web site at **http://www.socialstudies.org**

Historical Reenactments

GRADE LEVELS	NCSS CURRICULUM STRANDS
✔ 3–5	I Culture
✔ 6–8	II Time, Continuity, and Change
	III People, Places, and Environments
	VII Production, Distribution, and Consumption

INTRODUCTION

In a historical reenactment, students re-create a particular historical environment or a particular series of historical events in order to interpret what life would have been like in a different time and place. The reenactment is structured around historical or cultural events, allowing students to live one day in a time or place that is very different from their own. Because of their experiences in a reenactment, students can formulate higher-level questions about a historical event or experience. For example, they might ask why a character behaved in a particular way or what significant actions and interactions caused other events. Because their experience in a culture foreign to them causes them to disconnect from their own culture, their responses or reactions are inherently personal.

Students are often slightly uncomfortable with the reenactment experience; contact with a different culture causes them to question their own beliefs and practices. However, they are usually ready for the next reenactment. Younger students can learn what their community was like in colonial times or when the pioneers settled in the area. Older students explore a variety of subjects from military engagements and the home front to social life and customs. A reenactment requires a four- to six-week commitment for planning; thus, the procedural recommendations that follow are divided accordingly.

PROCEDURAL RECOMMENDATIONS

Four Weeks Before the Event

- Determine the objectives, the discussion questions, and the assessment guidelines.
- Contact volunteers to help with the reenactment. Many wonderful reenactors, teachers, historical society members, professors, and parents want to help students. Inform these volunteers about the learning objectives and what the students need.

- Construct a file about each character to give to a volunteer. Provide articles and photocopies that give each character a unique perspective on the issues of the day. List overall objectives, and highlight objectives particularly important to individual characters within the file.
- Create a master plan and a schedule showing all the classes, equipment, tools, and ingredients needed for each activity. Do not forget to accommodate restroom breaks and meals. Consider the time and space required for each experience; more time and space are required for activities that work best with large groups, such as meals. Likewise, when time and space are limited, smaller groups of students should rotate at set intervals. If there are opportunities for historical leisure time, schedule them as well. Students need to understand how people experienced leisure time and what they did for fun as well as work.
- Assign volunteers to the schedule. Send a prebriefing letter to the parent or guardian of each child containing a permission form to leave school grounds for the activity if such a form is necessary.

Two Weeks Before the Event

- Send letters to volunteers explaining what they need to bring to the reenactment. Provide a copy of the master plan and the schedule to all volunteer participants.
- If food is a part of the activity, send recipes to those who are cooking. Encourage these cooks to give the recipes a trial run.
- Arrange for a volunteer photographer to document the event.

One Week Before the Event

- Hold a meeting with the volunteers to create a storyline. Explain how each step of the reenactment might unfold.
- Review the important details of the day. Be sure volunteers know what they are to do, where they are to do it, and when they are to do it.
- Help all volunteers understand that they are not doing projects for students; rather, they are working with the students.
- If the event occurs outside, talk with the volunteers about any alternate rain plans when everything moves inside. Assign the areas where specific events are to occur; arrange for alternate indoor sites.
- If cooking is a part of the reenactment, arrange for hot plates and electric skillets to be available for the cooking sessions. Locate circuit breakers for outlets. Even if it is planned that students cook over open fires, have hot plates and electric skillets available in case of rain.
- Tell the volunteers the location of the central supply depot for the materials needed in their sessions. Acquire supplies ahead of time or arrange for the designated committee to do the shopping. Differentiate between the materials, ingredients, and tools provided and those that the volunteers need to bring with them. Specify the location of cold items because schools have multiple refrigerators. Even if the event occurs outside, modern sensibilities or safety precautions do not allow for prolonged periods of unrefrigerated food. Inform volunteers of any areas that are off-limits.
- Obtain firewood if necessary. Because firewood can be difficult to obtain and store and is bulky to transport, it requires special planning to get it from the right place at the right time. Hardwoods give the best cooking coals. Cooking fires should have low coals—not high flames.

Two Days Before the Event

- Shop for groceries. Sort all materials—ingredients, tools, and supplies—for each session into boxes marked for that session. Place a second copy of the schedule and recipe in each box.

The Day of the Reenactment

- Before people arrive, make sure that a first-aid kit and fire extinguisher are available.

- Tell the volunteers where to find the best location for washing utensils and completing other cleanup tasks. Remind them not to use steel wool on cast iron cookware. Tell volunteers the location of the vacuum cleaner and other supplies. Remind them to return all supplies to the supply depot clean. Also remind them to check the restrooms one last time before leaving.

- If period clothing is used, label each full costume in its storage bag by size. Label individual pieces by size. Put the bag and students' clothes on the students' desks so that all of their things are together. Have students don reenactment attire in the restroom and assist them with buttons, suspenders, and hooks. Assign three parents to help with this task. Make sure that large safety pins are available for fast alterations. Neatly put all clothes back in the garment bags when students return at the end of the day. Volunteers need to check the period clothing for mending and laundering.

Special Considerations

- Build all fires in dug fire pits. Fill in the fire pits at the end of the day. Leave no trace of charcoal exposed. Wear cotton, wool, or linen when working around a fire; those fabrics reduce the chance of catching on fire. Be alert to smoking grease; this generally means the pan is too hot. Always attend to open flames.

- Have a food service cater a historical meal or allow students to bring sack lunches to the event. This is the best way to accommodate fussy eaters and twenty-first-century tastes.

APPLICATIONS AND IDEAS

Upper elementary students participate in this reenactment of 1745 New France.

Reenactment Schedule

7:30 A.M. When the students arrive, they place their sack lunches on their desks and change into their historical clothing.

8:00 A.M. The teacher greets the students, divides them into small groups for the day, and provides them with a background story setting the time and place for the reenactment.

8:30 A.M. The students meet a voyageur and a Jesuit priest who make first-person historical presentations based on student-generated discussion questions.

9:00 A.M. Students listen as a French woman recounts four French folktales around her campfire.

9:30 A.M. Students participate in three different 20-minute rotating sessions on crafts or cooking.

10:30 A.M. Restroom break.

10:45 A.M. Students return to learn about the construction practices used in the oldest residence in the state, the Old French House, with slides of the home and a local historian from the community.

11:30 A.M. Students continue to explore the French language with song and dance. These reinforce counting, introductions, and games coupled with customs and manners.

12:00 P.M. Students eat lunch followed by a restroom break.

12:30 P.M. Students listen to a first-person historical presentation: A French woman from Ouiatenon talks about French settlements in the New World.

12:45 P.M. Students attend a first-person historical presentation by a Native American warrior, who gives a perspective about Franco–Native American relations that is different from that of the French woman.

1:00 P.M. Students and adults model their period clothing in a fashion show depicting farmers, officers, tradesmen, merchants, upper-class women, lower-class women, traders, priests, marines, and voyageurs.

1:30 P.M. Students participate in the second activity period, consisting of four different 30-minute rotating sessions on various topics.

2:30 P.M. Restroom break.

2:45 P.M. The second activity period occurs, during which students taste traditional foods.

3:45 P.M. Students listen to first-person historical presentations by a French marine and a French farmer.

4:15 P.M. In the debriefing session, the whole group responds to discussion questions that require students to reflect on the entire day.

4:30 P.M. Students assist with the cleanup and then change out of their period clothing.

4:45 P.M. French reenactment ends.

Reenactment Activities

During the reenactment, students do each of the following:

- Smoke and sample jerky.
- Pick up a canoe.
- Pack bundles to feel how much the French carried on a portage.
- Try on a bone corset.
- Sew an essential article of clothing—a pair of drawstring pockets.
- Wash, card, and spin wool.
- Learn rudimentary French words and phrases and French folk songs.
- Do some hard trading on the trade blanket with the French trader.
- Cook a pot of French onion soup, and prepare Indian fry bread over an open flame.
- Cook Canadian oatmeal shortbread, corn chowder, and common bread.
- Bake French marble cake and herb batter bread.
- Carry water from a spring and clean pans.
- Play ninepins and checkers, walk on stilts, shoot marbles, or roll hoops.

ASSESSMENT

At the end of the reenactment, the students write a reflection about their experience.

4 Points	3 Points	2 Points	1 Point
What would daily life be like for your character?	What would daily life be like for your character?	What would daily life be like for your character?	What would daily life be like for your character?
How did your character contribute to the economy?	How did your character contribute to the economy?	How did your character contribute to the economy?	
How did your character interact with one of the following: Jesuit priest, voyageur, French woman, French marine, or French farmer?	How did your character interact with one of the following: Jesuit priest, voyageur, French woman, French marine, or French farmer?		
What role did your character play in the contest for empire among the English, French, Indians, and Spanish?			

REFERENCES AND RESOURCES

Morris, R. V. (2000). A retrospective examination of the Clio Club: An elementary social studies and enrichment program offered as an extra-curricular activity. *Journal of Social Studies Research, 4*(1), 418.

Morris, R. V. (2001). How teachers can conduct historical reenactments in their own schools. *Childhood Education, 77*(4), 196–203.

Morris, R. V. (2002a). Third grade at Simmons Elementary School, ca 1900. *Social Studies & the Young Learner, 14*(4), 6–10.

Morris, R. V. (2002b). Presidents' Day in second grade with first-person presentations. *Gifted Child Today, 25*(4), 26–29, 64.

Morris, R. V. (2005). The Clio Club: An extracurricular model for elementary social studies enrichment. *Gifted Child Today, 28*(1), 40–48.

Web Sites

American Civil War Re-enactment Society
http://acwhrs.com./

Historical Re-enactment
http://www.reconstrucciohistorica.cat/en/Historical_Reenactment.php

The Lexington Minute Men Inc.
http://users.rcn.com/waynemccarthy/LMM2002/index.htm

Reenactor
http://www.reenactor.net/

World War II Historical Re-enactment Society Inc.
http://www.worldwartwohrs.org/

28

Home Living Centers

GRADE LEVELS	NCSS CURRICULUM STRANDS
✔ K–2	I Culture
	IV Individual Development and Identity
	V Individuals, Groups, and Institutions
	VII Production, Distribution, and Consumption

INTRODUCTION

Many primary classrooms have a center that includes child-sized home living equipment such as kitchen appliances. In their free and structured play, young students explore home-related situations, problems, and resolutions. Students use play as an entry point for discussion about real-life situations and interactions between people (Wassermann, 2000). Younger students can replicate jobs and roles, while older students can conduct economic exchanges or solve problems in their play.

PROCEDURAL RECOMMENDATIONS

- Set up the home living center to include a student-sized toy stove, refrigerator, table and chairs, sink, bed, full-length mirror, and hall tree.
- Select props for inclusion in the center. Provide a variety of occupational hats and uniforms on the hall tree for the students to try on and wear. Arrange a variety of dolls representing multiple ethnicities and ages on the bed. Supply pans for cooking and baking and plates for serving food at the table or washing in the sink. Store play food in the cabinets and refrigerator.
- Arrange for students' initial experience in the center to occur during playtime so that they become comfortable with the environment and explore the resources available to them in a

nonthreatening way. After play, ask probing questions such as "Can you tell me about how you have been playing this morning?" and "What will you do next?"

- Set up a series of center experiences. For example, remove all food from the home living center and ask, "What will we do if we do not have any food in the house?" Move all of the dishes into the sink and say, "Who left all these dirty dishes for us? What can we do to solve this problem?" Referring to the mirror and the hall tree, ask the students what job they want to do today. "What would you wear if you were a _____? What will you do to help your community?" Using the dolls in the center, students explore child care, empathy, and nurturing behaviors. "How can we take care of all of these children?" "How can we keep them all clean?" "How do we show children that we care about them?" "How will we get lunch ready for all of them?"

- Allow students ample opportunity to "play" in the center, carrying out various tasks or assuming various roles.

- After play time, gather students into the large group to report on the jobs they carried out during center play. Encourage students to pose new issues or questions to be explored in future center experiences.

- In the following days, ensure that there is an equal mix of student-initiated issues and play and teacher-initiated issues and play.

- To assess student performance in the home living center, use the performance checklist.

APPLICATIONS AND IDEAS

When primary students come into their classroom, their teacher tells them they are going to the store today. Students inspect the cabinets and determine what they need before making their list. They find coupons in the cabinets and discuss whether or not they need any of the products featured on the coupons and revise their shopping lists accordingly. Next, students find a teacher-made "newspaper" featuring simplified grocery ads. Students discuss the factors they will consider when they choose between two grocery stores. They calculate how much play money they have and determine what they need most. In each step, the teacher helps students examine both what they have and what they want, then guides them in making appropriate decisions.

The mail carrier delivers mail to the primary family in the home living center. When the family sorts through the mail, they find several different and simplified types: a personal letter, a postcard, a catalogue, an advertising flyer, and a telephone bill. Students decide how they will respond to each of the pieces of mail. They browse through the catalogue and make choices about what to purchase for their home based on their family budget. They decide to discard the advertising flyers because they do not feature items their family has decided to purchase. Members of the family use a globe to locate the city from which the postcard originated. Students read the letter, which asks a member of the family for an interview for a job. (This will provide a play topic for tomorrow.) Family members decide to form small groups to respond to the postcard and the letter. When they open the telephone bill, they find several unexpected charges. When they call the telephone company (the teacher), they learn that the student teacher has been playing with the telephone. Students then discuss how to use the telephone properly and decide what they will need to give up so that they can pay this bill. They learn how to read the simplified telephone bill, check the due date for payment, and fill out the form that came with the bill. Next, they use their simplified checkbooks to write a check to the telephone company, and they record their check in their check registry. Finally, they stamp and mail their payment after writing their return address in the proper place on the envelope.

ASSESSMENT

PERFORMANCE ASSESSMENT CHECKLIST FOR HOME LIVING CENTER		
Observable Behavior	**Observed**	**Comments**
Accurately identifies items in the center (e.g., household appliances, furniture, telephone)		
Correctly uses items in the center		
When questioned, articulates the issues/topics explored in the center		
When questioned, proposes and explains potential solutions to issues		
Peacefully resolves conflicts with others		

REFERENCES AND RESOURCES

Fromberg, D. P. (2002). *Play and meaning in early childhood education.* Boston: Allyn & Bacon.

Hyyonen, P. (2008). Teachers' perceptions of boys' and girls' shared activities in the school context: Towards a theory of collaborative play. *Teachers and Teaching: Theory and Practice, 14*(5–6), 391–409.

Lee, R., Gamsey, P. G., Sweeney, B. (2008). Engaging young children in activities and conversations about race and social class. *Young Children, 63*(6), 68–76.

Terpstra, J. E., & Tamura, R. (2008). Effective social interaction strategies for inclusive settings. *Early Childhood Education Journal, 35*(5), 405–411.

Wasserman, S. (2000). *Serious players in the primary classroom: Empowering children through active learning experiences* (2nd ed.). New York: Teachers College Press.

Web Sites

Early Childhood Research and Practice:
http://ecrp.uiuc.edu/v5n1/sandberg.html

Grounds for Play:
http://www.groundsforplay.com/playground-equipment/preschool-playground-equipment.html

Kaplan Early Learning Company:
http://www.kaplanco.com/children-dramatic-play.asp

National Association for the Education of Young Children:
http://www.naeyc.org/

School Outfitters:
https://www.schooloutfitters.com/catalog/default/cPath/CAT5_CAT126

29

Interactive Bulletin Boards

GRADE LEVELS	NCSS CURRICULUM STRANDS
✔ K–2	Any (Depending on Topic)
✔ 3–5	
✔ 6–8	

INTRODUCTION

Elementary and middle school classrooms typically include bulletin board space. Often teachers or students decorate the space with seasonal items or information related to a topic under study. Bulletin boards require substantial time to create, prepare, and display. Creating an interactive bulletin board that encourages student involvement is a wise use of that time. Interactive bulletin boards encourage students to intellectually and physically manipulate the information displayed, developing and testing hypotheses. They offer students an opportunity to further explore or examine one element or concept of the social studies topic under study and allow visual or kinesthetic learners to engage more fully with the curriculum. If pairs or small groups of students interact with the display, interactive bulletin boards encourage a discussion of issues and perspectives. Interactive bulletin boards are a good fit with Strategy 30. As a field of study, social studies is rich with artifacts, narratives, issues, and perspectives. Interactive bulletin boards are a space where these artifacts, narratives, issues, and perspectives can be presented in an enticing and engaging format.

PROCEDURAL RECOMMENDATIONS

- Examine your lesson or unit objectives to generate potential higher-order questions. For example, intermediate students studying westward migration in North America might be asked to examine the well-known westward trails, comparing climate, food sources, terrain, potential contact with other humans, and distance. Based on the information they accumulate, they can identify which route they believe to be the best. The bulletin board might contain U.S. maps from the era of westward migration that include political, topographic, population, and climate information. Students studying the Japanese and European feudal systems might be asked to arrange the various roles individuals had in a feudal society into a hierarchical display on the bulletin board. They might then compare and contrast the two feudal systems for classmates.

- Group questions according to the location and type of information needed to answer them. Doing so creates the potential for more than one interactive bulletin board focusing on the same topic. Multiple bulletin boards provide multiple interactions without all of the focus being in one place. This is particularly important when large numbers of students participate.

- For each group of questions, gather all of the information required for exploration and response. If the information can be used in its original form (for example, a map of the United States), set it aside. Determine how best to adapt and display other information for interaction. This may include photocopying quotations and using cardboard or foam core to strengthen frequently handled items.

- Determine design. Central questions should be prominent on the bulletin board. It should also be evident how the bulletin board relates to the social studies unit under study. Arrange all of the needed information in the available space. It may be necessary to create pockets for information; attach folders with information or directions, attach rulers or writing utensils, or include other information or materials necessary to interact with the bulletin board.

- Introduce the interactive bulletin board to students by relating it to the unit under study. Let students know that by interacting with the bulletin board, they will better understand the unit. Referring to the bulletin board questions and activities during social studies lessons helps students make the learning connection.

APPLICATIONS AND IDEAS

This interactive bulletin board in Ms. Rogers's classroom is connected to her unit on "New Wonders of the World." Students have been studying the reasons why people build monuments and the process they follow in choosing types and locations. In order to predict what new kinds of monuments or "New Wonders" should be built, students study "Ancient Wonders of the World." Using the spinner located on the bulletin board, students determine their groups and the focus of their inquiry. Ms. Rogers has arranged for all students to have specific experiences with all of the Ancient Wonders. For example, if a student lands on red, he or she locates pictures of the seven Ancient Wonders and reads about their physical properties (e.g., size, building materials) and geographic locations. Landing on yellow requires inquiry into the time period when and the reasons why the Ancient Wonders were built. Landing on blue requires exploration of interesting facts about the Ancient Wonders. This may include political or cultural significance, associated scientific innovations, or builders and designers. Landing on green requires inquiry into the appearance and use of the structure today.

Working in small groups, students use a variety of resources (e.g., globes, atlases, maps, Web sites) to answer questions. For example, students in the yellow group are asked, among other things, to find out for each Ancient Wonder when construction began and ended, how long the project took, who requested the building of the Ancient Wonder, and for what purposes it was constructed. Students record information on color-coded cards and then place the cards in the pockets on the bulletin board next to pictures of the appropriate Ancient Wonders. As other students begin their research, they can see what has already been discovered and recorded about each Ancient Wonder. After a specified time (no more than five devoted blocks of time), the groups get together to review and synthesize the information in the pockets. The goal of this task is to help students look at the Ancient Wonders for patterns. For example, the red group notes the enormous size of all of them. The photographs they examine indicate that all the Ancient Wonders can be seen from a distance. The yellow group discovers that most of the Ancient Wonders served as evidence of the wealth and strength of the political rulers of the time.

Using this information, the teacher divides the students into seven new groups, each representing one of the Ancient Wonders. This provides the first real opportunity for students to compare the different kinds of information they each researched. Each of these groups prepares a poster that synthesizes the four categories of information. The goal is not to just place the collected information on a poster. Rather, students are asked to relate the information and categories to one another. For example, how are the physical properties of the Ancient Wonder related to the social or political structure of the time? How is the belief system of the political leader connected to the belief systems of the population, and how is this portrayed in historical and current use of the Ancient Wonder? As the groups present their posters to the class, the teacher reinforces the patterns and themes for the purpose of reinforcing the connection telling why people build monuments and where they are placed.

ASSESSMENT

The bulletin board itself is not assessed; however, in some instances, the results of student inquiry may be displayed on the bulletin board and evaluated there. Depending upon the tasks assigned, a variety of assessment tasks would be appropriate.

REFERENCES AND RESOURCES

Isenberg, J., & Foster, D. (1987). *Beyond basic bulletin boards*. Logan, IA: Perfection Form.

Jackson, D. L. (1999). *Bulletin board ideas*. Charlotte, NC: Queens College.

Meagher, J. and Novelli, J. (1999). *Interactive bulletin boards*. New York: Scholastic.

Meagher and Novelli have several books about bulletin boards and interactive bulletin boards. None of them are specifically designated as social studies. However, they provide ideas for the interactive nature of bulletin boards.

Web Sites

Discovery Education has an entire section devoted to bulletin boards (**http://school.discoveryeducation.com/schrockguide/bulletin/index.html**). The options are a bit overwhelming, but keeping the *interactive* goal of a bulletin board in mind will significantly narrow the options.

The Web site *Bulletin Board Pro* has a specific site for social studies bulletin boards (**http://www.bulletinboardpro.com/socialstudies.html**). This site has photographs of several different bulletin boards. The examples change frequently and not all of the bulletin boards are interactive. This one (**http://www.bulletinboardpro.com/BB64.html**) is interactive.

Kinderhive.net (**http://web.archive.org/web/20060502011850/www.kinderhive.net/winterbb.html**) has several examples of bulletin boards. *Wild and Wooly* is a good simple example for the primary grades.

30

Learning Centers

GRADE LEVELS	NCSS CURRICULUM STRANDS
✔ K–2	Any (Depending on Topic)
✔ 3–5	
✔ 6–8	

INTRODUCTION

A learning center is an area in the classroom where students explore new concepts, themes, and skills independently or in small groups. Learning centers may include multiple lessons or stations through which students progress over a period of time. Centers enhance student learning by providing opportunities to practice a skill or review content, adding enrichment activities, or introducing a related concept. Traditionally, teachers set aside a specific time period each day for students to spend in learning centers. Each station focuses on one or more activities that students complete individually or in small groups. Many classrooms have two or three learning centers attending to different academic areas or different topics. For example, one classroom may contain separate social studies, science, and writing learning centers. Another classroom may contain separate learning centers on environmental stewardship, immigration, and peace movements, each one integrating appropriate academic areas. Well-developed learning centers encourage students to self-monitor their learning and cooperation. They can also accommodate the different abilities and learning styles found in a typical classroom.

As explained in the above description, it is easy to see why learning centers are particularly appropriate in social studies. Social studies is a conceptually rich discipline, and elementary students vary in their ability to grasp abstract concepts. By providing the opportunity to engage in some self-paced learning, as well as the opportunity to revisit challenging (and enjoyable) lessons, students have the additional time with the abstract nature of the curriculum. In addition, social studies units often include cultural elements such as art, music, and literature. An exploration of these elements is often more meaningful when students, individually or in small groups, experience and study the elements "close up," both literally and figuratively.

PROCEDURAL RECOMMENDATIONS

- Choose an appropriate topic, concept, or skill. The learning center can supplement the teacher-led unit, or it can stand alone as a unit of study, requiring only a teacher-led introduction and culminating activity.

- After determining the learning objectives, list all the activities that would help students master the unit's objectives. Select those activities that encourage individual or small-group learning or that may be readily adapted to the learning center environment.

- Consider activities that accommodate multiple learning styles: visual, auditory, and kinesthetic. And, consider multiple ability levels. For example, include listening, reading, writing, and observing activities as well as manipulatives.

- Also consider activities that encourage independent and small-group learning. Balance these opportunities throughout the different stations. For small-group activities, use heterogeneous groups to maximize academic and social benefits.

- If students will be learning a new concept or skill, develop different activities that help students learn the new concept or skill, apply the concept or skill, and extend their understanding by comparing what they are learning to previous knowledge or creating a new understanding.

- Gather a variety of resources for each station. Stations that include reading should have a variety of texts and trade books. Include books that are at various reading levels but still reinforce the topic, concept, or skill under study. For struggling readers, create audiotapes or CDs of each text so students can listen while following along in the book.

- Determine the order or approach for student participation. Will students rotate in small groups during a set time each day? Do students need to complete all or some of the stations in a specific order? Will everyone complete Station 1 on the first day, Station 2 on the second, and so forth? In making these decisions, consider which stations build on prior knowledge from other stations. If there is not room for students to physically move about the room, set up all of the materials in one place. This type of center dictates that large groups of students cannot work at the center itself.

- Organization is key to a successful learning center. If students are to physically move from location to location, several organizational tips are helpful.

- Set up tables or chairs or somehow distinguish one area from another. Reading areas may include comfortable pillows and chairs, but writing areas should have a table and chairs to make it easy for beginning writers to develop a comfortable writing form.

- Create station titles and prominently display them at each station. If students must work in a set pattern or order, it is best to arrange the stations in the order required. Also, make students aware of any specific time limits.

- Establish a checklist for students so they can keep track of their own progress. This should be something that students can carry around with them and that the teacher checks periodically. Avoid a classroom display that allows students to see one another's progress. A display of this type can reinforce a competitive environment, which is not conducive to a well-run learning center. A form listing all the activities and providing a space for both the teacher and the students to note completion is appropriate, as are more creative checklists that relate to the unit's topic. For example, students studying other countries or working on mapping skills may use a passport that the teacher can check periodically.

- Provide a place for each student or group to turn in the work the teacher will evaluate.

- If there are dimensional products or performances to be evaluated, create a sign-up sheet and space for students to present their work.

- Clearly arrange all of the necessary materials or directions for obtaining materials at each center. This includes reference materials, reading and writing materials, scissors, glue, study guides, audiocassette or compact disc players with headphones, and other equipment.

- After all of the materials have been gathered and prepared, introduce the learning center and its activities to the students. Stimulating interest in the learning center with an engaging lesson works well. Explain to students how their progress in the learning center will be monitored by the teacher and them.
- A learning center does not mean the teacher turns students loose. One must still monitor, encourage, evaluate, and participate in the learning center activities.

APPLICATIONS AND IDEAS

Ms. Jones created a world geography learning center for her sixth-grade class. With the exception of the first and last lessons, students moved through the different stations of the learning center in small groups or independently. Ms. Jones predetermined that students would need 30 to 45 minutes three times a week for 3 weeks to successfully complete the learning center. The sixth-grade social studies curriculum focused on world history, and this particular learning center, which was implemented early in the year, reinforced basic geography skills and built interest in places around the world by examining the famous "Ancient Wonders of the World." The first lesson was facilitated by the teacher and included a review of major geography themes and cocepts.

Students completed individual, small-group, and whole-group activities reviewing basic concepts such as cardinal directions, longitude and latitude, development of regions, and both human and environment interactions. Ms. Jones also introduced and explained how students would progress through the learning center. Each student was given a *Travel Journal* that included (a) student responsibilities and overall directions for the learning center, (b) a lesson completion checklist for teacher and student monitoring of progress, and (c) formats for Journal entries.

TABLE 30.1 ANCIENT WONDERS OF THE WORLD				
	JOURNAL ENTRY— STUDENT	JOURNAL ENTRY— MS. JONES	LESSON ASSIGNMENTS— STUDENT	LESSON ASSIGNMENTS —MS. JONES
Introduction Lesson	N/A	N/A		
The Great Pyramids (latitude and longitude exercise, readings, and three-dimensional building of pyramids)				
The Parthenon (examine topographic map of site, judge location of site in relation to purpose)				
The Taj Mahal (read stories of the relationship that inspired the monument, interpretation of specific parts of the site)				
The Great Wall of China (mapping of site, historical purpose, interpretation of photographs over time)				
The Leaning Tower of Pisa (computer research/report on attempts to preserve site)				
Add a new Wonder	N/A	N/A		

The Journal entries were one assessment task completed for each lesson. Students wrote which "Wonder" they were studying, why it was an important place, interesting things they learned and observed regarding the physical and human geography, plus one piece of advice to give to a future traveler. This Journal provided a quick way for the teacher to ensure that students were involved with the different lessons. Table 30.1 illustrates the checklist Ms. Jones used in her students' Journals to assess their progress. Each lesson/station also included different assessment tasks related to geography themes and concepts.

All lessons attended to absolute and relative location as well as human and physical characteristics. During the lesson on the Great Wall of China, students also examined the theme of movement of people and ideas. Students examined the themes of human and environmental interaction and regions. In addition, the different lessons accommodated the different abilities and learning styles of students. Students were involved in kinesthetic, visual, and auditory experiences.

The culminating lesson was facilitated by Ms. Jones and required students to synthesize their learning from the center. In the large group, students discussed what they learned at each site and why they believed that site was considered a Wonder. Students were then assigned to small cooperative groups and asked to nominate another landmark to receive the status of Wonder. The small groups examined a variety of international landmarks and built a case for why their particular landmark deserved Wonder status. The small groups made presentations to the entire class, a group discussion was facilitated, and consensus was achieved that Uluru (formerly known as Ayres Rock) in Australia was most deserving of Wonder status.

ASSESSMENT

Because a learning center contains a wide variety of activities, multiple kinds of assessment tasks and scoring rubrics are appropriate. Consider holistic and analytic scoring rubrics, as well as performance checklists.

REFERENCES AND RESOURCES

Brown, M. & Bergen, D. (2002). Play and social interaction of children with disabilities at learning/activity centers in an inclusive preschool. *Journal of Research in Childhood Education, 17*(1), 26–37.

Gardner, H. (1993). *Multiple intelligences: The theory into practice.* New York: Basic Books.

Gardner, H. (2000). *Intelligence reframed: Multiple intelligences for the 21st century.* New York: Basic Books.

Geographic Education National Implementation Project (GENIP) (1987). *K–6 geography: Themes, key ideas, and learning opportunities.* Skokie, IL: Rand McNally Educational Publishing Division.

Geographic Education National Implementation Project (GENIP). (1989). *7–12 geography: Themes, key ideas, and learning opportunities.* Skokie, IL: Rand McNally Educational Publishing Division.

Geography Education Standards Project. (1994). *Geography for life: National geography standards.* Washington, DC: National Geographic Research & Exploration.

Haas, M. E. (2000). "A street through time" used with powerful instructional strategies. *Social Studies and the Young Learner, 13*(2), 20–23.

Taylor, M., & Otinsky, G. (2006). Embarking on the road to authentic engagement: Investigating racism through interactive learning centers. *Voices from the Middle, 14*(1), 38–46.

Web Sites

The North Carolina Public School Web site:
(**http://www.ncpublicschools.org/curriculum/artsed/resources/handbook/dance/31learning**)
has an article on using learning centers.

This link to Find Articles
(**http://findarticles.com/p/articles/mi_qa3614/is_200501/ai_n13643984**) has an article
about the effective use of learning centers in the classroom.

Literature Book Clubs

GRADE LEVELS	NCSS CURRICULUM STRANDS
	I Culture
✔ 3–5	II Time, Continuity, and Change
✔ 6–8	III People, Places, and Environments

INTRODUCTION

Many adults have participated in book clubs over the course of their lives, realizing the joy that comes with exploring a good book and then having the opportunity to talk about it with others. Students, and some teachers, find some social studies material dry and uninteresting. The human experiences have been left out, thus making it difficult for students to connect to the lives of people in the past or in different parts of the world. Children's literature, both fiction and nonfiction, helps students explore the similarities and differences with other people and places. Quality children's literature integrates naturally with the social studies and, when done well, allows the teacher to meet both language arts and social studies learning objectives. Book clubs are standard practice in many elementary and middle school literacy and language arts programs, and book club procedures have been well documented (see McMahon & Raphael, 1997; Raphael, Pardo, & Highfield, 2002; Raphael, Pardo, Highfield, & McMahon, 1997).

As explained and expanded here, the focus of the book club strategy is on how to use literature to help students learn social studies. If the focus is just on literacy content and skills, social studies content and skills may not be learned. Using literature must include an explicit focus on the social studies content being addressed; learning objectives must address social studies so that teachers will connect literature with concepts, themes, or content related to the social studies. Specifically, teachers are cautioned that addressing literacy objectives without addressing social studies concepts, themes, and objectives is not quality integration.

PROCEDURAL RECOMMENDATIONS

- For the social studies unit under study, determine what will be best learned through a book club. It could be specific content (e.g., the experiences of Marco Polo, Harlem Renaissance) or themes and concepts (e.g., ordinary individuals in extraordinary times, movement, immigration, genocide, reconciliation). Then write measurable learning objectives.

- Assess the reading abilities of students. Based on those levels, choose a variety of quality children's literature that addresses the social studies learning objectives and that is appropriate to the students' various reading levels. If possible, choose a different book for each group of no more than five students. With larger classes that have relatively homogeneous reading levels, there may be multiple books at one level. The books may be historical fiction, biographies, autobiographies, informational text, and so on. As a variation, it is also possible to use primary source documents such as letters, diaries, newspaper articles, legal opinions, etc. Brief primary sources and segments of secondary sources (e.g., one section in a textbook) are a good adaptation if there is not enough time for students to read an entire book. The process is the same; the text is different.

- For students new to participating in book clubs, explain how book clubs work as well as the broader goals of reading and talking about what has been read. Explain that they will read a little, write a little, and talk about what they have read and written. They will do this multiple times over the course of completing the book. For older students chapter breaks serve as appropriate periodic goals.

- For students who have prior experience with book clubs, introduce the particular book club. This whole-group instruction includes any necessary background content and skills needed as well as the concepts or themes to be explored. This includes the historical, political, and social context, to the extent the teacher believes that this should be introduced at the beginning as opposed to discovered during the book club. Because of its basis in literacy, this is also the appropriate time to provide necessary background instruction in literacy (e.g., literary elements, comprehension).

- Introduce and display the writing prompts that students will be addressing in their later conversations. These prompts (social studies and literacy) reflect the concepts or themes, reinforce the learning objectives of the book club, and make students aware of the focus of the discussion.

- Provide quiet time for reading (i.e., sustained silent reading) in the class, with the teacher also reading. Attending to students' reading levels and preferences, recommend individual silent reading, partner reads, or other reading strategies. For some struggling readers, this may include a read-aloud in a corner of the room. Very few teachers have enough time for all of the reading to be done in class. If in a team setting, the social studies and language arts teacher may work together to find time. It is also appropriate to assign reading as homework.

- After the quiet reading time (or upon returning to school), the writing prompts are displayed and explained again. Students are given additional quiet time to provide individual written responses to the prompts.

- Students who have read the same book come together, with one student serving as the discussion leader. The discussion leader uses the writing prompts as conversation starters, noting that the conversation may go in many directions. As students discuss the books, they are encouraged to reference specific parts of the text that support their statements. Each time the group gets together to discuss a portion of the book, a different member of the group serves as discussion leader.

- During the small-group discussion, circulate among the groups clarifying issues, ensuring the groups are on track, and noting what each group is discussing.

- Gather the class for a brief period to synthesize the many conversations. This is an opportunity to reinforce the concepts and themes that were the focus of the learning objectives. From a literacy perspective, it also provides an opportunity to make predictions about what may be occurring next.

- The cycle is repeated until the books are completed.

APPLICATIONS AND IDEAS

The sources mentioned in the Introduction and cited in the References and Resources list provide excellent guidance in using book clubs to achieve literacy objectives and are highly recommended to teachers. These books also contain sample literacy-based writing prompts for a variety of children's literature and reflect a variety of thinking levels, from recall to evaluation. Provided as follows are some writing prompts that specifically address social studies concepts and themes.

Grade Level: Eighth
Concept: Citizenship
Theme: The Various Ways Individuals Exercise Their Citizenship
Whole-Group Instruction Focus: Legal and customary rights and responsibilities of citizens in a democracy, democratic ideals, gaining citizenship status
Books: All biographies (e.g., Rosa Parks, James Madison, Abigail Adams, Cesar Chavez, Jackie Robinson)
Social Studies Writing Prompts:

- What democratic ideals or values do you see displayed by the individual you are studying?
- In what instances do you see the individual acting in ways that are contradictory to democratic ideals?
- How did the individual connect his or her actions to the idea of citizenship?
- How did the individual express his or her rights as a citizen?
- How did the individual express his or her responsibilities as a citizen?

ASSESSMENT

A performance checklist similar to the one explained in Strategy 19 works well with *Literature Book Clubs.*

REFERENCES AND RESOURCES

Houser, N. O. (1999). Critical literature for the social studies: Challenges and opportunities for the elementary classroom. *Social Education, 63*(4), 212–245.

Krey, D. M. (1998). *Children's literature in social studies: Teaching to the standards* (NCSS Bulletin no. 95). Washington, DC: National Council for the Social Studies.

Sandmann, A. A., & Ahern, J. F. (2002). *Linking literature with life: NCSS standards and children's literature for the middle grades* (NCSS Bulletin no. 99). Silver Spring, MD: National Council for the Social Studies.

For book club, see:

McMahon, S. I., & Raphael, T. E. (with Goatley, V. J., & Pardo, L. S.) (Eds.). (1997). *The book club connection: Literacy learning and classroom talk.* New York: Teachers College Press.

Raphael, T., Pardo, L., & Highfield, K. (2002). *Book club: A literature-based curriculum* (2nd ed.). Lawrence, MA: Small Planet Publications.

Raphael, T., Pardo, L., Highfield, K., & McMahon, S. (1997). *Book club: A literature-based curriculum.* Littleton, MA: Small Planet Publications.

Web Sites

Literature Circles
(**http://www.literaturecircles.com/**) are similar to the book club process described above. Explore the Web site for more ideas.

Whatever the social studies topic under discussion, it is crucial that the literature selected reflect and enhance students' understanding of that topic and be authentic, nonbiased and nonstereotyped. Check out the following professional organizations and publishers for recommendations.

For further information, contact:

Booklinks:
http://www.ala.org/ala/aboutala/offices/publishing/booklinks/index.cfm

International Reading Association:
http://www.reading.org/General/Default.aspx

National Council for the Social Studies:
http://www.ncss.org

National Council for Teachers of English:
http://www.ncte.org/

Rethinking Schools:
http://www.rethinkingschools.org/

32

Media Literacy

GRADE LEVELS	NCSS CURRICULUM STRANDS
✔ K–2	I Culture
✔ 3–5	IV Individual Development and Identity
✔ 6–8	V Individuals, Groups, and Institutions
	VII Production, Distribution, and Consumption

INTRODUCTION

On any given day, citizens are bombarded with hundreds of advertisements intent on inspiring a purchase—whether it is needed or not. Children, who do not have the experience or expertise to separate fact from fiction, are particularly susceptible to these advertisements. Media literacy encompasses advertisements, print and visual media, the Internet, and entertainment. When students practice media literacy, they demonstrate discernment of propaganda and evaluate sources for reliability and validity. Because of the tremendous presence and potential influence of the media, it is important for students to be able to examine and validate the information presented as well as search for new information prior to making decisions.

It is certainly appropriate to take the idea of media literacy into other current applications such as political campaigns and policy initiatives or into historical applications such as the purchase of Alaska or the establishment of Israel. For these applications, students examine a variety of media sources such as newspaper articles and editorials, political cartoons, blogs, or television news in search of understanding.

PROCEDURAL RECOMMENDATIONS

- Generate with the students a list of the most popular new toys and games available that they neither own nor have played with.
- From this list, have students vote to determine which three or four items they will examine. Fewer items can be examined if this is pursued as a whole-class activity. However, if students are working in small, cooperative groups, a few more items may be necessary.

- Provide assistance to students in capturing television commercials that advertise the items to be examined. These advertisements may be on television, corporation Web sites, YouTube, or even Web sites that students frequently visit. Have students examine all of the information presented about each item.
- Have students create a descriptive profile of each item. Encourage students to be as specific as possible in their profiles. According to the information available:
  - What do the ads promise the item will do?
  - How well do they promise it will perform?
- Arrange the profile criteria in checklist fashion down the left side of the evaluation form.
- Gather the actual items the students have evaluated.
- Have students evaluate each item against its profile checklist.
- When all of the items have been evaluated, lead students through a discussion of what they found.
  - How did the items perform?
  - How truthful was the advertising?
  - Do certain kinds of advertising tend to be more or less misleading?
  - Does the advertising seem to be targeted to certain kids? Why might this be so?
- Link the evaluation and discussion of products with an introduction or reinforcing lesson on types of propaganda, such as "glittering generalities," "on the bandwagon," or an endorsement by a celebrity. Use advertisement language and pictures to create the discussion questions.

APPLICATIONS AND IDEAS

In the following example, Mr. Patel's students learn decision-making skills through examining a popular toy; they can then apply the same evaluation techniques when making decisions about larger purchases or about candidates for public office. This strategy, as described with a specific example, is one way to educate young citizens to become wise consumers and to discern propaganda. The following example focuses on a current application of analysis to items that children see advertised and want to possess.

Prior to the winter holiday, Mr. Patel's students generate a list of the most popular new toys and games available that none of the students either own or have played with. From this list, the students chose three or four items to examine. The students chose similar items; in previous years, his students examined a variety of dolls one year and video games a different year. Another year they chose several different items including a doll, a board game, and a piece of sporting equipment. Mr. Patel has his students vote on the most popular items and examine the items that receive the most votes. (He usually does this with fewer items as a whole-class activity, but the first year he needed more items when the students worked in small, cooperative groups.) With the assistance of the school media specialist, he captures television commercials advertising the items to be examined on computer or DVD. His students also gather print advertisements from catalogs, Web sites, and magazines; the students examine all of the information presented about each item.

The students create a descriptive profile of each item that includes the size of the item, its actions, longevity, movement, and appearance. The students determine the claims made by the advertisers. Mr. Patel encourages the students to be as specific as possible in their profiles. One student takes the claim "The doll is like a real baby" and breaks it down into specifics as to how the doll is like a real baby when she specifically says:

- The doll feels like a real baby.
- The doll cries like a real baby.
- The doll moves like a real baby.

Mr. Patel finds this particularly challenging for youngsters because many advertisements make vague promises, and statements such as "Zip is an awesome video game" and "Zap will become your favorite doll" require more critical evaluation. Students decide which advertising scripts are vague or unfounded and thus cannot go into the profile. Students also work to deconstruct such statements. Mr. Patel asks, "What makes an "awesome video game?" If there are certain characteristics that the students agree to make a video game awesome, those statements are listed in the profile. Through discussion, students also discover that what makes something "awesome" differs among students.

The students arrange the evaluation form in checklist fashion with names listed down the left side of the form. Across the top, the students list levels of performance or achievement from low to high. "Poor," "fair," and "excellent" work well as categories. Every year, Mr. Patel's students use different criteria lists specific to the item's advertising. The students' Truth in Advertising Evaluation Form developed for a miniature motorcycle racetrack consists of specific statements in the product's advertising, the packaging, and inferences the students drew from advertising graphics.

Motorcycle	Poor	Fair	Excellent
Catches big air			
Spins donuts			
Pops wheelies			
Travels 50 feet per charge			
Fast, 10-second charge			
Two motorcycles can run side by side			
Motorcycles have bright lights			
Motorcycles have flaming tailpipes			

The room parents help Mr. Patel gather the actual items for the students to evaluate. The room parents ask local retailers to donate the items and seek contributions from the manufacturer, the parent organization, the state economic council, or a school business partner to fund the purchase of the items. After Mr. Patel completes the unit, his students donate the items to a local charity.

Mr. Patel has the students evaluate each item against its profile checklist. The students look at the helicopter advertisement that says that the toy flies; they then observe the real toy and check to make sure the toy matches the advertisement. The students watch the television commercial for a robotic dog showing the dog perfectly performing a series of tricks. The students test the toy to see if it does the same series of stunts in the classroom. The students evaluate the toys by comparing them to their written statements in print or media advertising.

When the students finish evaluating all of the items, the teacher leads them in a discussion of what they found:

- How did the items perform?
- How truthful was the advertising?
- Do certain kinds of advertising tend to be more or less misleading?
- Are television advertisements more or less misleading than the packaging?
- Are there certain kinds of statements in advertising that students and parents should be more cautious of than others?

Mr. Patel links the evaluation and discussion of products with a reinforcing lesson on the types of propaganda, such as glittering generalities, on the bandwagon, common man, testimonial, or an endorsement by a celebrity. Using quotations from advertisement language and pictures from a toy motorcycle advertisement as an example, he creates the following discussion questions:

- Why is playing with this motorcycle track an experience "just like what real motorcycle racers have"? (transfer)

- How is this motorcycle track "technologically engineered" and "aerodynamic"? (glittering generality)
- How do you know that this motorcycle track is the "racetrack that 'serious' motorcyclists want"? (bandwagon)

ASSESSMENT

As a concluding activity, students prepare statements about their research. Students select an assessment product where they generate letters to the editor of the local newspaper, give presentations to other classes, or create displays for the stores that donated the items. Of course, the stores only want displays that help sell the items.

4 Points	3 Points	2 Points	1 Point
Do they make a judgment to purchase or not?	Do they make a judgment to purchase or not?	Do they make a judgment to purchase or not?	Do they make a judgment to purchase or not?
Do they justify their judgment by citing specific examples?	Do they justify their judgment by citing specific examples?	Do they justify their judgment by citing specific examples?	
Can they cite specific propaganda techniques used in marketing this product?	Can they cite specific propaganda techniques used in marketing this product?		
Do they identify another situation where this same propaganda technique was used?			

REFERENCES AND RESOURCES

Berson, M. J. (2004). Digital images: Capturing America's past with the technology of today. *Social Education, 68*(3), 214–219.

Hammer, R., & Kellner, D. (2001). Multimedia pedagogy and multicultural education for the new millennium. *Reading Online, 4*(10) http://www.readingonline.org/newliteracies/litindex.asp?HREF=/newliteracies/hammer/index.html

Mattioli, D. J., & Obenchain, K. M. (1996). *Instructional handbook for elementary social studies.* Boston: Houghton Mifflin Custom Publishing. This strategy is adapted from "Playing Is Believing," one of the lessons in the previously referenced text.

Murnane, J. R. (2007). Japan's Monroe Doctrine?: Re-framing the story of Pearl Harbor. *History Teacher, 40*(4), 503–520.

Tesar, J. E., & Doppen, F. H. (2006). Propaganda and collective behavior: Who is doing it, how does it affect us, and what can we do about it? *Social Studies, 97*(6), 257–261.

Wilkinson, G. (2006). Commercial breaks: An overview of corporate opportunities for commercializing education in U.S. and English Schools. *London Review of Education, 4*(3), 253–269.

Web Sites

Center for Media Literacy:
www.medialit.org

KQED Education:
http://www.kqed.org/education/digitalmedia/media-literacy.jsp

Media Literacy.Com:
http://www.medialiteracy.com/

The Media Literacy Clearing House:
http://www.frankwbaker.com/default1.htm

Propaganda:
http://www.propagandacritic.com

33

Mini-Society

GRADE LEVELS	NCSS CURRICULUM STRANDS
✔ 3–5	IV Individual Development and Identity
✔ 6–8	V Individuals, Groups, and Institutions
	VI Power, Authority, and Governance
	VII Production, Distribution, and Consumption
	X Civic Ideals and Practices

INTRODUCTION

In discussing the type of education democratic citizens should experience, John Dewey wrote: "A democracy is more than a form of government; it is primarily a mode of associated living, of conjoint communicated experience."(p.87). One way to bring the tenets of democracy into the classroom is to create a microcosm of our larger society in which students deliberate about the concerns adult citizens deal with on a daily basis. Everyone has rights and responsibilities that are discussed, agreed on, and clearly articulated. Students can determine necessary services to help the classroom run smoothly, apply for positions that provide those services, and then work to meet the needs of their community. They can establish private businesses to produce products needed in order to help their community flourish. In this mini-society (often called a token economy), students begin to see the interdependence inherent in every community and can examine how societies function.

    If monetary profit is a goal, students and teacher can create real classroom businesses, providing goods and services to classmates and the school at large. If the learning goal is to better understand how societies function, how individuals are interdependent, the role of power and authority, or the role of citizens, then a simulated society may better serve the purpose.

PROCEDURAL RECOMMENDATIONS

- To create a simulated society in the classroom, begin by brainstorming with students all of the different tasks that must be carried out to keep the classroom running smoothly. These can be as immediate and concrete as returning graded papers or watering classroom plants. They can also be more distant, such as providing water, lights, and ventilation in the classroom.

- Discuss the responsibilities of teacher and students. Prompt students to offer ideas about what each of them can contribute to the classroom society. Also discuss power and governance in their classroom society: To what degree will each member have a voice in the decisions of the classroom? How much more weight will the teacher's voice carry? Depending on the depth of these discussions, the teacher may wish to have students set some classroom rules (see Strategy 2).

- After students have brainstormed their list of tasks involved in keeping the classroom running smoothly, create jobs congruent with those tasks. This may take some creativity on the teacher's part. For example, students cannot provide or manage classroom utility services, nor can they pay the utility bills for the school. However, a student could calculate the classroom's prorated share of the utility bills as well as each class member's prorated share. Each month individual students could receive the utility bill that they are responsible for paying.

- Prepare necessary materials for the establishment and maintenance of a mini-society. This includes the monetary system ("KODs"—Kathy Obenchain dollars), job application forms, banking forms (deposit slips, withdrawal slips, ledgers), paychecks, student checks, payment forms, coupons, invoices, and so on.

- Arrange to have at least one job available for each student, and be sure to allow for choice among jobs. Then post a list of available jobs, each with an accompanying job description. You might also list a salary; beginning salaries should be equal. Have students review the list of jobs and decide which they are most interested in and which will best suit their particular talents or present a new area they would like to explore.

- Have students complete a form similar to a real job application. In addition to their name and age, students should list their education, special talents and skills, prior experience, and references. They should also list the jobs for which they are applying. Suggest that students list at least three options: in a class of 25, there is competition for some jobs.

- Sort through applications, check references, and interview prospective "employees." These processes need not take a great deal of time. A telephone call or visit to a reference (students usually list parents or other teachers) can be very brief, as can an interview with an elementary-aged child.

- After completing the interviews and job selection, arrange for training for the jobs that require specialized skills. Be advised that the set-up of a classroom society may take up to 1 hour each day for about 2 weeks. However, once the set-up is completed, student assistance in the classroom, as well as social studies and citizenship skills development, is ample compensation. Keep in mind that, in the mini-society, students do not neglect their roles as learners, nor do they focus only on performance of their own job. For example, the plant waterer's job is to care for classroom plants. That responsibility does not absolve the student from other common classroom responsibilities, nor does it absolve other students from being cautious when playing near the plants.

- Encourage students to apply for new jobs approximately once each grading period.

- If desired, arrange for students to earn a paycheck of simulated money. Schedule paydays once per week, and give raises to students who perform their classroom jobs well.

- As students earn paychecks, introduce basic concepts in economics. Teachers might develop lessons in scarcity, opportunity cost, supply and demand, banking, saving, and interest computation.

- If students are earning a salary, they will also incur expenses, such as desk and cubby rental and utilities. Of course, taxes will also be withheld.

- Develop a system in which students may spend their earnings during periodic auctions of goods and services. Items auctioned might include homework passes, a lunch date with the teacher, books the teacher purchased with extra book club points, or other items the students value. Students might also want to contribute auction items. Neither teacher nor students should purchase auction items.

- Keep in mind that, as described here, behavior management is not an explicit goal of a mini-society. Students who participate in setting rules and articulating rights and responsibilities have a better understanding of their behavioral responsibilities. However, a token economy that rewards students for appropriate behavior is very different from a mini-society, in which students earn rewards (classroom money) for performing a classroom job. We recommend that the two approaches not be combined because of their different goals.

APPLICATIONS AND IDEAS

Possible jobs for the classroom mini-society include the following:

1. *Paper passer*—distributes any papers or forms needed
2. *Greeter*—greets all classroom guests and escorts them to and from the main office
3. *Homework monitor*—gathers assignments and directions for any absent student
4. *Attendance taker*—prepares and delivers attendance forms requiring teacher signature
5. *Lunch monitor*—following school procedure, collects lunch information for the school cafeteria
6. *Safety monitor*—attends to potential safety concerns in the classroom (books in the pathways of others, unsafe play behavior, teetering objects, etc.)
7. *Recycler*—reminds classmates about recycling and collects materials; delivers recyclable materials to collection station
8. *Librarian*—keeps track of books, games, or other materials on loan to students
9. *Telephone attendant*—answers the classroom telephone
10. *Plant attendant*—cares for any plants in the room
11. *Zookeeper*—cares for classroom pets

If a classroom economy is also included in the mini-society, additional jobs include the following:

1. *Payroll clerk*—writes the student paychecks each week
2. *Bank teller*—handles students' financial transactions; students may choose either to cash their paycheck for classroom money or to deposit most of their paycheck in the bank
3. *Bank controller*—maintains an accurate record of each student's account balance
4. *Rent collector*—collects "rent" on desks and chairs from students earning a salary
5. *Utility clerk*—calculates the prorated share of each student's utility usage; bills each student on a periodic basis
6. *Tax collector*—calculates and deducts withholding taxes from each student's paycheck

If civics and government are also a function of the classroom mini-society, related jobs include the following:

1. *Mayor*—working with the teacher, assists with the management and coordination of classroom jobs
2. *Classroom council members*—are trained as peer mediators, resolve classroom conflicts

ASSESSMENT

Assessment aside from the costs and benefits of quality job performance is unnecessary.

REFERENCES AND RESOURCES

Dewey, J. (1944). *Democracy and education*. New York: Free Press. (Original work published 1916).

Indiana Department of Education. (1988). *The mini-economy: Integrating economics into the elementary curriculum*. Indianapolis: Author.

Indiana Department of Education. (1988). *Teaching economics in the mini-economy*. Indianapolis: Author.

Most mini-societies have an economics focus. The described strategy has a civics focus, but economics can be easily included. Both of the previously listed resources from the Indiana Department of Education connect the described mini-society to teaching basic economics. They also contain teacher directions and lessons with accompanying handouts and forms.

Kourilsky, M., & Ballard-Campbell, M. (1984). Mini-society: An individualized social studies program for children of low, middle, and high ability. *Social Studies, 75*(5), 224–228.

Laney, J. D. (1985). Hotdogaronia: Mini-society in a Texas classroom. *Southwestern Journal of Social Education, 15*(1), 15–18.

Web Sites

The National Council for Economic Education (**www.ncee.net**) includes information about token economies and mini-societies.

The following Web site provides information regarding a variety of mini-society programs:
http://www.clemson.edu/fyd/minisociety.htm

The following article from the University of Kentucky provides a classroom example of a mini-society and token economy:
http://www.ca.uky.edu/AGC/NEWS/2002/May/mini.htm

34

Mock Trials

GRADE LEVELS	NCSS CURRICULUM STRANDS
✔ 6–8	V Individuals, Groups, and Institutions
✔ 3–5	VI Power, Authority, and Governance

INTRODUCTION

Mock trials introduce students to the complexities of law and courtroom life in the United States. While students participating in mock trials learn the content of particular cases, the primary purpose is to understand courtroom processes and to improve higher-order thinking skills. These include listening and questioning skills and the analytical skills required of competent citizens. Mock trials also serve as engaging performance-based assessment.

In social studies classrooms, the preparation and participation in a mock trial that is focused on constitutional issues requires student understanding of the role of the judicial system, historical precedents, the rights of the accused, the jury system, and the rule of law. Understanding the rule of law in the U.S. constitutional system is a foundational principle in a civic education curriculum. In a typical mock trial, students assume the variety of roles represented in a typical court case: In essence, a mock trial is an elaborate and structured role-play activity. Whether mock trials are created by the teacher, purchased commercially, or are based on factual or fictitious circumstances, the basic participants and rules are the same.

PROCEDURAL RECOMMENDATIONS

- Gather necessary materials for the mock trial. These include procedural rules, fact statements, witness profiles and statements, evidence, a description of the case, and profiles of any victims. For example, witness profiles include any knowledge of the case, the relationship of the witness to any victims, and factual information regarding the reliability of the witnesses. Witness profiles do not have to be lengthy: A typed, half-page summary is usually sufficient. If possible, work with the local bar association. Many attorneys are familiar with mock trials, and some will be willing to work with students. Their insights and expertise are invaluable.

- Introduce and explain the mock trial process to students. If possible, attend an actual trial or view a video of one, noting for students the different roles and procedures. Provide a handout of the procedural rules and responsibilities for each participant.

- Introduce students to the particular case to be tried. Provide a general description of the incident and the exact nature of the case. What is the defendant accused of doing? What exactly are the charges? Students can try either civil or criminal cases. There are specific differences regarding the standard of proof—a preponderance of evidence is needed for civil cases and evidence beyond a reasonable doubt for criminal cases. Students must be clear on the type of case involved. In general, procedures are the same.

- Assign students to specific roles. Every student in the class should have a role. Suggested roles include judge, jury members, court artist, video operator, bailiff or clerk, timekeepers, attorneys for prosecution and defense, witnesses, defendant, and plaintiff. After assigning roles, have students more closely examine and prepare for their roles in the trial. Each witness must learn his or her character and what he or she knows about the crime. Attorneys must learn the role they are playing and its responsibilities, be familiar with the crime, and know the procedures for both opening and closing statements as well as for examining and cross-examining witnesses. After students have learned their roles, have the attorneys "prep" their witnesses. Because students do not read from a script during the trial, it is essential that they understand their roles and responsibilities. Practice is warranted.

- Mock trials follow a fairly standard procedure:
  1. Opening statements by prosecution, then defense (3 to 5 minutes each)
  2. Direct examination of prosecution witnesses (4 to 6 minutes per witness)
  3. Cross-examination of prosecution witnesses by defense (2 to 4 minutes per witness)
  4. Redirection of prosecution witnesses by prosecution, if necessary (1 to 2 minutes per witness)
  5. Direct examination of defense witnesses (4 to 6 minutes per witness)
  6. Cross-examination of defense witnesses by prosecution (2 to 4 minutes per witness)
  7. Redirection of defense witnesses by defense, if necessary (1 to 2 minutes per witness)
  8. Prosecution closing argument (3 to 5 minutes)
  9. Defense closing argument (3 to 5 minutes)
  10. Judge's instructions to the jury with dismissal for jury deliberation
  11. Return for a verdict

- If possible, have all students observe the uninterrupted deliberations of the jury. This allows all participants to see how the evidence was interpreted.

- After the activity, debrief with students regarding the mock trial process. What might each participant have done differently? What additional information (evidence or witnesses) would have been helpful? Trials are one way to resolve conflicts. What other ways could this conflict have been resolved?

APPLICATIONS AND IDEAS

Children like to tell and retell fairy tales; a good way to capitalize on this interest is to recast the fairy tale as a court case. Students learn courtroom proceedure, problem solving, and decision making while working with characters from their favorite stories and determining what was fair. Here are several examples of stories played out in court cases:

Story	Indicted	Charge
Cinderella	Cinderella	Curfew violation
Goldie Locks and the Three Bears	Goldie Locks	Breaking and entering
Hansel and Gretel	Hansel	Witchicide
Jack and the Bean Stalk	Jack	Theft
Little Red Riding Hood	Wolf	Murder
Rapunzel	Evil Queen	Criminal confinement
Snow White and the Seven Dwarfs	Evil Queen	Attempted murder

ASSESSMENT

At end of the mock trial, the students write a reflection about their experiences in which they address the following questions:

- What would you look for in selecting members of the jury?
  - Who would you try to exclude?
- What information would make a good opening or concluding statement?
  - What information would you try to leave out of the opening or concluding statement?
- Give an example of when to object.
  - Why is that important?
- Did you reach a verdict about the guilt or innocence of the person?
  - How did you reach that conclusion?
- Did the person under indictment receive a fair trial?
  - Why or Why not?

4 Points	3 Points	2 Points	1 Point
Define who they would include and exclude in jury selection.	Define who they would include and exclude in jury selection.	Define who they would include and exclude in jury selection.	Define who they would include and exclude in jury selection.
Determine the information to include and exclude in opening and concluding statements.	Determine the information to include and exclude in opening and concluding statements.	Determine the information to include and exclude in opening and concluding statements.	
Give an example of when to object and why it is important.	Give an example of when to object and why it is important.		
In the assessment rubric, the bottom left criteria should be in the present tense like the others, instead of past tense. It should read, "Reach a verdict and articulate how they reached that conclusion and determine if it were a fair trial."			

REFERENCES AND RESOURCES

Helgeson, L., Hoover, J. J., & Sheehan, J. (2002). Introducing preservice teachers to issues surrounding evolution and creationism via a mock trial. *Journal of Elementary Science Education, 14*(2), 11–24.

Joseph, P. R. (2000). Law and pop culture: Teaching and learning about law using images from popular culture. *Social Education, 64*(4), 206–11.

MacKay, C. (2000). The trial of Napoleon: A case study for using mock trials. *Teaching History: A Journal of Methods, 25*(2), 59–68.

Web Sites

American Bar Association:
http://www.abanet.org/

Bradley University:
http://www.bradley.edu/campusorg/trial

Center for Civic Education:
http://www.civiced.org

Constitutional Rights Foundation:
http://www.crfc.org/mocktrial.html

Est. of Hans Jensen v. The White Star Line:
http://www.andersonkill.com/titanic/home.htm

Nineteenth Judicial Circuit Court
http://www.19thcircuitcourt.state.il.us/bkshelf/resource/mt_conduct.htm

35

Model Factory

GRADE LEVELS	NCSS CURRICULUM STRANDS
✔ K-2	VII Production, Distribution and Consumption
✔ 3–5	VIII Science, Technology, and Society
✔ 6–8	IX Global Connections

INTRODUCTION

Students who think in concrete terms find it difficult to understand things that are remote in time, location, or concept. The question "Where does milk come from?" often elicits the response "The store." Citizens of any age rarely think about the complexity and interdependence of producers and consumers or the interdependence of workers in the levels of production. For young citizens to make informed decisions about the goods they consume, they must better understand means of production, working conditions, support industries, and environmental considerations. One way to assist students in developing these understandings is to simulate the production and/or distribution of goods in a model or simulated factory, using common classroom or household items.

Re-creating an assembly line process can encourage students to engage in thoughtful discussion about innovation, specialization, and cottage industries. Using two- or three-dimensional blocks, students might create an assembly line production process using raw materials to generate a particular product for distribution in order to better understand the interdependence of workers and materials. Students can "assemble" any product, as the blocks represent specific products with which students are familiar.

PROCEDURAL RECOMMENDATIONS

- Connect this strategy to an appropriate social studies lesson or unit. This might be Labor Day, career exploration, or an introduction to economics for primary-grade students. A unit on the Industrial Revolution or an introduction to economics is an appropriate context for intermediate- and middle-grade students. For older students, particularly those in middle/junior high school U.S. history, time spent in a model factory provides a concrete experience to help them understand the impact of Henry Ford, the assembly line, and the role of labor and the worker in society.

- In an introductory and separate lesson and/or field trip, introduce students to the concept of labor specialization by visiting a local factory or fast-food restaurant. Students might also visit a local craftsperson—someone who takes a good through the production process from raw materials to finished product.

- If possible, have students examine finished products in a retail setting. Direct them to examine how the product is displayed.

- Introduce students to the idea of setting up their own factory and producing an item. Students can brainstorm an item they would like to sell or select an item from their history curriculum that was popular during a particular era. Tell students that they will not create the actual item but rather a representation of the item with the blocks. For ideas on creating an actual item to sell, contact your local Junior Achievement representative.

- Gather a large number and variety of blocks to represent different stages of the assembly process. If you use three-dimensional blocks, collect enough sets of green, blue, yellow, and red blocks to represent raw materials. Distribute different colors of blocks at different stages of the assembly line process. For example, production of an automobile might begin with the large yellow block. Four small blue blocks are added as tires, and a red block is added to represent a steering wheel. Other products will use different combinations and assembly processes.

- If you prefer to create your own three-dimensional blocks, gather clean milk cartons, cereal and shoe boxes, copy paper boxes, and so forth. Paint, cover with paper, or label the boxes to represent different stages of the assembly line process. If you choose to use a two-dimensional strategy, prepare cutouts from heavy card stock or art foam of different sizes, colors, and shapes. If the blocks or shapes are to be connected, provide some sort of adhesive (e.g., tape, Velcro). If the blocks are to be manipulated (colored, labeled), provide any necessary materials.

- Have students watch as you create the item they decided on, arranging a specified number of blocks in a particular order. This will provide a model for them to follow.

- Train a specific number of students to make the entire item from start to finish. Begin with raw materials and end with packaging for distribution or retail display. Set up the students in this scenario with some or all of the needed materials in their own separate area. Time the students from start to finish (3 to 5 minutes). When students finish, set aside the completed products.

- Select a different group of students, and train each in one specific task in the creation of the product. Set up the students along an assembly line (line up classroom desks or tables), giving each student only the materials and/or tools needed for his or her specific task. Allow the same amount of time for product completion. Set aside the goods produced.

- At the conclusion, conduct a debriefing session in which students discuss and compare the processes.

APPLICATIONS AND IDEAS

It is essential that students debrief during the assembly line experience, but more importantly, they should debrief after the experience. If there is no structured and facilitated time to synthesize what they have learned, students are apt to view the experience as a fun activity, achieving little awareness or understanding of associated learning. Debriefing can occur in the whole group, in small groups, or individually. It may also be verbal, written, or illustrated. Several questions for discussion, written at various thinking levels, according to Bloom's Taxonomy (1956) follow.

Debriefing Questions

How many products did the first group create? (knowledge/comprehension)

Examine the completed products from the first group. How similar are they to each other? In what ways are they different? (analysis)

What accounts for the similarities and differences? (evaluation)

How many products were made by the second group? (knowledge/comprehension)

How similar are the products to each other? How are they different from each other? (analysis)

What could happen to the creation of products when one worker is pulled from the first production line? (synthesis)

What could happen to the creation of products when one worker is pulled from the second production line? (synthesis)

Does one set of products appear to be of higher quality? Who or what determines high quality? Can the definition of "high quality" differ across time and people? (evaluation)

Could any of the workers be replaced by a piece of machinery? (evaluation)

What would the machine have to do to replace the worker? What are the benefits of a human worker? A machine? What are the drawbacks of each? (evaluation)

How do students feel the same or different depending upon their work experience? How do those on the assembly line feel about their contribution to the final product? How do those who made the entire item feel?

What are the strongest assets of each group's product? (evaluation)

How might the products be marketed? (synthesis)

ASSESSMENT

As a follow-up and assessment to this activity, students might examine some common items like clothing, backpacks, and books. This assessment task checks student understanding of the concept (see Strategy 4) of assembly line by asking students to apply their understanding of the concept of assembly line to new examples. They can hypothesize whether the items examined were produced by an individual craftsperson or on an assembly line. Students can then find evidence to support their beliefs. Students can also mentally deconstruct a common item (like any of those previously listed). How many people do they believe were involved in its creation or construction? Would they all be working in one factory or on one assembly line? How "raw" are the raw materials in an assembly line? The raw beef patty is not the actual raw material. What is the source of the beef patty?

REFERENCES AND RESOURCES

Bloom, B. S. (1956). *Taxonomy of educational objectives, handbook I: The cognitive domain.* New York: David McKay.

Indiana Department of Education. (1995). *Play Dough Economics.* Indianapolis: Author.

Play Dough Economics is a comprehensive economics unit for elementary students. All lessons are taught using Play Dough, and one specific lesson examines specialization of labor and the assembly line. *Play Dough Economics* can be purchased through the National Council for Economic Education: www.ncee.net

Web Sites

The Henry Ford Museum at **http://www.hfmgv.org/** has information available for teachers related to Ford's contributions to the assembly line

Junior Achievement representatives assist teachers in structuring a business simulation for older students. Students participate in the business world as they envision, create, market, and sell a desired product to the public. Junior Achievement can be reached at **http://www.ja.org**

The websites below provide links to examples of classroom lesson plans on assembly lines in both an economic and historical context
http://www.bringinghistoryhome.org/third/unit-1
http://teachers.net/lessons/posts/312.html
http://www.emints.org/ethemes/resources/S00000484.shtml

36

Museum Exhibits

GRADE LEVELS	NCSS CURRICULUM STRANDS
✔ K–2	I Culture
✔ 3–5	II Time, Continuity, and Change
✔ 6–8	Others (Depending on Topic)

INTRODUCTION

Most of us, as well as our students, have visited history museums on school or family trips. Sometimes we even find them to be a refuge in a busy city. Sometimes they are a small and powerful discovery we stumble on. Whenever and wherever we visit museums, there are specific exhibits that deeply affect us. The U.S. Holocaust Memorial Museum in Washington, D.C., has numerous exhibits that take our breath away. The room with the display of shoes taken from prisoners at the camp in Majdanek can be overwhelming for the visitor. At the Emigrant Trail Museum and Pioneer Monument, located within Donner State Park in the Sierra Nevada, the video and audio story of the tragic experiences of the Donner party are enlightening. Also impressive is the Pioneer Monument, which features a statue of three pioneers looking westward. The statue is on a base that is 22 feet high, the depth of the snow the year the Donner party was stranded in the area.

These are not the kinds of exhibits that our students would construct. However, creating an exhibit that is accurate, informative, accessible, and engaging about an event, era, concept, or individual is something they can do. Creating a museum exhibit is an effective synthesizing and evaluative experience for students and is a novel product-based assessment task. Creating an exhibit requires students to take large chunks of knowledge or information and retell them in a form requiring print and visual sources. It is also evaluative, as students determine what is essential or what are the most representative parts of the topic. Museum exhibits are also meaningful assessment tasks because students are able to connect what they have done to what they see in the world outside of the classroom (Parker, 2009). While it may be an unfamiliar assessment format for students who are used to paper-and-pencil tests, it is a familiar format in the world.

PROCEDURAL RECOMMENDATIONS

* Determine which social studies units and learning objectives are complementary to a museum exhibit outcome measure. An exhibit could become a part of almost any social studies unit,

but it may not be an effective or appropriate way for students to demonstrate their understanding. For example, sixth-graders studying Ancient Greece would not have a difficult time obtaining artifacts. They could access photographs and write accompanying text, but that learning could be demonstrated in numerous ways. On the other hand, first-graders studying community helpers would have easier access to artifacts from firefighters, physicians, sanitation workers, and so on. An exhibit about sanitation workers could contain photographs, gear, maps of truck routes, text from interviews, and perhaps even some artifacts that were interesting discoveries made by the workers.

- Teach the unit as planned. Be sure to go beyond the textbook so that students see the connection between the topic and specific artifacts and primary sources. As appropriate, include primary source documents, guest speakers, photographs, audio recordings. Many of these sources may turn up in student projects. The museum project may be introduced at any time, but it is recommended that it not be introduced until about halfway through the unit. While it is important that students have time to think about the project, if they focus too early, they may just look for what they can use.

- Determine parameters of the project and exhibits. Reflect on the learning objectives and consider these questions:

  - As the teacher, what evidence do you need in order to know that students have learned the information? What do they need to show the teacher?

  - Are there any "progress points" during the project when you need to check or assess information?

  - Do you want any additional information beyond the exhibit? Paper? An oral presentation?

  - Is the size of the exhibits a consideration?

  - How much and what kinds of texts are required?

  - How many and what kinds of artifacts and primary sources are required?

  - How will students address issues of authenticity?

  - Who will be the audience for the exhibits?

- Determine how exhibits will be constructed and where they will be displayed. Exhibits may be attached to walls or bulletin boards. If the school has enclosed glass display cases, these might also be useful for the exhibits. Eliminate financial costs to students by utilizing classroom and school resources, such as computers to print text, covered cardboard to provide stable backing to text and photographs, and so on. The goal is for students to demonstrate their learning in an attractive, thoughtful, and engaging manner, not just to have the prettiest display.

- When the project is introduced, provide specific instruction on the purposes and structures of museum exhibits. If possible, arrange for a field trip to a museum or invite a curator or education specialist to explain the museum exhibits. Many universities have museum studies programs, and a faculty member or graduate student would be a good partner. These specialists assist students in learning some of the finer points of exhibit design, such as the use of item grouping, introductory text placement, the use of subheadings, item labeling, and object placement.

- Provide time and facilities for student work. If possible, have students with varying skills work in small cooperative teams. Begin with the task of writing a story that has a beginning, middle, and end. This becomes the basis for the exhibit. What is the story they want to tell the viewer, and why is it an important story? Addressing the importance of the story pushes students to higher-level thinking and should require both synthesis and evaluation. This story may become part of the introductory text, but it is most useful in guiding the students into thinking about what evidence and information will best tell the story.

- Based on the story, what are the items (photographs, newspaper articles, artifacts, audio recordings) that assist in the telling of the story?

- As students gather the items, they also work on using text to connect the items in their story. What should the introductory text explain? What brief information should be in the captions for each item? They also begin to think about the visual display. That is, what is the display order of the text item in the display? What should be first, and where should it be placed? Students are transitioning their story, with its beginning, middle, and end, from all text to a combination of visual and print media while retaining the story's chronology.

- Construct the exhibits, invite an audience for the opening of the exhibits, and have students at their exhibits answering audience questions. This step also serves as a celebration of the students' hard work and provides an opportunity to share their work and demonstrate what they have learned both through the exhibits and their conversations.

APPLICATIONS AND IDEAS

Museum exhibits may be used in a multitude of ways. The following examples, grouped by grades, address eras, events, concepts, and individuals.

	K–2	3–5	6–8
Eras	First Grade, Childhood	Colonial America, Westward Expansion	The 1920s, The Vietnam Era
Events	Moving Day, The First Day of School	Kwanzaa, Statehood	The Iraq War, Nationhood
Concepts	Family, Community	Migration, Interdependence	Conflict and Resolution, Innovation
Individuals	The President, Important People in the School	Civil Rights Leaders, The People Who Helped Build Our State	Noble Peace Prize Winners, People Who Made the World a Better Place

ASSESSMENT

A museum exhibit, typically the final product of this strategy, only displays a small portion of what a student has learned. A debriefing session or assessment period in which students process what and how they have learned is important. This may be done through an oral discussion (whole class or small group) or through a writing assignment, and many of the questions are reflective of questions students considered when designing their exhibits. Adjusting for topic and developmental level of the students, consider the following questions in such an assessment.

1. How well does the content of your exhibit tell your story?
2. What would you like to have included that you did not include? Why did you decide to not include it?
3. What is important about the arrangement of your exhibit?
4. What other ways could you have told your story?
5. How did you learn about your topic?
6. What new questions do you have?
7. What is the most important thing about your exhibit?
8. Who should see your exhibit and why? What do you want them to learn?

REFERENCES AND RESOURCES

Anderson, D., Lucas, K. B., Ginns, I. S., & Dierking, L. D. (2000). Development of knowledge about electricity and magnetism during a visit to a science museum and related post-visit activities. *Science Education, 84*(4), 658–679.

Cruz, B. C., & Murthy, S. (2006). Breathing life into history: Using role-playing to engage students. *Social Studies and the Young Learner, 19*(1), 4–8.

Diffily, D. (1996). The project approach: A museum exhibit created by kindergartners. *Young Children, 51*(2), 72–75.

Koetsch, P., D'Acquisto, L., Kurin, A., Juffer, S., & Goldberg, L. (2002). Schools into museums. *Educational Leadership, 60*(1), 74–78.

Martin, D. J. (2001). *Constructing early childhood science.* Albany, NY: Thomson Delmar Learning.

Mayfield, M. I. (2005). Children's museum: Purposes, practices and play? *Early Child Development & Care, 175*(2), 179–192.

Milligan, M. J., & Brayfield, A. (2004). Museums and childhood: Negotiating organizational lessons. *Childhood: A Global Journal of Child Research, 11*(3), 275–301.

Paris, S. G. (2002). *Perspectives on object-centered learning in museums.* Mahwah, NJ: Lawrence Erlbaum Associates.

Parker, W. C. (2009). *Social studies in elementary education* (13th ed.). Upper Saddle River, NJ: Pearson.

Rawlinson, K., Wood, S. N., Osterman, M., & Sullivan, C. C. (2007). Thinking critically about the social issues through visual material. *Journal of Museum Education, 32*(2), 155–174.

Web Sites

The following Web sites provide additional resources and background information to teachers who wish to create museum exhibits with their students and/or tour virtual museums.

The American Association of Museums has a Web site (http://www.edcom.org) that includes additional resource for museum educators. Several of the included resources may be applicable to teachers incorporating museums into the social studies classroom.

The website **http://www.indiana.edu/%7Earch/saa/matrix/mm.html** provides background information to a teacher on museum methods and should help him or her incorporate museums into the socials studies classroom in an accurate and authentic way.

This website **http://www.midgefrazel.net/fieldtrip.html** links to a clearing house of museum websites, lesson plans, and on-line museums.

37

Music History

INTRODUCTION

Music defines a period of time, an age, or an epoch. People often hear a song and remember what they were doing when they heard that song or who they were with when the song was playing. This immediate identification of popular taste with music of a particular decade allows students to build a mental musical time line that helps them identify a time with a particular style of music. Movie and television producers use musical clues all the time to help the audience immediately date the time and place where the story line is occurring. The music works as a chronological shorthand as dependable as showing fashion, cars, or the date centered on the screen.

In a similar manner, teachers can help students understand the context of the music that surrounds them. The teachers can guide the students to determine how the singer is looking at his or her life, what gives that person's life meaning, and what enduring problems the composer addresses in the song. The composer or lyricist often adds political overtones, expresses protest, or helps the students examine a slice of social history. When people write songs, they write from a point of view students can examine that provides a perspective from which to interpret meaning. Finally, composers pick up ideas from what happens around them in the music world, and those ideas also help to reference the music to a particular time.

Some musicians swear that they do not remember words unless they are connected to music; this leads some people to create songs to act as mnemonic devices. For many years teachers capitalized on this knowledge to help students learn facts by connecting those facts to music. In order to remember such things as the names of all of the states in alphabetical order, some people use the song *Fifty Nifty United States from Thirteen Original Colonies*. While it may not be the most sophisticated method of learning, many college students still recite the names of the 50 states in order because they learned this song in grade school. Other examples of linking content to music also exist. For instance, some people remember the preamble to the Constitution because of the Saturday morning cartoon *We the People* set to music in *SchoolHouse Rock*. While the lyrics and the tunes are catchy, students also remember the content knowledge equated with the songs. The information stays with the students in long-term memory. Students who remember information learned in this way do not see it as drudgery.

PROCEDURAL RECOMMENDATIONS

Build anticipation by playing samples of music from various periods for the students. Select five recordings so the students can hear the pieces more than once across multiple days. When selecting music, check the lyrics for appropriateness ahead of time and make sure the perspective and social issue are definable.

- Ask for student ideas about the types of music they like.
- Document roots of contemporary music by using a graphic organizer to show where their favorite music ties to the past and how it is connected to other types of music.
- Select three songs from each genre the students listed (e.g., rock, hip-hop) and provide student access. The students will know how to download them from the computer to their mp3 players. Select three songs from the 1970s at the same time.
- Ask the students to create a matrix that shows the names of the songs down one axis and the perspective and the social problem on the other axis.
- Ask students to compare how social problems have changed or stayed the same across time.
- If students bring in music to share but the teacher is not familiar with the tune, request that students wait 24 hours before sharing it. This gives the teacher time to review it to see if it is appropriate for sharing at school.
- Students build a PowerPoint musical history time line of the 20th century. The students identify an event for each decade, select a photograph that represents that event, and select a song that alludes to the event.

APPLICATIONS AND IDEAS

Mr. Fong has rock music playing as the students come into the classroom in the morning to unpack their book bags and hang up their coats. Mr. Fong asks his students to make a list of their musical preferences, which tend to cluster around rock, hip-hop, and country. Then on the chalkboard he draws a flow chart to show where their music had common roots. Using an mp3 player with a selection of songs downloaded from a computer, he plays clips of three examples to illustrate where the common roots branched away. He asks his students to download some selected current songs from the computer to their mp3 players. Mr. Fong asks the students to identify the point of view of both the composer and lyricist and tell what social problems emerge from the songs. Further, he asks his students to download some selected songs composed in the 1970s from the computer to their mp3 players. Once again, he asks the students to identify the point of view of both the composer and the lyricist as well as to tell what social issues emerge from the songs. He asks them to consider how current issues are addressed in songs written today and how those issues link to the historic study of songs. Mr. Fong asks his students if a song is a primary or a secondary source. Is a song a useful source for drawing historical conclusions? Why or why not?

ASSESSMENT

Listen to a piece of music.

4 Points	3 Points	2 Points	1 Point
Student identifies the social issue.	Student identifies the social issue.	Student identifies the social issue.	Student identifies the social issue.
How has this issue changed over time?	How has this issue changed over time?	How has this issue changed over time?	
How has this issue been expressed in other music?	How has this issue been expressed in other music?		
How has this issue been addressed through the political process in the past?			

REFERENCES AND RESOURCES

Bartel, V., & Hart, J. (2000). A preschool adventure: We're going to africa. *Social Studies, 91*(5), 235–38.

Maher, R. (2004). Workin' on the railroad: African American labor history. *Social Education, 68*(5), S4–9.

Otten, M., Stigler, J. W., Woodward, J. A., & Staley, L. (2004). Performing history: The effects of a dramatic art-based history program on student achievement and enjoyment. *Theory and Research in Social Education, 32*(2), 187–212.

Stiler, G., & Allen, L. (2006). Making connections with the past: (Un)masking African American history at a neighborhood community center. *Multicultural Education, 13*(4), 24–28.

Web Sites

"Fifty Nifty United States" lyrics: **http://www.sing365.com/music/lyric.nsf/Fifty-Nifty-United-States-lyrics-Ray-Charles/0AE98363D8B3BD3B48256C24000F4F7B**

Blues:
http://www.pbs.org/theblues/classroom.html

Digital History:
http://www.digitalhistory.uh.edu/audio/music.cfm

Federal Resources in Educational Excellence:
http://www.free.ed.gov/subjects.cfm?subject_id=156

Internet Modern History Sourcebook:
http://www.fordham.edu/halsall/mod/modmusic.html#Postwar%20Protest%20Songs

Rock and Roll Hall of Fame Museum:
http://www.rockhall.com/teacher/sti-lesson-plans/

School House Rock:
http://www.schoolhouserock.tv/America.html

38

Newspaper Making

GRADE LEVELS	NCSS CURRICULUM STRANDS
✔ 3–5	I Culture
✔ 6–8	II Time, Continuity, and Change
	V Individuals, Groups, and Institutions
	VI Power, Authority, and Governance
	VII Production, Distribution, and Consumption
	VIII Science, Technology, and Society

INTRODUCTION

Publishing classroom newspapers is an active, enjoyable, and creative instructional strategy. When skillfully facilitated by the teacher, student-made newspapers challenge students to interpret and demonstrate their social studies conceptual and content understandings in a nontraditional manner. Learning objectives and topics of study that focus on broad understandings of an event, a location, or an era are suited to student-made newspapers. Learning objectives that focus on broad understandings encourage the examination of the event or era from a variety of perspectives and in a variety of formats. Newspapers also provide an opportunity for students to focus on social and cultural history along with political and economic history when studying historical events and eras. Newspapers may explore multiple perspectives on a current issue or examine a current or historical event from the perspective of another country. For example, students might report on the American Revolutionary War from the perspective of the British or examine U.S. environmental policies from the perspective of Canada or Mexico.

PROCEDURAL RECOMMENDATIONS

- Be aware that student-made newspapers are usually culminating projects in a unit of study. As students progress through lessons and activities, assignments linked to the newspaper connect learning with the final product.

- Plan for students to work in cooperative groups, with each group responsible for generating an entire newspaper, or have them work as a large group to make one newspaper with small cooperative groups working on individual parts of the paper.

- Introduce students to the newspaper project early in the unit of study. If this is the first time students have created newspapers, this introduction should include an examination of a current newspaper. Have students analyze each section of the newspaper for content and focus: What kinds of stories are on the front page? What are the main topics on the editorial pages? Are these topics related to other stories in the newspaper? What is the difference between a news story and an editorial? Have students analyze the political cartoons. How do local, state, national, and international stories relate to each other? How big is the help wanted section? What are the types of companies advertising for help? How do employment opportunities relate to the industries or businesses in the community? What are people selling in the classified section? What does this tell us about life in the community?

- If time permits, bring in a guest speaker from the local newspaper. A conversation or question/answer session with a reporter or editor could help students see the role a local newspaper plays in a community such as informing, advising, selling, or entertaining.

- When students are familiar with the parts of a newspaper, begin the unit of study. Have students begin to gather information, note important events, read, and participate with the final project in mind. Assign groups at this stage or later in the unit. Early assignment provides focus; however, students may become focused too early in the unit if the teacher immediately assigns groups.

- Have students begin writing pieces for the paper at any point in the unit. If the unit topic is colonial life in British India and the current lesson covers the raw-material wealth and economics of British India, the students might work on a number of different types of articles. Agricultural reports could provide information on the different crops grown in the different areas of India. Help wanted advertisements might provide information about the jobs available and the types of workers sought. Business advertisements could provide a historical context to the types of products, inventions, appliances, farm implements, clothing, and services available to both British colonists and Indians. Have students divide these advertisements by geographic region or ethnic group to better understand climate and issues such as racism.

- Near the end of the unit of study, arrange for students to spend more class time putting their newspaper together. If they have access to desktop publishing software, they can create columns for their stories and use fonts similar to those used in documents of the era under study. If a scanner is available, have students scan student-created political cartoons and advertisements. Integration with language arts and/or technology objectives is appropriate at this stage.

- Encourage students to share the finished newspaper with other classes, the media center, the greater community, parents, and friends of the school.

APPLICATIONS AND IDEAS

Ms. Lee wishes to help her students understand the Trail of Tears, so she places them in groups of four. Each group takes on a different newspaper from that time, including newspapers reflecting: Abolitionist, British, French Canadian, Cherokee, Democrat, German, Shaker, Quaker, and Whig points of view. Each person writes one article about an interview or an eyewitness account concerning the main event from a global, national, or local perspective as well as one supplemental piece such as advertising, classifieds, or comics. This way, all of the students learn about the main events and also get to do the supporting tasks.

Finally, the students get to read the papers created by the other groups. The students analyze which newspaper was the most pro–Cherokee and which paper was the most pro–Jackson; in the process, they determine a continuum of papers. Students evaluate why the different newspapers had different perspectives and search for patterns for how religion or nationality impacted the perspective of the papers. Students examine how all of the papers represent the same time, but contain different opinions on the same events. Students discuss which newspaper does the best job setting the context of the time and how they can tell. Students discuss whether any of the newspapers showed both sides of the issues or multiple perspectives on the same issue. Ms. Lee asks the students if any of the newspapers looked at social history, which is the story of the common people, as opposed to major political or military figures.

ASSESSMENT

Creating a newspaper is a substantial project and is useful as a summative assessment task. Provided considerable time, research, and effort have been expended, the evaluation of a newspaper project is helpful for the students and the teacher. The checklist should be adapted to specific objectives and learning outcomes. It is also appropriate for the teacher to list his or her objectives in the assessment criteria. This provides valuable feedback for the teacher about whether students have demonstrated their mastery of unit content and related skills. The performance/product evaluation checklist shown here is intended for individual student evaluation; it must be adjusted if students are evaluated as part of a group.

Newspaper Evaluation Rubric

Criteria for Newspaper Articles	Content Accuracy	Historical Empathy	Controversial Issue	Multiple Perspectives
Weight	4	2	2	3
4 Points	The information in the articles and advertisement was historically and culturally accurate.	The student was able to describe an individual, time, and place in an authentic context in an article and advertisement.	Two points of view were clearly articulated within one article and expressed in two separate articles.	Four other voices represent minority positions, including such people as women, minorities, or religious dissenters.
3 Points	The information in an article and advertisement was historically and culturally accurate.	The student was able to describe two of the three: an individual, time, or place in an authentic context in an article and advertisement.	Two points of view were clearly articulated within one article or expressed in two separate articles.	Three other voices represent minority positions, including such people as women, minorities, or religious dissenters.
2 Points	The information in an article or advertisement was historically and culturally accurate.	The student was able to describe an individual, time, or place in an authentic context in an article and advertisement.	One point of view was clearly articulated within one article or expressed in two separate articles.	Two other voices represent minority positions, including such people as women, minorities, or religious dissenters.
1 Point	The information in the article or advertisement was historically or culturally accurate.	The student was able to describe an individual, time, or place in an authentic context in an article or advertisement.	One point of view was clearly articulated within one article.	One other voice represents a minority position such as women, minorities, or religious dissenters.

REFERENCES AND RESOURCES

Deveci, H. (2007). Teachers' views on teaching current events in social studies. *Educational Sciences: Theory and Practice, 7*(1), 446–451.

Henning, M. B., Snow-Gerono, J. L., Reed, D., & Warner, A. (2006). Listening to children think critically about Christopher Columbus. *Social Studies and the Young Learner, 19*(2), 19–22.

Passe, J. (2006). Sharing the "current events" in children's lives. *Social Studies and the Young Learner, 19*(1), 4–7.

Singer, A. J., Murphy, M. O., & Miletta, M. M. (2001). Asking the BIG questions: Teaching about the Great Irish Famine and world history. *Social Education, 65*(5), 286–91.

Wolk, S. (2003). Teaching for critical literacy in social studies. *Social Studies, 94*(3), 101–106.

Web Sites

Daytona Beach News-Journal:
http://www.nieworld.com/

Newspapers in Education:
www.nieonline.com

North West Arkansas:
http://www.nwanews.com/nie/

Omaha World-Herald:
http://nie.omaha.com/

Seattle Times:
http://services.nwsource.com/nie/times/

39

Oral Histories

GRADE LEVELS	NCSS CURRICULUM STRANDS
✔ 3–5	I Culture
✔ 6–8	II Time, Continuity, and Change
	IV Individual Development and Identity
	V Individuals, Groups, and Institutions

INTRODUCTION

The investigation of the social studies should connect students to their community, and the exploration of history should help students place themselves on a time line of events. As a teaching strategy, the oral history can facilitate both. Students can audiotape and collect oral histories from members of the community who share personal recollections of and reflections about specific events or time periods. Students can organize, write, edit, and rewrite the personal histories, thereby supplementing classroom texts. Students who use oral history chronicle and interpret events based on a variety of sources and perspectives. When students use oral history to examine an event or a time period from multiple perspectives, they recognize and value an important social studies goal.

Collecting oral histories takes a tremendous amount of preparation, training, research, and skill. Students will not be experts in the field of oral history, but opportunities for practice and research provide them with valuable experience.

PROCEDURAL RECOMMENDATIONS

- Refer to the objectives of the lesson or unit and explain to the students that collecting oral histories will enrich their understanding of a particular topic. Topics do not have to be limited to local history: Understanding the experiences and perspectives of local citizens during times of national or international crisis is important.
- Locate individuals who will provide oral histories. Begin by collecting oral histories from the students and the teacher as well as those from their family members and acquaintances. Always match experiences with the goals of the oral history project. Family members and acquaintances can connect you and your students to other individuals in the community.

159

- Other indirect sources include the local historical museum, county or city records, and newspaper archives. Ideally, a local historian trained in oral history collection can assist your students with training and question preparation. Compare these sources to the oral histories.

- Prepare students to conduct the oral history interviews. Achieve consensus on several general questions based on students' research of issues, events, and topics that they anticipate exploring through the oral history. Students document the responses of the informant by asking questions to which they already know answers to document the informant's perspective for their audience. Remind students that the purpose of the project is to learn how members of their community understand events of historical significance: How is the community member's perception of an event different from that in a history text?

- Emphasize to students that audiotaped or videotaped interviews provide more accurate records than do those in which the interviewer/student takes notes. A student who tries to accurately record the interview, think of follow-up questions, and actively listen to the interviewee will lose important details. In addition, taped interviews preserve the conversation, allowing others beyond the interviewee to hear the interview in its original form. Note that students will need to obtain written permission from the interviewee before taping any interview with him or her.

- Inform students about the process of taping, where the tapes and other equipment will be stored, who will have access to the tapes, and what form the final product will take.

- Arrange for students to practice interviewing before collecting the actual oral histories. They might interview in pairs with one student asking the questions and the other one jotting down notes and ensuring that the audio or video equipment is working properly. Students should demonstrate competency in both roles.

- Have students generate and practice delivering follow-up questions. Rarely does an interview strictly follow the general questions agreed on. It takes skill for students to recognize comments that they should follow up on while keeping the interview on track.

- Have students practice one interview as a class. Invite a guest into the classroom and have one or more students ask him or her questions. Have the rest of the students practice taking notes and managing the taping equipment. After the interview is complete, have students critique their experience. Were follow-up questions missed? Was everyone heard clearly on the tape? Do the questions need refinement?

- When the background research, question development, and interview practice are completed, students are ready to collect their oral histories. Invite speakers to come to class or send students into the community.

- When the interviews have been completed, have students transcribe their conversations. This step takes a great deal of time and provides an excellent opportunity to develop word-processing skills.

- Point out to students that oral histories may be organized in different ways. For example, each community member may have his or her own oral history presented in its entirety. A stay-at-home mother might remember the "Blizzard of '85," when all four of her children were at home for a week, and have her story recounted as a discrete piece of work. Another way to organize oral histories is by question or topic. For example, if students collect remembrances of the 1969 moon landing, they might record a number of interviewees' responses to one question: "How did this make you feel as a citizen of the United States?" The responses of individuals who were recent immigrants, children, members of the armed services, high school science teachers, and clergy in 1969 could be reported together.

- Whenever possible, work with a local historical agency. These agencies are often understaffed but provide a wealth of information. When the oral history projects are completed, these agencies can also serve as a site to house and display the projects. This allows the projects to be viewed by a larger number of people over a longer period of time.

- Have students send thank-you letters to all of the individuals who assisted in the project.

APPLICATIONS AND IDEAS

Three middle school history classes begin a unit on Vietnam. The teacher, Mr. Jones, is aware that students examine this topic again in their junior year of high school, and he is cognizant of his responsibility to connect world and U.S. history to the state and local community. He decides that his students will examine the war from the home front. This approach requires that his students research the war era and connect this distant and somewhat abstract event to the community, making it a more concrete experience for them. The approach also helps him meet his curricular responsibilities.

The first call Mr. Jones makes is to the local college, which houses an oral history department. He is able to connect with some college students willing to help with the project: They will identify prospective interviewees and train the middle school students.

Before the college students arrive, Mr. Jones and his students spend three class sessions preparing a chronology of the war and gathering information about the community during this era. The information collected includes data about area residents who served in the armed forces, a description of popular culture of the time, and an analysis of the local and national economy. Mr. Jones facilitates the research across all three of his classes, encouraging his students to share what they have discovered. With the general goal of understanding the effects of Vietnam on the local community, Mr. Jones and his students spend another two class sessions outlining some general questions, including "What was daily life like during the war? How was it similar to or different from life before or after the war?" and "Describe your favorite movies and TV programs. What made them special to you?"

With the general questions prepared, the college students begin regular visits to train the students and to help refine their questions and techniques. At the same time, Mr. Jones and all of the students begin their search for community members interested in participating. They get substantial assistance from family, other teachers in the district, the local Veterans of Foreign Wars chapter, and the local historical society.

With the refined questions, plenty of practice, and willing participants, the interviews begin. Mr. Jones and his class have decided to conduct the interviews in the school library over the course of a week. This allows them to set up and adjust the video equipment one time rather than transporting it to different sites around the community. Digital recording in one site also provides consistency from a lighting and background perspective. Viewers will focus on the oral content of the interview as opposed to any changing settings. This plan also provides a consistent format.

After students complete their interviews, they begin to transcribe, analyze, and edit the information. They decide that the best presentation format is to let each interviewee tell his or her story. This requires them to edit video as well as to create an accurate and interesting written narrative. Much time is spent on the project, and some students undertake additional research. Unfamiliar names, locations, and terminology are used in the interviews, and students must understand these in order to accurately present the stories.

This project takes a great deal of time and energy, and the families of many of the students become involved. With parental and school administration assistance, Mr. Jones's classes decide to present their project in an event open to the public with special invitations going to all of the interviewees. At the event, the entire crowd watches several selected video clips before each interviewee receives a copy of all of the collected and transcribed stories. The audience then moves in small groups through different stations. Small groups of students manage each station, presenting the information gathered through their research and interviews. The stations include video clips, photographs, and written narratives. The students donate the interviews and presentations to the local historical society so that the experiences of the citizens and the work of the students are available to the public.

ASSESSMENT

4 Points	3 Points	2 Points	1 Point
Student identifies where the narrative differs from the textbook.	Student identifies where the narrative differs from the textbook.	Student identifies where the narrative differs from the textbook.	Student captures an interview on tape and transcribes it into a narrative.
Student identifies where the narrative differs from the textbook.	Student identifies where the narrative differs from the textbook.	Student identifies where the narrative differs from the textbook.	
Student consults secondary sources.	Student consults secondary sources.		
Student consults other primary sources.			

REFERENCES AND RESOURCES

Errante, A. (2000). But sometimes you're not part of the story: Oral histories and ways of remembering and telling. *Educational Researcher, 29*(2), 16–27.

Lacourt, J., St. Clari, D., Kokotailo, P. K., Wilson, D., & Chewning, B. (2005). "Know your roots": Development and evaluation of an oral history curriculum for Native American middle-school students. *American Indian Culture and Research Journal, 29*(4), 59–74.

Langhorst, E. (2008). Golden oldies: Using digital recording to capture history. *School Library Journal, 54*(3), 50–53.

Lanman, B. A., & Wendin, L. M. (2005). *Preparing the next generation of oral historians: An anthology of oral history.* Education Blue Ridge Summit, PA: Rowman & Littlefield Publishers, Inc.

Ritchie, A. D. (2003). *Doing oral history: A practical guide.* Oxford, England: Oxford University Press.

Whitman, G. (2004). *Dialogue with the past: Engaging students and meeting standards through oral history.* Lanham, MD: Alta Mira Press.

Web Sites

The following websites all provide examples of oral histories. These are useful examples for students new to the process.

The History Channel:
http://www.historychannel.com/classroom/classroom.html

Library of Congress:
http://lcweb2.loc.gov/ammem/wpaintro

National Archives:
http://www.archives.gov

Oral History Association:
http://www.oralhistory.org/

The Whole World Was Watching:
http://www.stg.brown.edu/projects/1968

40

Pen Pals

GRADE LEVELS	NCSS CURRICULUM STRANDS
✔ 3–5	I Culture
✔ 6–8	II Time, Continuity, and Change
	III People, Places, and Environments
	VI Power, Authority, and Governance
	V Individuals, Groups, and Institutions
	IX Global Connections

INTRODUCTION

Social studies pen pals offer an opportunity for students to connect with others on a more personal level while adding to their store of knowledge about places and people. For many years, individual students and entire classes have written to and exchanged information with pen pals of similar ages and interests around the nation and the world. They compare cultural norms, leisure activities, community life, and the physical environment.

PROCEDURAL RECOMMENDATIONS

- Establish connections with teachers in other communities who are also interested in social studies pen pals. If students are studying a certain part of the country or the world or a certain type of community, contact a school or school district in that area. Membership in professional organizations, attendance at state and national conferences, and participation in electronic list-servs may provide an avenue for initial contacts.
- Establish parameters for the project. These include how often students will communicate, who will begin, how long the exchange will last, curriculum and learning goals, topics to cover, and other parameters specific to each project. This includes addressing topics or language to avoid. For example, using foul language or exchanging personally identifiable information (e.g., phone numbers) is not allowed.

- Identify instructional goals and objectives for the activity, and determine the topics you want students to explore. Potential goals and topics include learning how geography affects industry, economics, and leisure; examining population demographics to learn about predominant ethnic groups, religions, celebrations, and patterns of migration; and examining issues related to racism and ethnocentrism. History goals and objectives might relate to how a community changes politically, physically, socially, and culturally over time. It is important that both senders and recipients learn through the letter exchange. Senders learn about their community as they prepare responses. Senders also conduct an initial exploration of the recipient community in order to determine appropriate questions. Recipients learn from the information received. Teachers may also integrate curriculum goals for the language arts in the pen pal exchanges.

- In order to protect the privacy of students, have correspondence sent to and from a school address—whether using traditional or electronic mail—and use only first names of students. Teachers should also review all correspondence sent between pen pals. This is an extremely important component of all communication exchange projects. Nothing should be sent or read by students that has not been reviewed by the teacher. In addition to very real concerns about privacy and safety of students, it also provides an opportunity to ensure that correspondence is consistent with the learning goals.

- Introduce students to the goals of the pen pal project. To generate excitement, have each class prepare an introductory package to send to the other class, explaining who they are and where they live. Enclosing small artifacts or souvenirs representative of the class and its interests is appropriate and can generate interest for future communication. One might wish to include an introductory videotape or DVD that gives a tour of the classroom and community—a lively and personal way for the two classes to connect. Be sure to review traditional letter-writing format and etiquette with the students before they begin correspondence.

- Deal with ongoing communication as a class project. Decide with students what information should be included in the letters as well as what information will assist their learning. Brainstorming a list of topics, questions, and ideas assists those students having difficulty generating ideas for the content of their letters. It also allows you to ensure that you are addressing the necessary curriculum and the agreed-upon topics.

- Establish a tracking system to note the dates letters are sent, to whom they are sent, and the dates answers are received. This assists the teacher in finding a new pen pal to replace someone who is nonresponsive—at either end of the exchange. This system may be included on the student checklist, but a teacher-monitored checklist is also recommended.

APPLICATIONS AND IDEAS

There are specific benefits and drawbacks to making the decision to use snail mail or e-mail.

	Benefits	Drawbacks
Snail Mail	Easier to monitor, easier to reinforce language arts objectives, packages and letters are cultural artifacts (e.g., stamps)	Takes more time to send and receive exchanges, more costly
E-mail	Quick, inexpensive, exchanging photos and movies is easier; easier to construct/edit group communication; possible exchanges with multiple schools at once, with information shared to everyone; possibility of chats and bulletin boards	Potentially more difficult to monitor; students may want to use "text talk"

TABLE 40.1 PENPAL LETTER PERFORMANCE CHECKLIST

CRITERIA	SELF-CHECK	TEACHER-CHECK
Social studies content of the letter was accurate and reflected relevant social studies curriculum.		
All elements of a personal letter were included in the appropriate places. These include the return address, the date, the salutation, the body, the closing, and the signature.		
The body of the letter answered all questions asked by the pen pal in the previous letter.		
The body of the letter introduced and addressed the new social studies class topic.		
The letter asked questions that the recipient can answer and relate to the social studies themes and topics under study.		
Spelling and grammar are correct.		
Date the letter was sent		
Date a response was received		
Comments or notes by student or teacher		

ASSESSMENT

To encourage students to become more responsible for the completeness and accuracy of their work, use self-assessing performance checklists for each letter written. Choose criteria that are aligned with the curriculum and learning objectives. When appropriate, arrange the items in the order they appear in the letter. The social studies content will differ from class to class, so the checklist should be modified as needed. The language arts skills may be more consistent, as noted above. A sample is provided in Table 40.1.

REFERENCES AND RESOURCES

Barksdale, M. A., Watson, C., & Park, E. S. (2007). Pen pal letter exchanges: Taking first steps toward developing cultural understandings. *Reading Teacher, 61*(1), 58–68.

Kiernan, H. W., & Mosther-Ashley, P. M. (2002). Strategies to expand a pen pal program from simple letters to a full intergenerational experience. *Educational Gerontology, 28*(4), 337–345.

Lemkuhl, M. (2002). Pen-pal letters: The cross-curricular experience. *Reading Teacher, 55*(8), 720–722.

Levine, J. (2002). Writing letters to support literacy. *Reading Teacher, 56*(3), 232–234.

Liu, P. (2002). Developing an e-pal partnership: A school-based international activity. *Childhood Education, 79*(2), 81–88.

Stanford, P., & Siders, J. A. (2001). E-pal writing! *Teaching Exceptional Children, 34*(2), 21–24.

Teale, W. H., & Gambrell, L. B . (2007). Raising urban students' literacy achievement by engaging in authentic, challenging work. *Reading Teacher, 60*(8), 728–739.

Web Sites

There are a large number of Web sites offering to arrange pen pals, both e-mail and snail mail, for students. Most are legitimate; some are not. Be very cautious when choosing Web sites and when arranging communication for students. The sites below are well known and are used by a large number of teachers. Epals.com (**http://www.epals.com**) is a Web site devoted to facilitating electronic pen pals for classroom projects.

Contact the National Council for the Social Studies through their Web site for links to social studies teachers and an electronic discussion board:
http://www.socialstudies.org

The Peace Corps has a special page for teachers that includes a link for writing to a Peace Corps volunteer:
http://www.peacecorps.gov/wws/

41

Readers' Theater

GRADE LEVELS	NCSS CURRICULUM STRANDS
✔ 3–5	I Culture
✔ 6–8	II Time Continuity, and Change
	IV Individual Development and Identity
	V Individuals, Groups, and Institutions
	VI Power, Authority, and Governance

INTRODUCTION

Readers' theater is defined as "minimal theater in support of literature and reading" (Shepard, 1996). It is often described as theater without memorization, elaborate costuming, or props. Readers' theater transforms the reading of a literary work from a solitary and silent experience to a collective and verbal one. A staple in many language arts classrooms, readers' theater is used less frequently or less deliberately in social studies classrooms. The integration of this language arts medium with the social studies curriculum is natural. The goal for effective integration is to create a meaningful learning experience that values and teaches in both curricular areas. Similar to traditional theater, readers' theater performances include well-prepared and -rehearsed scripts. Teaching the process and mechanics of good script writing is assigned to the language arts curriculum, but the content integration is appropriate in the social studies classroom.

An expressive voice and facial expressions create the readers' theater character rather than elaborate props or costumes. Although the parts are well rehearsed, they are not memorized. In social studies classrooms, readers' theater should focus on a central social studies theme or concept such as change, patriotism, power, or interdependence. Scripts must be historically and culturally accurate; they may be created by the students or the teacher, or they may be purchased commercially.

The procedures that follow relate to a teacher-created script.

PROCEDURAL RECOMMENDATIONS

- Choose a social studies concept or important event to incorporate into the readers' theater format. Consider the conceptual understanding appropriate to the developmental levels of your students.

167

- Examine age-appropriate picture books, historical fiction, journals, biographies, and autobiographies for passages that clearly illustrate the concept or event under study.
- Choose a portion of the selected passage that has dialogue between two or more characters.
- List all of the characters featured in the passage you have selected. These will be the parts students read. Also include the role of narrator to provide the "framework for dramatic action" (Shepard, 1996). The narrator reads everything except the actual dialogue. If there is a great deal of additional text, arrange for multiple narrators; multiple narrators' roles can be divided by character, so that each narrator reads the supporting narrative of a specific character. They can also be divided by type of narration: One narrator reads the supporting character narrative; another reads the transitional or background narrative, such as doors opening, leaves rustling, and so forth.
- Prepare the script. Usually, a narrator begins with the scene setup, followed by character dialogue. The portion of the text chosen should be included in its entirety.
- Be aware that not every student will have a part. Be conscious of the attention span of your audience. For primary-grade students, prepare a narrative of approximately 5 minutes. For intermediate- and middle-grade students, prepare approximately 10 minutes of script.
- Create debriefing questions to further examine the concept or theme under discussion. These higher-order questions should examine how characters and their dialogue reflect the concept under study. Also ask about non-examples of the concept. These questions might ask students to compare characters to one another or to describe how they respond to a situation in the scene. The debriefing questions should include only recall-level questions if they provide a foundation for higher-order thinking.
- Although not every student will have a part in any one script, prepare all students. Have students practice reading parts, experimenting with a variety of facial and vocal expressions; discuss with students the impact of these expressions on the audience. Encourage students to study characters to determine what the appropriate emotions are for each. Discuss how students can convey those emotions to the audience without elaborate props or bodily movement.
- Choose readers for the presentation. Arrange for rehearsals to help students feel comfortable with expressive dialogue and with performing in front of an audience.
- For the performers, set up a semicircle or row of chairs in the front of the room. Students can remain seated as they read, or they might stand in order to be seen and heard more clearly.
- After thanking participants at the conclusion of the performance, begin the debriefing with teacher-prepared questions. This may be done verbally with the entire class or in small groups. This provides another opportunity for students to access the content, reinforcing the objectives of the lesson. Part of the debriefing may also be done in writing, although this method does not allow the teacher to use student-generated questions as a springboard for additional discussion.
- As students become more familiar with the readers' theater format, student-created scripts challenge them in another way: They become responsible for generating a concept or theme as well as making decisions with regard to script development.

APPLICATIONS AND IDEAS

Children's picture books are a great resource for teacher- and student-created scripts. They can be relatively short and they simplify very complex concepts for students. Characters are typically limited and language is straightforward. Consider some of the following topics and texts.

Holocaust: Bunting, E., & Gammell, S. (1989). *Terrible Things: An Allegory of the Holocaust* (Paperback). Philadelphia: Jewish Publication Society of America.
Homelessness: Bunting, E., & Himler, R. (1996). *Fly Away Home.* New York: Clarion.
Civil Rights: Rappaport, D. (2001). *Martin's Big Words.* New York: Hyperion.
Human Rights: Rocha, R., & Roth, O. (1990). *Universal Declaration of Human Rights: An Adaptation for Children.* New York: United Nations Publications.

Famous speeches and texts may also be turned into readers' theatre scripts. Rather than students memorizing words, they can focus on the meaning and making an impact with voice and expression. They can also consider multiple voices, even when the speech or text was written by one individual. When carefully chosen, they have tremendous impact. Consider some of the following when addressing citizenship and civic education topics:

- Preamble to the *Declaration of Independence,*
- Preamble to the *United States Constitution,*
- Excerpts from: King's *I Have a Dream speech, Lincoln's Gettysburg Address,*
- *Pledge of Allegiance,* and
- *Oath of Allegiance.*

ASSESSMENT

Readers' theater is based in large part on the performance of or reading by students. Table 41.1 features a simple performance checklist that can be adapted to different texts. A separate checklist or other assessment instrument should be created to evaluate students' understanding of the social studies concept(s) under study. Table 41.2 features a performance checklist that works with guided discussion. Writing prompts, illustrations, and traditional assessments also work.

TABLE 41.1 PERFORMANCE CHECKLIST FOR READERS' THEATER PARTICIPATION		
KEY ELEMENTS	**POSSIBLE POINTS**	**POINTS EARNED**
Appropriate volume	5	
Appropriate inflection	5	
Followed along and spoke at appropriate places	5	

TABLE 41.2 PERFORMANCE CHECKLIST FOR READERS' THEATER CONCEPTUAL UNDERSTANDING		
KEY ELEMENTS	**POSSIBLE POINTS**	**POINTS EARNED**
Identified the social studies concept(s) in the script	5	
Defined the social studies concept(s)	5	
Described additional examples of the concept(s)	5	
Distinguished between examples and non-examples of the concept(s)	5	

REFERENCES AND RESOURCES

Black, A., & Stave, A. M. (2007). *A comprehensive guide to readers theatre: Enhancing fluency and comprehension in middle school and beyond*. Newark, DE: International Reading Association.

Coger, L. I., & White, M. R. (1967). *Readers' theatre handbook: A dramatic approach to literature*. Glenview, IL: Scott Foresman.

Dixon, N., Davies, A., & Politano, C. (1996). *Learning with readers' theatre (Building connections series)*. Winnipeg, Manitoba, Canada: Peguis.

Fennessey, S. M. (2000). *History in the spotlight: Creative drama and theatre practices for the social studies classroom*. Westport, CT: Heinemann.

Flynn, R. M. (2007). *Dramatizing the content with curriculum-based readers theatre, grades 6-12*. Newark, DE: International Reading Association.

Laughlin, M. K., Black, P. T., & Loberg, M. K. (1991). *Social studies readers theatre*. Santa Barbara, CA: Greenwood Publishing Group.

Lord, B. B. (1986). *In the year of the boar and Jackie Robinson*. New York: Harper Trophy.

McKay, R. (1997). Essential ways of knowing: Drama and the visual arts in social studies. *Canadian Social Studies, 31*(3), 116.

Morris, R. B. (1973). *Seven who shaped our destiny: The founding fathers as revolutionaries*. New York: Harper Torchbooks.

Naylor, D. T., & DeWitt, S. W. (1999). Using trials to enrich social studies curriculum. *Update on Law-Related Education, 23*(1), 32–34.

Shepard, A. (1997). *Readers on stage: Tips for readers' theater*. (ERIC Document Reproduction Service No. ED413623).

Shepard, A. (1996). *What is RT? And how do you really spell it?* Retrieved July 17, 2002, from http://www.aaronshep.com/rt/whatis.html

Shepard, A. (1993). *Stories on stage: Scripts for reader's theater*. New York: H. W. Wilson.

Sierra, J. (1996). *Multicultural folktales for the felt board and readers' theater*. Phoenix, AZ: Oryx Press.

Young, T. A., & Vardell, S. (1993). Weaving readers' theatre and nonfiction into the curriculum. *Reading Teacher, 46*(5), 396–406.

Web Site

http://www.literacyconnections.com/ReadersTheater.php is a website that is literacy (as opposed to social studies) centered. However, it provides information about using readers' theater in the classroom.

42

Role Playing

GRADE LEVELS	NCSS CURRICULUM STRANDS
✔ K–2	IV Individual Development and Identity
✔ 3–5	VII Production, Distribution, and Consumption
✔ 6–8	VIII Science, Technology, and Society

INTRODUCTION

Students become involved with the actions, words, and ideas of others when they take on roles in the classroom. This strategy provides students with a concrete and whole-body opportunity to analyze and interpret different views and perspectives about events or issues. Students must predict what will happen in a given situation based on how they feel as the persons whose identities they have assumed. By portraying different characters with competing views, students analyze how and why views differ. Students must also create connections from the past to current events and world situations. While younger students might take on roles exploring the exchange of goods and services, older students might role-play more complex roles such as Jewish citizens of Germany being stripped of their civil rights in the 1930s.

PROCEDURAL RECOMMENDATIONS

- First, identify the concept for the lesson—for example, supply and demand. The large numbers of available laborers kept the wages low at the mills in Lowell, Massachusetts. The arrival of immigrants lowered the prices of labor, while management also kept wages low.

- Next, create a measurable learning objective. An example of a well-stated objective is the following: The student will be able to explain to his or her peers why the price of labor stayed low at the mills in Lowell.

- Research accounts that illustrate people working toward a resolution or description of the concept under study. For the mills scenario, choose stories that illustrate individuals who are working for social justice.

- Plan the role-playing vignette, including how you will use the space in the classroom and how students will move about in that space. Identify the characters needed and provide any helpful props. Props assist in identifying the character; they may be handmade signs, books, cultural symbols, or other artifacts. For the Lowell scenario, signs expressing the ideals of the main characters are appropriate.
- Brainstorm ideas about what students need to say and the questions the teacher will ask to help students predict what happens next. In role-playing, there is little, if any, scripted dialogue. Rather, the teacher and students are familiar enough with the concept that teacher facilitation through questioning guides the role-play.
- Consider ways to help the students create verbal and physical mnemonics to go with their parts.
- Contemplate times to cue the students when connecting the action to events in the present.
- Ask students to evaluate the motivations of the characters, the conditions of society, and the results of the actions of the characters.

APPLICATIONS AND IDEAS

An upper-elementary class role-played the Industrial Revolution in Lowell, Massachusetts. Students created signs that were worn by the students in their roles; each sign bore the name of the character on the front. The mill owner and entrepreneur signs had "New ideas, money, and knowledge" written on the back. The worker signs had the word "Strike" written on the back. Immigrants were provided with signs as well.

To begin the role-play, one student assigned parts, a second passed out signs for the characters, and a third chose three mill owners and entrepreneurs and their workers. The teacher guided the mill owners to an open space in the room and helped them move apart. The students used mnemonics: They pointed to their heads when the mill owners had new ideas, rubbed their fingers together when they discussed money, and moved into the thinker position when they talked about knowledge. When the owners hired workers, the workers moved their bodies toward the factories and owners. The workers made hammering motions when they built the mills and digging motions when they dug the canals for the waterpower. The teacher helped the students graduate their heights in a line past the three separate mills to show the falling water. Students acted as if they were pulling levers when they built the mill machinery.

There were three workers for each mill. The bobbin winder rotated one finger around another finger on the other hand. The weaver threw the shuttle from hand to hand. The spinner moved his or her left hand in a circle and pulled it toward his or her body with the right hand. The teacher asked the owners, "Are you content?" Then the teacher followed with the prompt "Why?" Next, the teacher asked the workers if they were content—why or why not? At least one of the workers wanted more money; he or she rubbed his or her fingers together. The teacher asked the students to tell why they wanted more money. Two mill owners said, "No way!" as they folded their arms. The teacher inquired as to why they said that. The other mill owner said, "Yes." What will the workers do?

Workers walked to the other mill. The teacher asked them why they were going to work for the other mill. The mill owners got together and talked. The teacher asked the students to speculate— "What do they say?"—and to predict—"What do they decide?" The teacher also had students make the connection to the present: "What is this like today?"

This time, when the mill workers rubbed their fingers together and said they wanted more money, the mill owners all folded their arms and said, "No way!" The mill workers raised clenched fists and went on strike by marching in a circle around the mills chanting, "Higher wages!" The mill owners asked the immigrants to come in and take the jobs. The teacher asked the immigrants if they were content and why. Next, the teacher asked the owners if they were content and why. Addressing the old workers, the teacher asked if they were content and why. The teacher asked all the students to make the connection to pertinent present events. The teacher asked all the students, "What are the strikers going to do now? Why do you think they will do that?"

Now the mill owners demanded that their employees work longer days. What did the workers think? What did the workers do? The teacher ended the lesson by asking the students to make the connection to a similar situation in today's international economy.

ASSESSMENT

To debrief from the role-play, the students group in quartets to create panel discussions consisting of a mill worker, a member of the town government, a town member not hired by the mill, and a mill owner.

4 Points	3 Points	2 Points	1 Point
Each student must explain what his or her character wants by presenting both a problem and a potential solution.	Each student must explain what his or her character wants by presenting both a problem and a potential solution.	Each student must explain what his or her character wants by presenting both a problem and a potential solution.	Each student must explain what his or her character wants by presenting both a problem and a potential solution.
Each student must explain how his or her solution would help himself or herself and another person in the quartet.	Each student must explain how his or her solution would help himself or herself and another person in the quartet.	Each student must explain how his or her solution would help himself or herself and another person in the quartet.	
Each student must evaluate whom his or her solution would hurt and whom it would help in the quartet.	Each student must evaluate whom his or her solution would hurt and whom it would help in the quartet.		
Each student must evaluate whether his or her solution could work today. Why or why not?			

REFERENCES AND RESOURCES

MacArthur, C. A., Ferretti, R. P., & Okolo, C. M. (2002). On defending controversial viewpoints: Debates of sixth graders about the desirability of early 20th-century American immigration. *Learning Disabilities: Research & Practice, 17*(3), 160–172.

Monahan, W. G. (2002). Acting out Nazi Germany: A role-play simulation for the history classroom. *Teaching History: A Journal of Methods, 27*(2), 74–85.

Morris, R. V. (2004). The nation's capital and a first grade classroom: Role-playing a trip to Washington, DC. *Social Studies, 94*(6), 265–269.

Morris, R. V. (2002). Presidents' Day in second grade with first-person presentations. *Gifted Child Today, 25*(4), 26–29, 64.

Patterson, J. (2002). Slavery revisited: Using economic reasoning to teach about the past and present. *Social Studies, 93*(1), 40–43.

Web Sites

BBC News:
http://news.bbc.co.uk/1/hi/education/4223842.stm

Interact:
http://www.teachinteract.com/

National History Education Clearinghouse:
http://teachinghistory.org/best-practices/examples-teaching/14947

The Simulating History Project:
http://www.simulatinghistory.com/

Sand Table Map

GRADE LEVELS	NCSS CURRICULUM STRANDS
✔ K–2	III People, Places, and Environments
✔ 3–5	VII Production, Distribution, and Consumption
✔ 6–8	VIII Science, Technology, and Society

INTRODUCTION

Students use an interaction among play, map making, and model building to create new understandings about geographic issues. Young students naturally play in the sand at home, park, or school. By using a sand table map of their world, students can explore a variety of historical and current issues (Perry, 2001). Wise educators harness this natural interest to design experiences that help the students to learn social studies content and skills. Tactile experiences should not be reserved exclusively for the young. Adult learners in university military officer training programs also use sand tables to demonstrate landscape, military positions, and transportation routes.

PROCEDURAL RECOMMENDATIONS

- Supplies are easy to locate for this activity. A yellow-orange-brown colored sand with a high feldspar content has larger grains and is preferable to white silica sand. Usually both are available at hardware stores with building supplies. Add a few drops of water to settle the dust. Inexpensive kitty litter can also be substituted if large-grained sand is difficult to procure.
- Each child can have a plastic dishpan on his or her desk as a mini-sandbox. This desktop sandbox gives students an opportunity to replicate geography after the teacher models it.
- A commercially manufactured sand table is ideal for this activity, but the teacher, janitor, parents, or shop class can make one inexpensively. Place a heavy plastic drop cloth or gardening plastic on the floor under a large rectangular table. Cut 2′ × 4′ boards to the size of the perimeter of the table; fasten the corners with screws and elbow brackets, creating a frame. Use C-clamps to attach the 2′ × 4′ frame to the top of the table. This forms a box and the 2 × 4s become the sides. Cover all of this with an additional layer of strong plastic to keep the box watertight. Secure the plastic with the C-clamps. To avoid poking holes in the plastic,

make sure to push the plastic all the way down, even in the corners. Fill the sand table only half full in order to keep the sand on the table. The teacher might also use an inflatable or plastic wading pool as a sand table.

- Once the sand table is assembled, turn to the content. Enlist the help of parents by having them show students evidence of utilities around their homes.
- Have the students place objects representing their homes and school on the sand.
- Add a model of the compass rose.
- Have the students examine the utilities that operate the school by searching for boilers, steamlines, meters, and access panels. The school custodian can offer assistance in this phase of the activity.
- Have students construct water treatment plants and reservoirs for drinking water as well as storm sewers and sanitary sewers. Direct students to determine the placement of wells and underground water sources in rural areas.
- A natural gas plant, an electrical power plant, electrical relay stations, and a telephone company should also be placed on the map.
- Have students construct electrical, natural gas, and water lines plus storm sewers and sanitary sewer lines as well as telephone, Internet, and television cables. Direct them to lay or bury colored yarn representing each of these. In laying the multiple lines that may overlap, students learn the importance of calling before digging.
- Throughout the activity, have students respond to questions such as the following: Who is responsible for providing this service? How are they paid? How do we make sure they do a good job? What happens if they do a poor job? Why does one company usually do this for a community? How many companies should do these things?

APPLICATIONS AND IDEAS

Younger students might determine how to cut roads that serve the most people with the least disruption of the land. Older students might explain how rivers and land forms found in their community affected the way their town developed and how people in the town changed these land forms. Using critical analysis skills, students can use the maps to develop a multifaceted rationale to justify the use of land for parks at the local, state, and national levels. Students can determine the differences in the missions of recreation areas, reservoirs, forests, parks, and monuments and further justify land usage by looking at the differing roles of state and federal properties. To improve the quality of life in urban areas, students might consider the use of green space when planning neighborhoods, esplanades, green corridors, landscaping, and parks.

Students can look at how people interact with the environment. In southern California, which is semi-arid land, people build homes on hills with thin layers of topsoil and slate. Students can re-create this geographic pattern in the sandbox using a matchbox for the house; when they add water representing heavy rains, the results help them understand how precarious some real estate remains. It helps to explain why insurance companies do not wish to insure these houses. Students can then evaluate who has the responsibility for paying to clean up natural disasters.

The Grand Kankakee Marsh once stretched from South Bend, Indiana, to Chicago, Illinois. In the late 19th and early 20th centuries, the swamp was drained and a canal constructed to contain it, which allowed land to be developed for housing and agriculture. Students re-create this in their sandbox and demonstrate how winter rains find the basements of houses when the water table rises to nearly that of the level of the former swamp. Students can evaluate the advantages and disadvantages of creating the canal. Students can also create areas that integrate farms, suburban communities, and restored swamplands.

Students can illustrate the differences among rural, suburban, and urban neighborhoods using the sandbox. In rural neighborhoods, there are no crowds or traffic problems, but people are not close to services. In suburban neighborhoods services are close, but traffic is heavy and people must drive everywhere. In urban areas people are close together, there are fewer places for cars, and people walk or take mass transit. In each of these neighborhoods, students must evaluate the advantages and disadvantages of their locations.

Students can determine how sprawl works by simulating it in their sandboxes. First, the land is covered with trees; then people come to cut down the trees, haul them away, and cut them into wood products. Next, farmers plant the land in crops and build houses in which to live. One year after the harvest, the land is developed to include a school; in the next year after the harvest, the land is developed to include a grocery store. A gas station follows quickly after that. A post office and bank are raised, and after yet another harvest, the farmland is developed into apartment buildings. From working with this model in their sandbox, students see how land is developed through the process of suburban sprawl. They evaluate the development pattern to determine the advantages and disadvantages of this process to the community.

Some parts of the world have been occupied by many different cultures. The modern country of Turkey shows evidence of many cultures including the Persian Empire, Hellenistic Era, Roman Empire, Byzantine Empire, and Ottoman Empire. Students can use their sandboxes to show structures being added and the towns growing with each of these occupations. In addition to the physical changes to the location, each new empire brought new ideas and religions to the people. Students need to consider whether each empire would wipe out all of the culture of the previous empire or allow some of the past to survive. Students also determine what they might see from the past when they travel to Turkey.

ASSESSMENT

A primary-grade class used a sand table map to display their model homes and school along with a steel mill. The map featured strip mines and deep mines from which the mill obtained iron ore, limestone, and coal. Students also created a water reservoir and cooling towers so the mill would not discharge hot water into the local water source. In doing so, they condemned several homes. Some of the students became angry when the power company tried to remove their houses. The company settled out of court. They gave candy to the homeowners to compensate them for their property. The reservoir faced additional problems caused by farmers who did not practice contour plowing: The runoff from their fields filled up the reservoir, necessitating that the power company perform expensive dredging operations. When students closed the coal mine, it left an unusable mess for community members, but when the iron mine closed, the company converted it into a sanitary landfill. Students drove trucks through their sand community to collect trash from the homes and school for the landfill. They brainstormed ideas about what else they could do with a former mine, such as converting it into a recreation area.

Problem Solving Checklist:

_____ Need a place to live—build a house

_____ Need a place (to go) to learn—build a school

_____ Need a place to work—build a steel mill

_____ Need raw materials for the steel mill—dig mines

_____ Need more room for the power company—pay for the property

_____ Need to process the water used to cool the machinery in making the steel—make a water reservoir and cooling tower

_____ Erosion filling up reservoir—conduct dredging

_____ Iron mine closed—turn it into a sanitary landfill

_____ Making trash at houses and school—take it to the landfill

_____ Problem with a former coal mine—convert it into a recreation area

REFERENCES AND RESOURCES

Elkind, D. (2006). The values of outdoor play. *Exchange: The Early Childhood Leaders' Magazine Since 1978, 171*, 6–8.

Kern, P., & Wakeford, L. (2007). Supporting outdoor play for young children: The zone model of playground supervision. *Young Children, 62*(5), 12–18.

Maynard, T., & Waters, J. (2007). Learning in the outdoor environment: A missed opportunity? *Early Years: An International Journal of Research and Development, 27*(3), 255–265.

Moyles, J. (Ed.). (2005). *The excellence of play.* (2nd ed.). Columbus, OH: Open University Press.

Perry, J. P. (2001). *Outdoor play.* New York: Teachers College Press.

Walsh, P. (2008). Planning for play in a playground. *Exchange: The Early Childhood Leaders' Magazine Since 1978,* (183), 88–92.

Web Sites

Fire and Cop Shop:
http://www.fireandcopshop.com/Products-Sand_Table_Apparatus.html

NexTag:
http://www.nextag.com/sand-and-water-table/search-html

Stream Table:

Wildland Fire Leadership Development Program:
http://www.fireleadership.gov/toolbox/documents/sand_table_showroom.html

Service-Learning

GRADE LEVELS	NCSS CURRICULUM STRANDS
✔ 3–5	VI Power, Authority, and Governance
✔ 6–8	X Civic Ideals and Practices

INTRODUCTION

Service-learning is an approach to teaching and learning that combines needed service to the community with the academic curriculum. More than any one or even a set of strategies, service-learning is an approach, a way to think about teaching and learning. When done well, service-learning meaningfully involves students in all phases of the process, including identifying, researching, and taking action on a community need. Service-learning projects are challenging and rewarding experiences for students and teachers and should be approached by knowledgeable teachers. Because of the teacher-facilitated, student-centered nature of service-learning, many teachers and students will find the approach unfamiliar. Teacher preparation is essential.

There are two main approaches to service-learning. The first approach is to begin with a community need. The links to the academic curriculum are created and facilitated by an effective teacher who weaves the curriculum in where appropriate. The second approach is to begin with the curriculum and encourage the exploration and identification of a community need that also meets the curriculum requirements. The community need approach is described in this strategy.

PROCEDURAL RECOMMENDATIONS

Prior to any classroom discussions, you should learn as much as possible about implementing service-learning in the classroom. There are several references at the end of this strategy. These, as well as others, will provide you with a solid base.

- On the day the project begins in the classroom, start by defining the community of interest. Is it the classroom, school, city, or global community? Different service-learning experiences can attend to different communities, and it may be easier for younger students to define more concrete communities such as the classroom or neighborhood.

- Ask students to identify some community needs. This can be a brainstorming session, or students can decide to interview others in the defined community to ascertain what they believe are needs or issues that should be addressed. If an interview is appropriate, prepare a short interview format. Both *A Kid's Guide to Social Action* (Lewis, 1991) and *Project Citizen* (Center for Civic Education, 2006) have useful templates that include the names of the interviewer and interviewee, questions asked, and responses. Students can also watch the local news and read the newspaper to determine community needs. They may also wish to invite guest speakers who could provide details about a particular need.

- Through a teacher-facilitated conversation, synthesize all of the information students have gathered. In the school community, it is possible that overflowing trash bins and wasteful use of paper are related. List all of the issues identified. Look for relationships among the issues identified and adjust the list, if necessary. Determine the issue that seems to be most pressing.

- More fully research the most critical need. This may involve conducting interviews, library or Internet research, surveys, or attending policy meetings. Be certain that you identify those who have the need and agencies that are already addressing the need. These individuals and agencies must be involved to more fully understand the issues related to the need as well as desirable solutions to meeting the need. At this juncture, the teacher should also be thinking about curriculum connections.

- Facilitate dialogue in which students as service providers determine specific solutions to addressing the community need (with service-recipient representatives, if possible). Ask questions like the following: What is the need? Why does this need exist? Are there policy, resource, or communication issues that impact this need? Who would be served by addressing this need? Have we consulted them? What are potential ways of meeting this need?

- Work with students to determine what the class can do to address this need. It is important that students tackle "doable" projects. That does not mean simplifying a need; rather, it means understanding the talents, skills, and classroom realities that students and teachers must keep in mind. Most community needs are addressed through multiple small steps. For example, animal shelter space issues can be addressed by raising funds to add more space, educating the community on pet overpopulation, and holding "adopt-a-pet day." The class members must determine what they can realistically do to address the community need.

- Break down the steps required to implement the solution. These include securing any necessary permission forms, arranging for guest speakers and field trips, soliciting materials and resources, and so forth. Create a flow chart of responsibilities and a time line. These responsibilities are shared between you and the students to support student voice and involvement.

- Determine with the class what knowledge and skills are needed by students in order to complete the project. This is a perfect opportunity for you to connect the service project to the social studies curriculum. Service-learning is also a good strategy for integrating across other curriculum areas such as writing and math.

- Arrange for students to carry out the project and implement their solution to the problem.

- Conduct structured reflection at every stage of the process. Teacher-created and -facilitated structured reflections ensure that students are thinking about the process in which they are engaged. These reflections attend to both the academic and the affective curricula. Reflections can include written, verbal, or artistic expressions, including small- and large-group discussion.

- As a final step, celebrate the achievement of the students with a pizza party, certificates of merit, media coverage, a field trip, or a guest speaker. Celebrations can be simple and inexpensive.

- A caveat: Some service-learning projects do not come to fruition. Students may meet with community or school resistance or may not be able to get needed permissions or materials. This is not a cause to give up but rather an opportunity to creatively work through the problem. If necessary, return to the initial list of community needs and choose a different need to address through a service-learning project.

Applications and Ideas

During a brainstorming session on community needs, two seventh-grade students asked their teacher, Ms. Polowski, why their community had so many homeless residents. This lead to broader conversation about the needs of the community, the needs of the agencies that work with the homeless, and the needs of the homeless. This topic also came up in a related manner through the results of community surveys in which many people expressed safety concerns about walking at night in the downtown area. It seemed that some local residents feared the homeless population, believing they were responsible for recent criminal activity.

With effective facilitation by Ms. Polowski, the class members decided that they should do something to help the homeless and could hopefully find a way to educate the community about this issue. The class interviewed the directors of two local homeless shelters, some homeless citizens, and the assistant police chief to see if they believed a project was needed. All agreed. After additional discussion, it was decided that students could best help the homeless by direct service. Both shelters needed volunteers to make and serve meals. The need for community education could be best met through the creation of a video that could be shown on the local cable access channel and distributed by local agencies to interested parties. The video would explain homelessness from historical, economic, political, and personal perspectives.

The students then enumerated the skills and resources they possessed. They had computer skills, reading and writing skills, and oral history skills. Their resources included a large number of students and a centrally located school, which made travel to and from the shelters quick and easy. Before proceeding, a committee of students met with the principal and Ms. Polowski to ascertain what permission they needed to leave school property and borrow school video and audio equipment. There was some reluctance on the part of the principal, but she finally agreed to the project, provided all of the students obtained parental permission and there was one adult volunteer for every seven students. She also requested written lesson plans from Ms. Polowski detailing how this project met the district's academic curriculum guidelines.

With Ms. Polowski's facilitation, the students then determined what they needed to learn before proceeding with the project. They decided they did not have enough knowledge about local, state, and national political and economic policies on homelessness. Students also wanted to confront their own stereotypes about homelessness before creating interview questions—and that required an examination of other stories about homeless citizens and homelessness in general. One stereotype that students shed during this process was the belief that one day a person has a home and literally the next day he or she is homeless. Through research, students learned that, in most cases, becoming homeless is a process that happens over time. All of this inquiry provided the social studies curriculum connection Ms. Polowski needed.

The class decided that there were two main tasks to focus on for this project: the direct service to the homeless population and the community education project. The students divided into two groups to begin work on the two projects. Each group assessed its skills and talents, identified additional needs (resources, knowledge, etc.), set up a time line, and allocated work to be done. Students were responsible for making contacts, setting up work schedules, conducting interviews, getting any necessary permissions, and doing the work. Ms. Polowski's responsibility was not to direct the projects but rather to make curricular connections, supervise projects, and facilitate the structured reflections. In this case, the reflections were carried out during whole-class discussion and individual journaling. The reflection questions targeted both affective and cognitive learning. Questions such as "How does it make you feel?" and "What were you thinking when . . . ?" addressed affective learning. Tasks that addressed the academic curriculum include: "Compare the size and profile of the homeless population currently to the homeless population of 20 years ago"; "Evaluate the effectiveness of current government policies dealing with homelessness"; "Explain how government funds are distributed to address homeless issues"; and "Reflect on the social and economic reasons persons become homeless."

The projects followed different time lines but consumed the entire school year. (Other social studies curriculum requirements were met as well.) The community education project began with preparing presentations and producing the video. The rest of the school year involved community education presentations. The direct service at the shelters continued on a routine schedule for the entire school year. A celebration in recognition of the students' work occurred at the end of the school year. Ms. Polowski contacted the local newspaper and arranged for a human interest story featuring the service projects. In their final reflections, students discussed what they learned and what they believed they contributed. Some students continued to volunteer their time. Others saw a termination of the project but, because of the effective facilitation by Ms. Polowski, they understood that the needs of their local homeless population continue.

ASSESSMENT

A service-learning project contains many smaller projects and opportunities for multiple traditional and nontraditional assessment tasks. Each service-learning project is so different that there is no single assessment task or set of tasks that are appropriate. Rather, a teacher should consider the academic learning objectives and the multiple tasks that provide evidence of that learning.

REFERENCES AND RESOURCES

Abernathy, T. V., & Obenchain, K. M. (2001). Student ownership of service-learning projects: Including ourselves in our community. *Intervention in School & Clinic, 37*(2), 67–76.

Center for Civic Education. (2006). *Project citizen: Citizenship portfolio process.* Calabasas, CA: Author.

Constitutional Rights Foundation. *Service-learning in the social studies.* Chicago: Authors.

Constitutional Rights Foundation & Close Up Foundation. (1995). *Active citizenship today: Field guide.* Los Angeles: Authors.

Hart, S. (2006). Breaking literacy boundaries through critical service-learning: Education for the silenced and marginalized. *Mentoring & Tutoring: Partnership in Learning, 14*(1), 17–32.

Howard, R. W. (2006). Bending towards justice: Service-learning and social capital as means to the tipping point. *Mentoring & Tutoring: Partnership in Learning, 14*(1), 5–15.

Lewis, B. (1991). *A kid's guide to social action.* Minneapolis, MN: Free Spirit.

Soslau, E. G., & Yost, D. S. (2007). Urban service-learning: An authentic teaching strategy to deliver a standards-driven curriculum. *Journal of Experiential Education, 30*(1), 36–53.

Wade, R. C. (2007). Service-learning for social justice in the elementary classroom: Can we get there from here?" *Equity & Excellence in Education, 40*(2), 156–165.

National Council for the Social Studies.(2001). Service-learning: An essential component of citizenship education. *Social Education, 65*(4), 240–241.

Web Sites

The Constitutional Rights Foundation provides, free of charge, a newsletter titled *Service-Learning NETWORK.* You can contact the foundation and subscribe to the newsletter via the Web site: **http://crf-usa.org**

Additional service-learning Web sites include the following:

National Youth Leadership Council: **http://nylc.org**

National Service-Learning Clearinghouse: **http://servicelearning.org**

45

Story Board

GRADE LEVELS	NCSS CURRICULUM STRANDS
✔ K-2	II Time, Continuity, and Change
✔ 3–5	III People, Places, and Environments

INTRODUCTION

A story board allows students to map the progress of a story in much the same way a cartoon illustrates multiple events in multiple frames. The purpose of the story board is to help students sequence events, clarify the roles people played, and determine how the land changed across time. Story boards are different from time lines in that they visually sequence the major events in a story with illustrations and captions. Students can use story boards to examine causes and effects, to explore chronology, to compare past and present, to study geography or local history, and to develop a multicultural perspective (Bage, 2000). Younger students can work in small groups to recount the events of a story with simple artwork.

For example, a story board about the California Gold Rush of 1849 could include drawings of the discovery at Sutter's Mill, the news spreading, people leaving for the gold fields, boom towns, fortunes being made overnight, vice, legacies, and maps of routes to the gold fields. Students could write a caption for each picture, mount and display their work, and explain their story board to the class. Individual students might also independently explore the story board to find out how the story unfolds. Older students can create story boards by interspersing their illustrations with reproductions of information from primary sources (see also Strategy 16).

PROCEDURAL RECOMMENDATIONS

- Determine whether students will work independently, with partners, or in small groups. If students work in groups, assign appropriate cooperative roles.
- Have students select a specific story or event related to the topic under study. Work with them in determining the appropriate sequence of events in the story.

- Provide a variety of media. Have students create a picture for each event in the sequence. Mount these pictures on poster board in chronological order.
- Have students interpret each picture with an attached caption. The caption should move the story along, present information, and explain the events in the picture.
- Provide time for students to present their story boards to the class, read their captions, and explain their illustrations. Allow students to review the story boards in their free time.

APPLICATIONS AND IDEAS

A teacher read a story about child labor to her primary-grade students. The students then made simple drawings depicting the beginning, middle, and end of the story. The students also generated captions to go with their pictures. They presented their story boards to their classmates. Later they compiled these retellings into one large book that the librarian catalogued as part of the school library collection.

After reading about the Lewis and Clark expedition, upper-elementary students created story boards depicting contemporary world and national events, the Louisiana Purchase, the Corps of Discovery, the land along the way, and the Native Americans. They used a photocopy machine and computer graphics to cut and paste images into collages, each featuring at least two ethnic groups. These collages showed what the students learned about the Lewis and Clark expedition. Captions included student interpretations and primary source text from Thomas Jefferson and the diaries of Lewis and Clark. Students next looked at the Lewis and Clark expedition from the perspective of the Indians whom Lewis and Clark met along the way.

Another upper-elementary teacher used video clips from *The Patriot* to inspire interest in the exploits of Francis Marion. Students read about the Swamp Fox and the war for independence in the South before making a story board about him. They used pastels to illustrate two story boards: one retold the movie and the other one recounted the actual events of the Revolutionary War in the South. Their captions compared the tactics used in the American Revolution to those used by guerilla soldiers in the Vietnam War. Students evaluated why these tactics succeeded against the United States.

ASSESSMENT

An elementary class used video clips from *Gladiator* to compare modern arenas to the arenas of ancient Rome. Students generated two parallel story boards: one illustrated events from the movie and the other illustrated what actually occurred in these arenas. Students used colored chalk to make their drawings and typed their captions on the computer.

4 Points	3 Points	2 Points	1 Point
Students compare the movie depiction with historical events. Students compare a modern arena to ancient Rome in their visual and caption.	Students compare the movie depiction with historical events. Students compare a modern arena to ancient Rome in their visual and caption.	Students compare the movie depiction with historical events. Students compare a modern arena to ancient Rome in their visual and caption.	Students compare the movie depiction with historical events. Students compare a modern arena to ancient Rome in their visual and caption.
In their captions, students compare amusements in ancient Rome to entertainment of the 21st century in the United States.	In their captions, students compare amusements in ancient Rome to entertainment of the 21st century in the United States.	In their captions, students compare amusements in ancient Rome to entertainment of the 21st century in the United States.	
Students evaluate what the American people's passion for "big-money sports" says about the American people.	Students evaluate what the American people's passion for "big-money sports" says about the American people.		
Students evaluate whether the interest in 21st-century stadiums is merely a distraction Americans use to avoid facing social problems.			

REFERENCES AND RESOURCES

Bage, G. (2000). *Thinking history 4–14: Teaching, learning, curricula and communities.* New York: Routledge/Falmer.

Web Sites

Amnesty International:
http://www.amnestyusa.org/education/index.html

Peace Corps:
http://www.peacecorps.gov/wws

Teaching Tolerance/Southern Poverty Law Center:
http://www.tolerance.org/teach/index.jsp

United Nations Global Teaching and Learning Project:
http://www.cyberschoolbus.un.org

World Wise Schools (Peace Corps):
http://www.peacecorps.gov/wws/educators/index.html

46

Time Lines

GRADE LEVELS	NCSS CURRICULUM STRAND
✔ K–2	II Time, Continuity, and Change
✔ 3–5	
✔ 6–8	

INTRODUCTION

An essential understanding in the social studies, particularly history, is chronology (National Center for History in the Schools, 1996; National Council for the Social Studies, 1994). In order for students to understand issues of continuity, change, and cause and effect, they must know what events occurred and the order in which those events occurred. Historically, culturally, and politically significant events can be examined through revolutions, progress, and cause and effect. For example, the Renaissance was partly a reaction to the Middle Ages. Its effects changed the art world forever. The Industrial Revolution began with a handful of inventions that mechanized the production of certain products. Its effects on industry and transportation changed access to products and places. Time lines can contain different types of information and span different lengths of time (Hoge & Crump, 1988). Students can create time lines with dates, pictures, and events. Primary-grade students might begin with a single day of their own life in order to grasp the concept of the passage of time.

Because they can grasp more abstract concepts, intermediate- and middle-grade students might examine events that are more distant. A time line might even be acted out: Students can be assigned the "role" of an event and asked to place themselves in chronological order along a line of tape on the floor. Classes might also tier or stack time lines examining different parts of the world simultaneously. Alternatively, they might examine different aspects of society during a particular era by stacking time lines that represent economic cycles, political movements, social issues, technological advances, and so forth. A caution with time lines is to remember that they are a tool to assist with learning; they are a type of graphic organizer. They help students synthesize and evaluate their learning. Time lines are not the total of student learning about a topic.

PROCEDURAL RECOMMENDATIONS

- Select a lesson or unit for which chronology is an essential element. Be sure to instruct students—especially younger ones—in the concept of chronology. For a link to literacy, the term *sequence* may also be used.
- With students, determine the breadth and depth of the time line to be constructed. This encourages students to remain focused as they continuously evaluate the relevance of information gathered.
- Determine what time increments will be marked on the time line (e.g., every 10 years; 100 years; 1,000 years) and evenly space them on the chalkboard, whiteboard, or paper being used. This is important for students just beginning to understand the concept of the passage of time. For example, if you are using 10-year increments, be sure the space between 1940 and 1950 is the same length as that between 1920 and 1930. These marks serve as a framework for the rest of the time line.
- Structure questions related to the lesson or unit objectives that encourage students to think critically in choosing items for the time line or in evaluating items on an existing time line.
- If students create the time line, encourage the use of mixed media. Incorporating words, pictures, photographs, and so forth adds depth to the display.

APPLICATIONS AND IDEAS

Introducing chronology to young children may be difficult because their understanding of time and the passage of time is different from adult understanding. Kindergarten students are introduced to time lines by making a time line of one school day. This is done late in the day so that students may recall and reflect on the day.

Each student is given one sheet of paper with the words "This Morning" written across the top. Students are directed to write or draw what they had for breakfast on the paper. This is set aside and students are given a sheet of paper with the words "Morning Recess" across the top. Students are directed to write or draw what they did during recess. This is set aside and students are given a sheet of paper with the words "Today at Lunch" across the top. Students are directed to write or draw what they ate for lunch and who sat at their lunch table. If time permits, additional papers with "Afternoon Recess," "Afternoon Snack Time," or other easily identifiable blocks of time may be included.

Once each student has completed all of the papers, talk about sequencing events in the order in which they occurred. Ask students if they had breakfast or went to morning recess first. Direct students to place the paper that shows what they did first to the left (connect this to how they read and write a word, beginning at the left). Ask them to place the paper that shows what they did next to the right of the first one. Repeat this for as many papers as the students have completed. Ask students questions that connect chronology to cause and effect. For example, did what they had for breakfast affect or influence what they had for lunch? Did the game they played during morning recess affect or influence what they decided to do for afternoon recess? Not every scenario will reflect cause and effect, but hopefully enough will so that students begin to see the connections among events.

As students become more familiar with the idea of chronology, have them create a time line of their life—using words and pictures. Older students may place significant local, national, and international events on their personal time lines, particularly if they recall reactions to these events or the effects of these events on their lives. Examples might include moving to a new community because of a devastating hurricane or being very scared for their family when they watched a television broadcast of the September 11, 2001, terrorist attacks. In later years, students will connect how the experiences under British rule influenced the wording of the Declaration of Independence and the Bill of Rights.

During school construction, workers poured and scored a sidewalk into 35 evenly spaced blocks, marking the path from the transportation zone to the school's front door. Using sidewalk chalk, fifth-grade students converted this walkway into a walk-on time line depicting events leading up to the American Revolutionary War. In class, students studied the American colonial and revolutionary eras. The teacher facilitated a discussion on what students perceived to have been the critical or most important events leading to the outbreak of the war. Students then placed these events in chronological order, noting that in some cases, multiple events occurred in the same year. In those instances, students tried to determine beginning dates (month and/or day) and any relationships among the events.

The sidewalk blocks were divided among the students (one block one year). Students began the design process by creating black-and-white rough sketches. These rough drafts featured a picture, date, and text—a caption of approximately five to seven words that interpreted the block. This was particularly challenging in those years in which many important things happened. The teacher worked with the students to synthesize these multiple events into a single caption. Students transferred the design on their drafts to pieces of poster board approximately the size of each cement block. They then refined and colored their designs.

Outside, students arranged themselves along the sidewalk according to the chronology their designs followed. They transferred their images onto the sidewalk, noting the date(s) depicted in the upper left hand corner of the block. To reinforce the scholarship and creative endeavor involved, each student also signed his or her name in the lower right hand corner. The posters were displayed in the classroom for instruction, while the sidewalk time line serves as public art with an educational focus.

ASSESSMENT

Although the topic of time lines differs according to the lesson, there are some essential characteristics of all time lines that may be evaluated with a performance checklist.

Element	Yes/No	Comments
Are events accurately recorded?		
Is scale used accurately (e.g. 1″ = 5 years; 1″ = 1 day) throughout?		
Is the student able to translate events on the time line into a narrative (oral or written)?		
Is there evidence that the time line includes important events and not every event?		
Is the student able to explain significance for inclusion of events on the time line?		

REFERENCES AND RESOURCES

Alleman, J., & Brophy, J. (2003). History is alive: Teaching young children about changes over time. *Social Studies, 94*(3), 107–110.

Bechtol, W. M. (1988). Three-dimensional timelines make history more concrete. *Social Studies Texan, 4*(3), 26–29.

Donahue, M. L., & Baumgartner, D. (1997). Having the timeline of my life! *Teaching Exceptional Children, 29*(6), 38–41.

Hoge, J. D., & Crump, C. L. (1988). *Teaching history in the elementary school.* Bloomington, IN: Social Studies Development Center.

Hoone, C. J. (1989). Teaching timelines to fourth, fifth, and sixth graders. *Social Studies & the Young Learner, 2*(2), 13–15.

Munro, R. (2000). Exploring and explaining the past—ICT and history. *Educational Media International, 37*(4), 251–256.

National Center for History in the Schools. (1996). *National standards for history.* Los Angeles: Author.

National Council for the Social Studies. (1994). *Curriculum standards for social studies: Expectations of excellence.* Washington, DC: Author.

Nesbitt, D. (1998). Developing a mental timeline. *OCSS Review, 34*(1), 57–59.

Simsek, A. (2007). The improvement of chronological perceptions among fifth grade students: A quasi-experimental study. *Educational Sciences: Theory and Practice, 7*(1), 610–615.

Web Sites

The Massachusetts Studies Project has a page explaining time lines and links to different kinds of time lines:
http://www.msp.umb.edu/LocHistoryTemplates/MSPTimelines.html

The Ohio Department of Education provides a sample lesson for teaching time lines to second graders:
http://ims.ode.state.oh.us/ODE/IMS/Lessons/Content/CMA_LP_S05_BC_L02_I03_01.pdf

For computer assistance in designing time lines, contact Tom Snyder Productions, Inc., for the Timeliner program. This program creates and prints a variety of time lines.

Tom Snyder Productions, Inc.
80 Coolidge Hill Road
Watertown, MA 02172-2817
1-800-342-0236
http://www.teachtsp.com

Timelines of History (**http://www.timelines.ws/**) is a Web site offering a variety of time lines across time and space.

47

Trash Trail

GRADE LEVELS	NCSS CURRICULUM STRANDS
✔ 3–5	III People, Places, and Environments
✔ 6–8	V Individuals, Groups, and Institutions
	VII Production, Distribution, and Consumption
	VIII Science, Technology, and Society
	IX Global Connections
	X Civic Ideals and Practices

INTRODUCTION

A trash trail follows a manufactured good from raw materials to product, focusing on the trash or waste produced in the production cycle. This instructional strategy has a distinct link to environmental issues and is well-suited to an integration with the science curriculum. For social studies, the purpose is for students to understand the global interconnectedness of the goods they possess, the environment, and the world. In addition, there are important connections to economics and technological advancement. Science education has a growing emphasis in science, technology, and society (STS). Social studies is the society component. Students might choose a favorite toy, video game, or other manufactured good and trace the entire manufacturing cycle of the item, trying to determine the types and magnitude of the pollution generated in making the item as well as where the pollution is directed. For example, if electric power is used to manufacture a toy and the electricity is generated by a coal-fired generator, polluted water and air may result. Students are asked to trace all of the components of their item to see the net cost of producing the item and to determine the value of the item compared to the pollution generated.

PROCEDURAL RECOMMENDATIONS

- At an appropriate time and place in the social studies curriculum (e.g., industries in communities around the world, Industrial Revolution, Progressive movement, Earth Day), ask students to bring their favorite toy or possession to the class with parental permission.

If possible, also have them bring in any available manufacturer's information. The manufacturer's information is very important because it typically provides content and production information. The item needs to be in the classroom for only one day. If this is to be a whole-class project, bring in a popular item for the entire class to examine and research.

- On the day the item is in the classroom, lead students through an examination and analysis, initially asking questions about where the item was manufactured and what materials were used in its production. Have available any resources students might need in this process. Globes and atlases are two standard resources. Identifying what the items are made of may be more difficult. If possible, arrange for adult guests who could help with materials identification. Local manufacturing plants may be able to assist you. This step will require inferences. Students will not be able to exactly identify a manufacturing plant and sometimes even a country. However, once they identify the raw materials, they can make informed, reasonable inferences as to where the raw materials are from.

- Arrange for a field trip to a local manufacturing plant (see Strategy 18 in this text for ideas for successful field trips). Students often do not realize the complexity of the interactions among workers, materials, and machines that occur in the manufacture of a good. The field trip provides a concrete experience during which they observe directly how an item is produced.

- During the field trip, direct students to focus their attention on how the item produced is manufactured and on the by-products of the manufacturing process. Upon returning to the classroom, have students focus their research on those same issues in relation to the item brought to class. This can become somewhat like solving a mystery; access to the Internet, helpful adults, and other needed resources are a must.

- After students have discovered the materials and manufacturing by-products involved in the production of their item, assist them in identifying and analyzing any pollutants released during the manufacture of the item. This is an appropriate link to most science curriculums. Natural and synthetic components, combined with the necessary processes used in producing an item, will create by-products. At this stage, have students identify those by-products and their effects on natural resources.

- As a culminating activity, have students illustrate on a map, time line, or some form of graphic organizer the production chronology of their favorite item. Be sure that students note what kinds of pollution are generated, where pollution occurs, and what the effects are—both real and potential—of that pollution.

RELATED IDEAS

- Have students examine the packaging of a selected item in the same way they examine the item itself.
- Have students analyze the distribution trail of an item. What pollution is generated by transporting the item from the manufacturing site to retail distributors? What pollution do retailers generate?
- Have students analyze the raw materials of the item and/or packaging. What are they? Where do they come from?
- Have older students overlay economic factors in analyzing their item. That is, in addition to completing an environmental cost-benefit analysis, students could speculate about what would happen to the economy of a community if a particular factory was removed. They could also determine what the financial and human costs and benefits might be of modifying the factory to substantially reduce or eliminate pollution.

- Convert an academic activity into social activism. If students believe they have discovered a problem, have them research and propose reasonable solutions. These solutions could then be presented to those with the authority or power to effect change: company owners, legislators, and the media.

APPLICATIONS AND IDEAS

Eighth-grade social studies students had been studying international treaties and U.S. trading partners. Through discussion, it became apparent that students did not comprehend how many of the goods that are a part of their everyday lives are imported or the level of production involved with a single good. The teacher decided to explore the construction, distribution, and disposal of cellular telephones. Having just purchased a new one herself, she brought in her phone along with all of the packaging and information that accompanied the telephone when she purchased it. Several of the students were able to examine their own telephones. They noted the materials used (e.g., plastic) and the source of those materials (e.g., petroleum based). They also noted the country of manufacture and/or country of assembly. They also noted the company that produced the telephone and any of its components if this information was included. For example, telephone batteries are often produced by another company in a different country.

Once students had figuratively deconstructed the telephone, they began to search for as much additional information as possible about each of the telephone components. What company produced the battery, where was the company located, and what else did it produce? What were the by-products of production and how were they handled? What were the batteries made of, and where were these resources found? What were the by-products of battery production, and how were they handled? These questions focused on the purchase of a new product and the role of producer. Students learned that different components were made in different countries—and none in the United States. They also used the Internet (visiting the Web sites of corporations, governments, and environmental groups) to explore and determine the production process, the modernity of the production facilities and process, and any associated environmental issues.

The teacher then turned to the consumer. How did the product get to her city for her to purchase it? Where did he or she purchase it? Where did all of the packaging that accompanied the telephone when purchased end up? How much of the packaging was recyclable or reusable? Could the packaging be reduced? How? Where did discarded phones and discarded batteries end up? What were the consequences of these forms of disposal? Through this process, students refined their research skills, became more adept at asking questions, and became more aware of the sources of the goods in their lives, all of which should have helped them become wise consumers and educated citizens.

The questions in Figure 47.1 provide a general outline to follow when examining items. Depending on the specific age and ability of students, the questions should be refined or modified.

ASSESSMENT

A variety of performance or product assessments are suitable to evaluate student understanding. Performance checklists, holistic rubrics, and analytic rubrics, of which there are multiple examples in this text, may be used. In addition, the discussion questions above could be modified into a traditional short-answer writing task that would be evaluated for accuracy and critical thinking.

FIGURE 47.1 Tʀᴀsʜ Tʀᴀɪʟ Aɴᴀʟʏsɪs Qᴜᴇsᴛɪᴏɴs

Where?

- Where was the item manufactured?
- Is there only one manufacturing site, or are different components manufactured in different places?
- What is a reasonable way for the different components to travel to a further manufacturing or assembly facility?

What?

- Of what materials is the item composed?
- Which components are the most highly refined and processed?
- Of those highly refined, what are the ingredients or components?
- How and where are all of the necessary components acquired?

How?

- Is pollution or waste a by-product in acquiring the necessary components?
- What is the process required to make the item?
- What equipment is involved in the process? Include equipment involved in moving the components to the site.
- How is the equipment powered?
- What kinds of pollution does the equipment produce?

Is It Worth It?

- Is the amount of pollution and/or waste created to produce the item worth the enjoyment of the item?
- What criteria should be considered in answering this question?
- Have we considered all of the criteria?
- Is it possible to reduce pollution and/or waste and still get the desired product?

REFERENCES AND RESOURCES

This is a context-specific strategy. The resources used to carry it out depend on the item(s) analyzed. Community connections through the local Chamber of Commerce or Rotary International are suggested.

National Council on Economic Education. (1996). *Civics and government: Focus on economics.* New York: Author. Lesson 9—"How Are Economic Solutions to Pollution Different from Political Solutions?"—can be adapted and used to extend the strategy described.

National Council on Economic Education. (1997). *Voluntary national content standards in economics.* New York: Author.

Web Sites

The American Chemistry Web site has an article on how plastic, a common component in many items, is made:
http://www.americanchemistry.com/s_plastics/doc.asp?CID=1571&DID=5972

How Products are Made
(**http://www.madehow.com/index.html**) is a Web site that provides information on how a wide variety of things are made (e.g., aluminum foil, toy wagons). It provides students some examples of all of the individual components of many common items.

48

Traveling Ambassador

GRADE LEVELS	NCSS CURRICULUM STRANDS
✔ K–2	I Culture
✔ 3–5	VI Power, Authority, and Governance
	IX Global Connections
	X Civic Ideals and Practices

INTRODUCTION

Classroom traveling ambassadors are paper cutouts of people or stuffed animals that are mailed—or actually travel—around the state, nation, or world accompanied by a list of questions related to the curriculum. These traveling ambassadors make the journey that a classroom full of students cannot make. Traveling ambassadors are often staples of geography curricula; they make it possible for large numbers of students to travel vicariously to distant (and sometimes not-so-distant) locales to learn about a region and its people. One commercially produced ambassador, Flat Stanley (a paper cutout of a man), travels all over the world, collecting cultural and geographic information, and reinforcing literacy skills.

Traveling ambassadors can also be used to reinforce other segments of the social studies curriculum, specifically citizenship education, which is the primary purpose of the social studies curriculum (National Council for the Social Studies, 1994). A well-developed approach to citizenship education, including a classroom traveling ambassador, creates meaningful, cross-cultural, and concrete learning opportunities for students to develop citizenship skills and dispositions as well as content knowledge.

PROCEDURAL RECOMMENDATIONS

- Decide which aspect of the social studies curriculum the traveling ambassador should reinforce. Citizenship as a central focus does not exclude history, geography, economics, or other social studies areas. Selecting one concept simply gives direction to the project.

- Introduce the idea of a traveling ambassador to the class, referring to the difficulty of the entire class's traveling in their desire to learn about people and places. Link the idea of vicarious travel to social studies curriculum goals, particularly those related to citizenship. Have students brainstorm a list of all the ways they can learn about others. Among other things, they will probably note that they hear stories about and see pictures of other people's travels.

- Purchase or create a traveling ambassador. The ambassador should not be so large that the costs of mailing it are prohibitive or that it becomes unmanageable for the person hosting it. However, it should be large enough to be readily apparent in photographs with people and landscapes. Be sure to give the ambassador a name.

- Brainstorm with students a list of people and places that they believe would help them learn about citizenship. Include local, state, national, and international sources. Referring to the list, discuss with students what they think the people or places included could contribute to their learning about citizenship.

- Make initial contact with individuals or sites. Prepare a concise letter that introduces the class, the project, and the goals for the desired visit. Send all of the letters early in the school year; it will take time, several contacts, and negotiation to set up some visits. In many cases, the ambassador begins its travels close to home. It is easy to get the ambassador into a school board or city council meeting. However, it may take several months to arrange a visit with the U.S. ambassador to the United Nations.

- As each visit is confirmed and scheduled, set aside time with students to prepare a list of questions to be answered during the visit. This requires that students research the person or place being visited. Caution students to avoid questions that they can easily answer themselves with basic research (e.g., What is your full name? Where do you work? Are you married?). Encourage questions that link the person or place to the curriculum. For example: What has been the hardest decision you have made as vice-president of the United States? How does being a member of the city council relate to good citizenship? What are the challenges of being a citizen of both Hawaii and the United States? If desired, have students also create a list of activities they would like the ambassador to experience.

- Make travel arrangements for the ambassador. Will it be traveling with someone? If so, make sure there is room in the suitcase or car. Convey the ambassador and its travel belongings to the carrier. If the ambassador is traveling through the mail, enclose it in a sturdy box. Allow plenty of time for arrival and give directions for return mail; include postage. Attach a lost-and-found tag directly to the ambassador.

- Pack all necessary supplies for travel. The ambassador should travel with a digital or disposable camera, lists of questions, any gifts for the host, and any items that the ambassador needs for comfort.

- If possible, have a telephone conversation with the host or the host's representative prior to the ambassador's arrival. A local school board member will probably take the ambassador on his or her travels; however, a U.S. congressperson will most likely direct a staff member to coordinate and host the ambassador. Discuss with this person the questions students are enclosing as well as the overall purpose of the citizenship ambassador.

- While the ambassador is traveling, introduce questions or comments about the journey. Links to geography can be established by having students calculate travel distance, time taken to get to a destination, time zones, and so on. Literature, history, science, and civics links can also be made, depending on the person or place visited.

- When the ambassador returns, prepare photos for viewing (digital or film). Set aside a time for the class to read responses to the questions posed and to look at all of the pictures. If the host is a local resident, ask him or her to speak to the class regarding the ambassador's trip. Link the ambassador's travel experience to the citizenship curriculum or citizenship concepts such as justice, truth, the common good, and the individual rights and responsibilities of citizens. For primary grades, the travels may just be to students' homes to learn about how citizenship is practiced in the family.

APPLICATIONS AND IDEAS

Rover the (small stuffed) Citizenship Dog lives in Mrs. Roush's fifth-grade classroom, although he is rarely in residence. Rover roves the world, learning about citizenship—specifically how people in different places practice good citizenship in their different roles. In the last 10 years, Rover has made numerous trips: He has visited Washington, DC, his state capital, the local mayor's office and the city council, New Orleans, Cape Kennedy, the concentration camp Dachau, Hawaii, and the United Nations in both New York and Geneva.

On each trip, Rover has traveled with a list of teacher-facilitated, student-developed questions regarding citizenship. On a trip to see a space shuttle launch, Rover asked how the job of an astronaut relates to good citizenship. On a trip to Dachau, Rover asked how citizens allowed and participated in the extermination of so many fellow human beings. In Hawaii, Rover asked about the relationship between native Hawaiians and mainlanders and how each group interpreted good citizenship. The answers to these and many other questions inspired many thoughtful discussions back home about history, culture, economics, and geography—all in the context of citizenship.

The pictures of Rover on his travels have been both humorous and inspirational. Photos of Rover playing on the White House lawn with Socks (the Clinton family cat), getting his "wings" on his first airplane ride, and having his duffel bag inspected by large Secret Service dogs are quite funny. Pictures of Rover assisting in serving Thanksgiving dinner at a Washington, DC, homeless shelter, beside a U.S. congressperson in an important committee meeting, and outside the gates of Dachau have been much more moving and have led to important classroom discussions about the rights and responsibilities of citizens, particularly with the effective facilitation of Mrs. Roush.

Rover travels in a small duffel bag with all of the necessities for long trips. He carries a camera, a small dog toy (in case he gets bored), a hat (to keep the sun off his face and to provide a place for souvenir pins), care and feeding instructions, a little money for any travel necessities, and the list of student questions. A letter of introduction accompanies the questions.

Rover is an integral member of the class. He brings the problems and possibilities of the local community, the state, the nation, and the world into a single classroom in a small midwestern city.

ASSESSMENT

Specific assessments would be tailored to assignments related to the traveling ambassador's adventures and will differ dramatically with each teacher. A combination of traditional and nontraditional assessment is appropriate.

REFERENCES AND RESOURCES

National Council for the Social Studies. (1994). *Expectations of excellence: Curriculum standards for the social studies*. Washington, DC: Author.

Destinations for citizenship travel include the following:

School district central administration offices

City or town government offices, including social services and public works

State government offices—the local assemblyperson is a good contact for a comprehensive visit; a direct contact with the governor's office is appropriate for a visit to the executive branch

Federal government offices—the local representatives or senators are good first steps

Contact colleagues, parents, and friends prior to their planned vacations—these vacations may provide some unplanned opportunities.

Web Sites

Rover is a civic education version/adaptation of Flat Stanley®, a well-known geography and literacy project. The official Web site for Flat Stanley® is **http://www.flatstanley.com/**. The academic goals of the two projects are different, but they share a common goal of connecting children to people and places they cannot typically visit in person.

49

Video Productions

GRADE LEVELS	NCSS CURRICULUM STRANDS
✔ 3–5	II Time, Continuity, and Change
✔ 6–8	III People, Places, and Environments
	IV Individual Development and Identity
	V Individuals, Groups, and Institutions

INTRODUCTION

Students make video productions using a digital video camera to document and interpret historical topics. These projects allow students to demonstrate their research while showing how local history topics form connections with national or international events. Students blend their evidence from interviews with authorities, historical photos, and other primary sources to get a final product. Students share their work with community members in service clubs such as the Exchange, Lions, Rotary, and Optimists. Students create an authentic product that demonstrates what they have learned (see also Strategy 16, Strategy 45).

PROCEDURAL RECOMMENDATIONS

- Have students form small groups. Have the groups brainstorm and select the content they wish to interpret from an experience, story, primary source, interview, or combination of these.
- Prompt students to select the approach they wish to take with their audience. Will their production include only their point of view? Will it show both sides of an issue? Who is the intended audience? Will the production let the audience members decide at the end what position they will take?
- Provide basic instruction on proper shooting of video footage, including the selection of subject matter, camera angle, and composition. Look for a photographer in your community who can volunteer to teach these and other photography fundamentals.

- Suggest that students use both close-ups and broad views.
- Have students sort their images by quality, retaining only the best images and sequences.
- Suggest that students use the historical markers from field trips, site gift-shop publications, primary and secondary sources, information learned from docents, informational flyers, and other available information as resources to construct a script.
- Be sure to check on copyright issues if students are using music and photographs to accompany the program.
- Students take on tasks for the group through the following activities:
  - One student locates authorities and films and transcribes the interviews.
  - One student writes a narrative with an introduction, body, and conclusion that is congruent with the content and central theme of the proposed video production. Encourage students to use primary source material and establish historical context by including quotations from famous persons of the era as well as from common people with dissenting perspectives.
  - One student scans historical images from historical societies and libraries.
  - One student locates and films background footage, sets up reenactment sequences with historical sites and reenactors, records students reenacting events at the historical site, and edits the production using a software package such as Final Cut Pro. Students film the historical sites as they look today, trying to capture the exact time of day, season, or weather as dictated by historical records and library collections of photographs and historical illustrations of the events.
  - One student finds music for the project and creates the captions and credits.
- Invite parents to the premiere showing of the project.

APPLICATIONS AND IDEAS

One group of students created a 10-minute video on the National Road. They interviewed a college professor and the director of the state National Road Association, then created a script from those interviews. In the county historical museum, students found images of the road that they scanned into the video. They shot video of modern traffic and commerce on the National Road as well as historic sites along the road. The video focused on the controversy between preserving the historical qualities of the road and developing the road for modern commerce.

ASSESSMENT

A group of students decided to create videos to illustrate primary sources associated with the Whitewater Canal. Students found primary source accounts of building and traveling on the canal. They found illustrations and photographs of life along the canal, which they scanned to use as digital images. They found volunteer actors to read the primary sources and used their voices for the soundtrack. Each of these 1-minute, illustrated primary sources gave voice to a person who lived along the Whitewater Canal 150 years ago.

4 Points	3 Points	2 Points	1 Point
Student locates and narrates a primary source about a person who lived, worked, or traveled along the Whitewater Canal.	Student locates and narrates a primary source about a person who lived, worked, or traveled along the Whitewater Canal.	Student locates and narrates a primary source about a person who lived, worked, or traveled along the Whitewater Canal.	Student locates and narrates a primary source about a person who lived, worked, or traveled along the Whitewater Canal.
Student selects a visual image that supports the content of the primary source.	Student selects a visual image that supports the content of the primary source.	Student selects a visual image that supports the content of the primary source.	
The primary source reveals more about the social, economic, or transportation history of the time and place.	The primary source reveals more about the social, economic, or transportation history of the time and place.		
The primary source reveals more about the national context of the time.			

REFERENCES AND RESOURCES

Escobar, D. (2001). *Creating history documentaries: A step-by-step guide to video projects in the classroom.* Waco, TX: Prufrock Press.

Howard, M. (2001). Team up with digital video and iMovie for social studies excitement. *Library Talk, 14*(5), 18–20, 22.

Ranker, J. (2008). Making meaning on the screen: Digital video production about the Dominican Republic. *Journal of Adolescent & Adult Literacy, 51*(5), 410–422.

Wassermann, S. (2001). Curriculum enrichment with computer software: Adventures in the trade. *Phi Delta Kappan, 82*(8), 592–597.

Web Sites

ESL Video.com:
http://www.eslvideo.com/svp_phrasalverb.php

Making Movies:
http://www.bham.net/bieff/guide1.htm

The Internet TESL Journal:
http://iteslj.org/Techniques/Brooke-Video.html

50

Webquests

GRADE LEVEL	NCSS CURRICULUM STANDARDS
Any	Any (Depending on Topic)

INTRODUCTION

As more and more classrooms and students have relatively easy access to the Internet, WebQuests are increasing in popularity. Developed in 1995 by Dr. Bernie Dodge at San Diego State University (http://www.webquest.org/index.php), a WebQuest is an interesting mixture of electronic learning center, self-paced learning, inquiry experiences, and, sometimes, a bit of a scavenger hunt. They are completely self-contained, and students find everything they need through electronic links in the WebQuest. In particular, WebQuests are designed to encourage student inquiry and higher-level thinking. Given the increasing availability of primary sources, interactive maps, and news information on the Internet, a WebQuest is a great way to organize a high-quality learning experience in social studies. A good WebQuest is a unique delivery method that should utilize classroom best practices. A poorly conceptualized or designed WebQuest is no more educational than a poorly conceptualized or designed traditional lesson or unit. The strategy outlined here is a brief overview. Detailed examples of WebQuests, as well as instructions for creating WebQuests, are widely available on the Internet.

WebQuests are designed for individual and small-group use. Students access a pre-determined web page (a home page) that introduces the topic under study and learning objectives. The home page has a variety of links on it that include, at minimum, an introduction, task, process, conclusion, and resources. Each of the subpages contains additional links. These may include readings, maps, dictionary definitions, and printable worksheets, to name a few. WebQuests may be designed for students to work individually, collaboratively, or in multiple configurations as they progress. They are not designed for students to spend hours staring at a computer screen; rather, they organize the experience for the learners.

PROCEDURAL RECOMMENDATIONS

- Determine the learning objectives for the lesson or unit.
- Consider how a WebQuest will advance student learning as well as how best to utilize the strategy. WebQuests could be used in a variety of ways:

- A single lesson (mini-WebQuest)
- One station in a traditional learning center
- An entire unit of study
- A student-created assessment task (more suitable for older students)
- An optional enrichment center or project
- Decide if an existing WebQuest will work or if you need to create one.
  - Existing WebQuests are widely available with a simple Internet search (e.g., see http://webquest. org/index.php). Some school districts provide standards-based, district-approved WebQuests that may be useful even if you are in a different school district. However, as with any classroom resource, existing WebQuests should be carefully examined for accuracy and applicability.
  - For teachers with software that supports Web site creation and use and who have the skills and time to create a WebQuest, an original WebQuest may be the best option because it can be tailored specifically for your students' learning objectives. There are many Web sites (e.g., http://webquest.org/index.php) that provide step-by-step directions and support.
- Prepare necessary computer hardware and software. For example, if you want students to view a high-quality video, be sure that compatible viewing software is on the computer. Is a printer necessary? If students will access the WebQuest in your classroom, how many computers are available? If students are to work in small groups, will they all work on the WebQuest at once? That is, consider that only two to four students can reasonably see and work through an activity with one keyboard and computer screen.
- Whether using an existing WebQuest or designing a new one, work through it a few times on your own, or have someone navigate it to be certain that all of the links work and it is easy to navigate. Although WebQuests vary in complexity and style, they typically contain all of the following components:
  - The **Home Page** is the first page the students see when they access the WebQuest. It provides an overview of the entire WebQuest and contains all of the links to subsequent sections of the WebQuest.
  - The **Introduction** poses the problem or introduces the inquiry. It provides the dilemma or problem to be explored. Essential questions may be included in this portion and/or in the Task section.
  - The **Task** explains what is expected of the student or students. It details the student outcome of the WebQuest. It could be a brochure, video presentation, museum exhibit, or skit.
  - The **Process** outlines the steps and stages students will work through. It gives them a time line to follow. For some students used to heavily directed classroom experiences, a WebQuest, or any multistage/multistep project that does not provide the time line may result in students putting off early work and then being unable to complete the task. The process helps students develop time management skills.
  - While students may choose different Tasks in order to learn the required material, there is typically one **Evaluation** for all students. It is aligned with the learning objectives and details an assessment task and provides the scoring criteria.
  - The **Conclusion** references the learning goal and what students should have learned and may include a series of reflective questions, new ideas or next steps that students could pursue.
  - The **Resources** page includes links to a large number of teacher-reviewed and -approved links that can be used to complete the required task.
- Establish clear procedures for computer use. Consider using some elements of cooperative learning. If students work in groups, have each be sure that each group member has a clearly defined role. Only one person at a time can operate the keyboard and mouse. How will the other students be intellectually engaged in the lesson?
- Monitor student progress throughout.

APPLICATIONS AND IDEAS

Dr. Bernie Dodge and his team have a rubric for evaluating WebQuests. It can be found at http://webquest.sdsu.edu/webquestrubric.html

Dr. Bill Martin also created a rubric to evaluate how well a WebQuest encourages higher-level thinking. It can be found at http://drwilliampmartin.tripod.com/s_WebQuest_Rubric1.html

This site provides a rubric that students can use to evaluate their own, as well as one another's WebQuests. It can be found at http://www.pampetty.com/webquests/evaluation.htm

ASSESSMENT

Assessment tasks in WebQuests are often evaluated through analytical scoring rubrics and many examples are available on the Internet, as well as throughout this text.

REFERENCES AND RESOURCES

Johnson, L. E. (2004–2005). Using technology to enhance intranational studies. *International Journal of Social Education, 19*(2), 32–38.

Kahl, J. D. W., & Berg, C. A. (2006). Acid thunder: Acid rain and ancient Mesoamerica. *Social Studies, 97*(3), 134–136.

Kennedy, S. (2004). The well-constructed WebQuest. *Social Studies and the Young Learner, 16*(4), 17–19.

Lipscomb, G. (2003). "I guess it was pretty fun": Using WebQuests in the middle school classroom. *Clearing House, 76*(3), 152–155.

Milson, A. J. (2002). The Internet and inquiry learning: Integrating medium and method in a sixth grade social studies classroom. *Theory and Research in Social Education, 30*(3), 330–353.

Milson, A. J., & Downey, P. (2001). WebQuest: Using Internet resources for cooperative inquiry. *Social Education, 65*(3), 144–146.

Pohan, C., & Mathison, C. (1998). WebQuests: The potential of Internet-based instruction for global education. *Social Studies Review, 37*(2), 91–93.

Thombs, M. M., Gillis, M. M., & Canestrari, A. S. (2009). *Using WebQuests in the social studies classroom: A culturally responsive approach.* Thousand Oaks, CA: Corwin.

VanFossen, P. J. (2004). Using WebQuests to scaffold higher-order thinking. *Social Studies and the Young Learner, 16*(4), 13–16.

Wennik, S. (2004). Reporting on the process of legislation: A civics WebQuest. *Social Studies and the Young Learner, 16*(4), 1–14.

Web Sites

Due to the rapid development and modification of WebQuests, the links below, while all active when this text was published, may or may not remain active. The same is true for the links within each Web site.

The Center for Teaching History with Technology includes links to some middle and high school WebQuests:

http://thwt.org/webqueststhinkquests.html

http://teachingtoday.glencoe.com/howtoarticles/developing-a-social-studies-webquest-project is a link to an article on how to develop a social studies WebQuest.

http://www.emints.org/webquest/3-5soc.shtml is an example of an elementary social studies WebQuest.

http://webquest.org/index.php is entirely devoted to providing access to a variety of WebQuests for classroom use, as well as supplying WebQuest design, evaluation, and resources. It is maintained by Dr. Bernie Dodge, creator of WebQuests. This Web site is well-developed. Topics and grade levels vary.

http://www.kathimitchell.com/quests.htm is an educator-created Web site that includes numerous links to social studies WebQuests.

http://www.suelebeau.com/webquests.htm is an educator-created Web site that includes numerous links to social studies WebQuests as well as links for directions on how to build your own WebQuests.